GEORGE ROBEY

& THE MUSIC-HALL

GEORGE ROBEY

& THE MUSIC-HALL

James Harding

Hodder & Stoughton
LONDON SYDNEY AUCKLAND TORONTO

British Library Cataloguing in Publication Data
Harding, James *1929*–
    George Robey and the music-hall.
    1. Great Britain. Music-hall. Robey, George 1869–1954
    792.7028092

ISBN 0-340-49955-9

First published in Great Britain 1990

Published by Hodder and Stoughton,
a division of Hodder and Stoughton Ltd,
Mill Road, Dunton Green, Sevenoaks, Kent TN13 2YA
Editorial Office: 47 Bedford Square, London WC1B 3DP

Typeset by Hewer Text Composition Services, Edinburgh
Printed in Great Britain by St Edmundsbury Press, Bury St Edmunds, Suffolk

To the memory of

BILLY MILTON

– actor, composer, singer, dancer, pianist

The modern theatre is worn out; it never was so worn out as it is today. The music-hall, cherishing as it does so much creative talent of a somewhat exaggerated order, is very much alive. Half, if not more, of the music-hall turns may be called creative.

EDWARD GORDON CRAIG

The music-hall song was, and is, a necessary part of our civilisation. Those old music-hall ditties . . . supply a gap in the national history.

RUDYARD KIPLING

CONTENTS

Acknowledgments

When my old friend Billy Milton agreed reluctantly, at the age of eighty-three, to move into Denville Hall, the theatrical retirement home, he made one proviso. This was that he should take with him the cherished piano which had been a gift from Cole Porter in the high noon of the 1930s. It was a typically stylish gesture. He also took with him a wealth of memories that covered sixty years on the musical stage in London, Paris and New York. Many of these memories he was kind enough to share with me, for Robey had given him generous help both at the start of his career and during it. So had Blanche Littler. He was, besides, Robey's partner in the comedian's final stage appearance. The dedication of this book is an expression of gratitude.

I am grateful as well to Mr David Drummond, animator of *Pleasures of Past Times*, for valuable documentation; to Miss Monica Gough, who appeared with Robey in the film of *Chu-Chin-Chow*; to Miss Julia Keen, who disclosed Robey's talent for verse; to Mr R. B. Marriott, lately of the *Stage*; to Mr Hugh Palmer, the expert on recorded sound; to Mr Shaun Prendergast for topographical information; and to Mr Ken Woodward, dedicated archivist.

My special thanks go to Mrs Pauline Skinner for her adroit secretarial skills.

xi

ILLUSTRATIONS

(between pp. 78 and 79)

'My hat's a brown 'un'
Robey and his first wife, daughter and son
Robey in 1906, in top hat
Robey as pantomime dame, as Queen of Hearts and as Shakespeare
'Spoof' caricature of Robey
'The Simple Pimple'
Self-caricature
Robey as the German Music Professor
Wilkie Bard
Billy Bennett
Dan Leno
Marie Lloyd (The Estate of J. C. Trewin)
Vesta Tilley
Little Tich (Raymond Mander and Joe Mitchensen Theatre
    Collection)
Robey as Lucifer Bing
With Violet Loraine
As Bold Ben Blister (The Estate of J. C. Trewin)
Poster featuring Robey's Falstaff (The Estate of J. C. Trewin)
Still top of the bill in 1940
Sir George Robey at eighty-four, with his second wife, Blanche
    Littler

Many of the pictures are from the author's own collection. It has not always been possible to trace copyright. The publishers apologise for any inadvertent infringement and will be happy to include an acknowledgment in any future edition.

FOREWORD

George Robey scintillated at the top of the bill for close on fifty years. He outlasted all his great contemporaries in the tough world of music-hall and became, in the end, something of a national monument as 'The Prime Minister of Mirth'. Everyone knew his famous catch-phrases – 'Well, I meantersay!', 'Fancy that!', 'I'm amazed!', 'In other words . . .', 'I *am* surprised at you!' – which were delivered in the ripe sub-Cockney growl that reached, without a microphone, the furthest corner of the theatre. 'Desist!' he would sternly command when he had convulsed the audience with the most flagrant double meanings. 'Desist! Let there be merriment by all means. Let there be merriment, but let it be tempered with dignity and the reserve which is compatible with the obvious refinement of our environment.' There would be silence for a while and then more laughter would burst out. 'Desist!' he would say again. 'Kindly temper your hilarity with a modicum of reserve . . . I did not come here to be laughed at. I am surprised at you, Ag-er-ness!' The rebuke, delivered with an offended glare, the huge black eyebrows arched in disapproval, only made his audience laugh that much louder.

Habited in the grotesque costume of a red-nosed, unfrocked clergyman, Robey dominated his audience. From the moment he made his entrance, rushing on stage as if pursued by unknown enemies in the wings, he created an air of urgency that immediately transfixed the attention. He held it thereafter with the basilisk stare of his eye, the tortured wriggle of his crescent-shaped brows and, above all, the haughty demeanour of a bishop shocked by the levity of his congregation. No one knew better than Robey how to play an audience, how to lead it on and up through ascending degrees from chuckles to outright hysteria. His technique was

xv

impeccable, his method of attack unparalleled. When Bernard Shaw was rehearsing *The Apple Cart* he told Cedric Hardwicke: 'Attack the first lines like a music-hall artist, like Robey. Try to get the Robey touch and then you can come back to my lines.'

But Robey was more than a music-hall performer. He went on the halls at the end of a golden period, just before the moment when the music-hall began its decline into 'variety'. He survived the transformation and retained his public. As a pantomime dame he was adored throughout the country and judged second only to Dan Leno. Keenly aware of the way the wind was blowing, always eager for novelty, he adapted to the discipline of straight plays, revues and night-clubs. Then he took to operetta and scored more success. His most daring adventure was an excursion into Shakespeare as a memorable Falstaff. The old saying about clowns wanting to play Hamlet was true in his case – he really did harbour that ambition. His crystal-clear diction, he once said, he had learned in his youth by memorising and reciting long passages from *Hamlet*. He also made a valiant attempt with films, though few of them are worth a second glance, became a popular broadcaster and even appeared on television.

The paradox of Robey is that, although the stage personality he created was vulgar, subversive, anarchic even, in private life he was the most conventional of men. Appointed a Commander of the British Empire for his charitable works and eventually a Knight, he aspired to gentility, respected the established order and loathed trades unions only a little less than he did Communists. He was an autodidact who made himself a connoisseur of oriental art, an Egyptologist and a skilled painter in watercolours. His collection of Chinese porcelain was built up over years of shrewd forays into the auction rooms. He knew a great deal about postage stamps and Persian armour. As a craftsman he learned to make violins which were played and admired by Kreisler and Menuhin. He spoke German fluently and well, having been partly educated in the country. At the same time he was an enthusiastic cricketer and member of Lords, and a doughty inside right who played in professional football teams. As an all-round athlete he prided himself on the stamina that propelled him through four turns nightly on the music-hall stage and, at the age of sixty-eight, sixteen performances during thirteen hours out of the twenty-four in non-stop revue. A win by Chelsea Football Club gave him as much pleasure as a *famille rose* plate of the Ch'ien Lung period.

I have tried in this book to set Robey in the context of the music-hall system and to show him at work among friends and colleagues who give flavour to the period: Dan Leno, Little Tich, Marie Lloyd, Wilkie Bard, Billy Bennett, Nellie Wallace and all the others whom the long-lived veteran outlasted. We should remember that Jacques Tati needed only to see that short film clip of Little Tich to hail the tiny virtuoso of the big boots as a great forerunner. We need only hear Robey's gramophone records and see the brief films of him in his music-hall persona to realise that he was a comedian of inimitable genius.

J.H.

CHAPTER I

'PERADVENTURE, SIR, TO MITIGATE THE DAMP'

[i]

'The 'ouses in between'

Except for a slight curve at either end, the Kennington Road in south-east London offers a drab vista extending relentlessly for a mile or so into the distance. It rambles through the heart of Lambeth parallel with the Thames and expires soon after reaching the trees and shrubs of Kennington Park. Not far from its other extremity is the Lambeth Walk and the ceaseless clank of trains bound for Waterloo. When, beginning in the 1820s, the terraced houses that line Kennington Road were being put up, it was still possible to view some of the fields that once enclosed the area. These remnants of greenery soon vanished under bricks and mortar, and the inhabitants might have echoed Gus Elen's wry lament for his East End views:

> Oh! It really is a werry pretty garden,
> And Chingford to the eastward could be seen,
> Wiv a ladder and some glasses,
> You could see to 'Ackney Marshes,
> If it wasn't for the 'ouses in between.

By the 1860s the neighbourhood was richly populated with superior artisans, bank clerks, respectable tradespeople and laborious craftsmen. This was the land of Mr Pooter, of genteel persons who, on an income of only a few hundred a year, were nonetheless able to maintain a cook and a housemaid. At number 334 Kennington Road, a small house on three floors, lived Mr and Mrs Charles

I

Wade and their family of two sons and two daughters. Mr Wade, a civil engineer, worked on the building of tramways, and since that new mode of transport was becoming very popular he often found himself moving from town to town for the installation of bigger and better systems. His family came originally from Hampshire, and his Uncle George, as the family Bible recorded with some pride, had married a real live aristocrat, a Lady Frances Kerr. When she died Uncle George took as his second wife a spouse with the more plebeian name of Miss Larkin. But the memory of a tenuous connection with nobility lingered on, and it was perhaps in honour of his uncle's achievement that Mr Wade decided to christen his first-born son George.

George was born at 334 Kennington Road on 20th September, 1869. Unlike Charlie Chaplin, who first saw the light of day in the same thoroughfare twenty years later and who experienced miserable poverty at a time when the area had become seedy and run down, the infant George knew a childhood that was happy and secure. Meals appeared at regular intervals, life was agreeable and a loving circle of aunts and uncles surrounded him with affection. When he was four or five his father had to move, and the family with him, to Hoylake, near Birkenhead, where Mr Wade was involved in the construction of the Mersey Tunnel. Here George had his earliest glimpse of the sea. At first it did not impress him. Then, one day, he wandered over the sand dunes and came across a wreck. It enthralled him. 'I magnified it as youngsters do,' he later recalled, 'but it seemed perfectly awful. It conjured up visions of dead sailors in a way that was extremely fascinating. I am certain that Hoylake with its stretches of sand, its view of water and sky, and its wreck helped to give me that love of the sea and all that belongs to it which has remained with me all my life.' On growing to manhood he would from time to time feel an irresistible nostalgia to smell the sea. 'When that feeling comes,' he said, 'I simply have to obey it, chuck everything, and take the quickest train to some place when I can stroll on a beach, breathe the keen salt air, and listen to the talk of the waves. After a few hours thus spent I always return to work rested, refreshed, and a new man.'

A year or so later the family man came back to London, this time to Peckham where Mr Wade engaged on building yet another tramway to fill with its clangour what W. S. Gilbert ironically called 'an Arcadian Vale'. Peckham and its neighbour Camberwell were to George's liking, but the place he loved best was New Cross. There dwelt one of his doting aunts in a venerable house filled with china, old furniture and antiquities. He enjoyed his visits to her for she would gravely conduct the small boy on inspections of her treasures, point out their beauties and teach him to appreciate them. Her tuition nurtured an interest in antiques and helped him develop into a lifelong collector. One day his mother announced that she was going to call on the aunt but that George must stay behind. Disappointed, frustrated, he submitted to her farewell kiss and saw her catch a passing tram. He resolved that he would not be denied his visit to New Cross. Since he did not know the way he followed his mother's tram and jogged behind at a safe distance. As the tram drew near his aunt's house he found his bearings and ran ahead. Once through the back door he erupted into the kitchen. 'Lawks!' ejaculated the cook. 'Lawks!' squeaked the housemaid. After they had recovered from the shock he swore them to silence, though at the sound of his mother ringing the front doorbell his nerve gave way. He slipped out at the back and ran home behind a Peckham-bound tram. When his mother returned a few hours later she found George tranquilly asleep on a sofa, looking, she told him afterwards, like an angel.

He learned to read and write at what he later described as a dame's school, although such an establishment must have seemed out of date even then. Before the days of universal primary education there existed elderly ladies of a pedagogic turn who gave, in their back parlours, elementary instruction to small boys and girls. To one of these 'dames' went George, a bright boy who quickly absorbed his lessons and picked up knowledge with ease. 'I was born with a rather large head,' he was to remark, 'and it fairly teemed with ideas.' While his slower classmates were still grappling with new concepts George had already absorbed them and his restless mind was seeking further stimulation. This he found in drawing caricatures of his teacher in his copybooks, or in placing a pin, sharp end uppermost, on the seat of a pupil who had risen momentarily to answer a question. Sent outside to be birched by authority, he occupied the time spent waiting by mixing up his fellow pupils' caps and coats in the cloakroom and, at the end of the day, enjoyed the scenes and angry confusion when their outraged owners accused each other of playing tricks.

A good eye was another of the attributes he discovered at school. No one could flip an ink pellet more truly or at a greater distance than George. He became famous for this accomplishment. One pupil in particular he disliked, a boy with whom he had fallen out over a prospective deal concerning pet mice, a boy, worse still, who was an industrious worker. During scripture lessons George made him a favourite target for his pellets of blotting-paper juicily soaked in ink. Each time he scored a bull's-eye and his victim would start up with a cry. 'Harold! No fidgeting!' the dame would thunder. George sat, a picture of bland innocence, while the seething Harold glowered vindictively at him.

He had great energy and self-confidence. At home he dominated his brother and two sisters and organised them willy-nilly into games they did not much want to play. When he became too demanding his mother would try to keep the peace. If her efforts failed his father, as the last court of appeal, gave sentence and chastised his bouncy eldest. George remained irrepressible. Not content with mere toy soldiers of lead, he needed a flesh-and-blood army to command, so he marshalled brother and sisters, threatened them with a spear and prodded them mercilessly if they fell out of line. From major-general he changed to highwayman and prowled, in imagination, the wastes of Hounslow Heath. Armed with a toy pistol he would lurk behind a blasted oak (in reality a kitchen chair), jump out on his victims, roll his eyeballs and scream, 'Hands up, caitiff! Money! – or you shall welter in your gore!' Loth to welter, the children disgorged toffees and acid drops which the kindly robber shared with them. He always found the highwayman scenario useful when his pocket-money ran out. Sometimes he even frightened himself with the force of his imagination. One moonlit night he stood by the bedroom window and suddenly began to dance about. The Man in the Moon was alive, he shrieked. The Man in the Moon was about to fly through that window and carry them all to live in the clouds. Soon he became even more upset than those whom he had tried to alarm. He dived into bed and hid under the blankets howling with fright while the others laughed. Finally his mother came in and held his hand until he wept himself to sleep.

Bright, imaginative, he was always eager for new experiences. One day he smoked his first cigarette. There were no ill effects and he enjoyed it enormously. He thought he would extend his researches and borrowed, in secret, one of his father's cherished pipes. The upshot was not so pleasing, for Mr Wade quickly found out and punished him severely. He did not smoke again for a long time after that. Eventually, as a grown man, he found the courage to try again. Ever afterwards he was a confirmed virtuoso of not only pipes and cigarettes but of cigars also.

One day (he was eleven years old at the time) his mother drew him aside and spoke anxiously. 'Georgie,' she said, 'would you mind very much if you changed your home?'

Had they, he wondered fearfully, been banished?

'We are all going to Germany,' she added. 'Your father has business in Dresden, so we are all going to live there – and you will be pleased to hear that there are very nice schools in Germany.'

The thought of Germany pleased him, though he did not believe that schools anywhere could be 'nice'. Yet in Dresden, while his father once again deployed his tramway experience, he did well at his studies. For three years he was the only foreigner in a German school and mastered the language so well that twice he came second in the class lists for composition. Art and science appealed to him, and his Latin and Greek flourished. He enjoyed most things except mathematics, a subject which, he was to say, 'I hated in any language'. His taste for practical jokes grew. Seeing a 'House to let' notice he added to it the name of a well-known local politician. A flood of unwanted callers disturbed the irate victim who summoned the police. George was let off lightly when they found that the culprit was a foreigner, an eccentric English lad into the bargain. On another occasion, impelled by scientific curiosity, he experimented with gunpowder. Only by a hair's-breadth did he avoid blowing up the family home. At school he established a football club well patronised by the English colony in Dresden. Its matches, both home and away, were keenly followed. With his mother he visited the art galleries and museums and discovered a talent for painting. He spent hours copying the pictures that hung there, absorbing the rules of perspective and colouring from the old masters he studied. Here, too, he enlarged the connoisseurship of old china which his aunt had encouraged in him at New Cross. There were evenings at the historic royal opera house where he saw *Rienzi* for the first time, and *Tannhäuser* and the standard works in the German repertory. Although he had no formal musical training he possessed a good ear and, having once heard a tune, could sing or play it afterwards with reasonable accuracy. He became a devout Wagnerian and revelled in the lush sonorities of *Die Meistersinger*. There his musical tastes ended, for he could not listen with pleasure to more modern works.

At the age of fourteen he was sent by his parents to lodge with a clergyman in the country, presumably to improve his German and also to give his host's family the benefit of English conversation. On long rambles through the countryside he learned to enjoy the charms of nature. His favourite flowers were the rose, the lily of the valley and the forget-me-not. He once remarked that he could even get enjoyment from looking at a blade of grass.

This, he afterwards said, was one of the happiest periods of his life. There followed eighteen months at school in Leipzig. Carried away by the romance of it all, he claimed to have fought a duel with a German youth who had insulted him. Graphically he evoked the clash of rapiers, vividly he described the gush of blood when steel penetrated neck and shoulder. It made a good after-dinner story. Here spoke the boy who had once frightened himself to death with tales of the Man in the Moon.

What is certain is that at the age of sixteen he was already a mature and confident young man. A group photograph of the time commemorates the opening of the Magdeburg Steam Tramway which his father had helped to build. Before a tram decked in bunting, plump gentlemen wearing shiny top-hats and luxuriant beards pose in frock-coats next to officials in peaked caps and uniforms with glinting brass buttons. George stands among them, bowler-hatted, one hand negligently in his trouser pocket. With his other hand he carries a walking-stick. The face, above its winged collar, stares with adult assurance at the camera.

Germany gave him culture and a love of painting, of art objects and of music. He now spoke the language with a fluency that impressed even natives. Two world wars failed to shake his admiration of a country to which he owed some of his happiest memories. And anyway, he used to say in the 1930s, had not Hitler done 'a great job' in pulling the nation together?

By 1885 trams were circulating in the streets of Dresden and his father's work was done. The family returned to London and there was talk of George going to university. Cambridge was hinted at. No one doubted his ability. The only problem was how to finance his studies. At that moment, according to George, Mr Wade experienced a 'streak of bad luck', or a speculation that went wrong. Cambridge, or any other university, was out of the question. Yet although he was denied the prospect of further education, for the rest of his life he went on teaching himself, picking up, like an inquisitive bower-bird, nuggets of information about exotic religions and philosophy, painting in watercolours, reading classical literature, amassing a rare knowledge of postage stamps, Ming plates, Chinese porcelain and Zulu war weapons.

Meanwhile he needed to earn a living. His father decided that he should become a civil engineer like himself. He must, ruled Mr Wade, start at the beginning and learn the tramway construction business from bottom to top. So he went to Birmingham as a tyro clerk of the works on the building of a new cable tramway. In the office he was punctual and assiduous. He had presence. His hair was always sleekly brushed, his dark suits were businesslike, his stand-up collars ever crisp and spotless. People often noticed his eyebrows, which were unusually thick, black and well arched, as if raised in a permanent mood of questioning. His employers congratulated him on the clarity and neatness of the plans he drew and proposed them as models for other workers. From time to time he went home to London bearing satisfactory reports of his progress. This was the period when Jack the Ripper haunted the main streets of the city. George's visits home, by a coincidence, seemed to occur at each new murder, and he would be greeted on his arrival with the remark: 'Hello, at it again?'

Model employee that he was, he soon decided that he could not face a lifetime of routine, of blueprints for tram systems, of files, of the same talk, the same hours, the same walls each day. He took up painting again and startled his family with vague talk of becoming an artist. More reassuringly, he joined Handsworth Football Club and soon became a leading player. There were also congenial friends in Birmingham, young men like himself who were interested in art and music. They all looked forward to the evenings when they gathered together and talked and played after a day's boring duties in some dusty office. Among them was an amateur guitarist with whom he struck up a friendship. George had brought with him to Birmingham a mandolin, an instrument not common then, and had acquired a passable mastery of its twangling tone. At impromptu after-dinner entertainments he would play duets with his guitarist friend, and then the others would sing or recite or act little sketches. The atmosphere was friendly, uncritical.

The duettists made their first public appearance at a charity concert held in a church hall. It adjoined the local church and had, he remembered, an ugly corrugated iron roof. The audience was numerous. George walked calmly on to the platform accompanied by his guitarist partner. They embarked on their duet, George's only fear being that here and there they might forget the next note. Neither of them did, and they brought their performance to its brilliant finale with a spectacular trilling on both instruments. There was much applause. Hand in hand they gracefully acknowledged the ovation and retired. Not then, nor at any other time in his career except towards the end, did George feel the slightest nervousness. Stage-fright was unknown to him. They went on playing at amateur soirées and parties and assembled quite a large repertory.

One evening in 1890 they turned up as usual for a charity concert in St Ambrose Church School, Edgbaston. The night was wet and stormy, though this did not alarm them so much as the fact that their friends who were to entertain the audience with songs had neglected to attend, fearing, perhaps, the effect of bad weather on their voices. How could they vary the monotony of an evening made up solely of guitar and mandolin duets? George, it was recalled, had sung before at one of their private gatherings. He was persuaded, after some hesitation, to 'oblige' with a burlesque Irish number. 'Let us hope for the best!' he muttered as he was thrust back on to the platform. The ditty, chanted in a thick Irish brogue to the accompaniment of thunder from outside, went down well, so well that the audience asked for more. They were not satisfied until he had given them three other songs, the extent of his repertory. The storm ended, and, with it, his enthusiasm for the mandolin. He had discovered something much more rewarding than playing duets and sharing the glory with a partner. He had captured an audience by his own efforts, amused them and made them laugh. Their applause at the end was directed at him alone. There was no sweeter, no more welcome sound than the noise of laughter and clapping. It was music to his ears. He wanted more of it. He could never, he realised, have enough.

His reputation as a comic vocalist spread throughout Birmingham and he added more songs to his collection. Perhaps one day he might be able to give up tramways and office work to become a professional entertainer? Birmingham was a pleasant city, he had acquired many good friends there, and in later years he was always glad to go back as a pantomime star. But London, at this point in his life, offered greater possibilities. Early in 1891 he returned for good to the capital and installed himself with his family who were now settled on Brixton Hill. The area, by chance, was propitious, for there lived many stars of the music-hall who found it convenient for the good bus and tram services that carried them late at night to and from various places of entertainment. Prudently, though, he kept on his office job with an engineering firm.

His social life flourished as it had in Birmingham. One of the organisations he joined was a whimsical body called the Thirteen Club where members deliberately tempted fate by going out of their way to spill salt, walk under ladders and patronise 'unlucky' numbers. He sang at their suppers and took other engagements which brought him an occasional guinea. Payment meant that he was no longer an amateur. It also might, he reflected, cause embarrassment to his family. As his professional soubriquet he adopted the name of a firm he had known in Birmingham called Roby. A little later, when a misprint gave it as Robey, he so liked the look of it that he used it permanently. In a similar way did Ronald Hutchinson, who worked for the sugar refiners Henry Tate, turn himself into Harry Tate the famous comedian.*

The London George knew in the 1890s is today as remote in history as Nineveh. Hansom cabs dashed along Regent Street past horse-drawn omnibuses on iron wheels that struck out a deafening

---

* Reuben Weintrop, it is said, took his stage name from Bud Flanagan, a bullying sergeant who had given him a rough time in the army. He planned to get his own back by turning the name of the man he hated into a laughing-stock.

thunder from cobblestones and macadam. There were still crossing sweepers like Jo in *Bleak House*. One of them, an aged female in a clean white apron, preserved the neatness of St James's Square. She was always accompanied by three cats, and when one of them came to maturity it would vanish, probably, so the legend went, to provide pies and fur hats, its place taken by another, younger animal for fattening up. Over Berkeley Square presided a crossing sweeper of devout Catholic faith. One Sunday a neighbouring Duchess, on coming back from mass, heard that he had not yet been to church. She despatched him to Farm Street and, while he was at his devotions, swept the crossing herself and on his return handed him the broom and what takings there had been. Street entertainers abounded. At the corner of Suffolk Street there was a man with a large wheeled cage wherein canaries, white mice and cats lived amicably together. The canaries and the mice did tricks on a pole and the cats gave boxing displays. By the National Gallery in Trafalgar Square sat a crippled dwarf who squeezed out eerie moans from an asthmatic concertina.

'All 'ot! All 'ot!' shouted the hot potato man on frosty nights, cutting open a floury potato that steamed in the cold air and dabbing it with butter. The coffee-stall owner pushed what looked like a chest of drawers up to his pitch. From its capacious depths he produced walls and roof. Then came jugs, cups, mugs and even a stove and a coffee urn. He conjured up from inexhaustible depths an array of loaves, cakes, butter and tins of milk. In the light thrown by a tavern window sat the trotter woman, an old lady wearing a neat mob cap who displayed fresh cooked pigs' trotters on a napkin spread out over her basket.

Through Bond Street and Piccadilly strolled gentlemen in top-hats and ladies, smartly coiffed, making their way to the carriages that awaited them. You might, if you could afford it, buy a dozen bottles of the finest champagne for less than five pounds, or rent a six-roomed house at fifty pence a week. Two people could enjoy a four-course luncheon including a bottle of champagne at Romano's for seventy-five pence. Partridge were twenty pence a brace, pheasants thirty pence and chicken seven pence. These luxuries were for the rich. Yet even the poor could have a good night out at a music-hall for no more than twelve pence or so. This included the price of ten cigarettes, a few beers, seats in the balcony, a programme and a hot supper.

A popular resort was Anderton's Hotel in Fleet Street. One of George's friends in the Thirteen Club organised a smoking concert there, and, having heard him sing at one of their gatherings, invited him to appear. Through clouds of tobacco smoke so thick that the walls disappeared from view George hurled in a stentorian voice that piece of inane doggerel called 'Where Did You Get That Hat?'* For the occasion he had rigged himself out in a garb that resembled the dress of Mr Stiggins, the prim-faced, red-nosed parson with 'a semi-rattlesnake sort of eye' in *The Pickwick Papers*. A shabby black coat like a cassock hung down beneath his knees and was left unbuttoned at the neck. A wig gave him a domed bald forehead, and his eyebrows arched blackly in surprise. He wielded a rusty umbrella and a worn top-hat. The effect was of a priest who had been unfrocked for some unsavoury misdemeanour. His father, who had been dragged, reluctantly, to see the performance, muttered under his breath, 'Can that disreputable-looking tramp be my boy?'

It was, and the boy now began to earn many a guinea. Performing on its own was reward enough. To be paid for doing what he enjoyed was an unbelievable privilege. On 28th April, 1881, he appeared at a smoking concert in Kennington, the eleventh on a bill of thirty-six and next to a 'fantasia on the clarionetum'. By now he was adding patter to his songs and developing his turn into a fully-fledged number. Later that year he visited the Royal Westminster Aquarium which stood on the site of what is now Central Hall round the corner from Parliament Square. It had been opened in 1876 with the vague intention of providing moral and educational uplift for the public. In the basement was a huge tank containing six hundred gallons of water. It housed, for a while, a dispirited crocodile. A pair of whales succeeded him but died soon afterwards, and even a talking walrus failed to liven up the mournful atmosphere. Performing seals brought a

---

* A curious example of the survival of old music-hall songs was recently given in the TV soap opera *Coronation Street* (1989), when Vera and Ivy burst out into an improvised version of 'Where Did You Get That Hat?' inspired by the pub landlord's exotic shirt.

touch of vivacity, as did, later, Pongo the gorilla and a kangaroo that boxed. There were billiard galleries and restaurants and cafés too. What finally drew the crowds, however, were giants, dwarfs, fasting men, and the women who lurked purposefully in the shadow of the aquaria. The establishment did better with 'Lulu', a beautiful girl (in fact a boy) who was shot from a cannon on to a platform way up in the roof. Another attraction was the acrobat Zaeo, whose daring somersaults were as thrilling as the scanty costume which failed utterly to conceal her ample charms. An evening's entertainment at the Royal Westminster Aquarium lasted five hours and, between musical interludes by organ and orchestra, offered Professor Frederick and his performing cats, Blondin the hero of Niagara, la Belle Fatima and her troupe of Tunisian beauties, and the Champion Jumper of the World. The last named could jump over twenty chairs ten feet apart and clear thirty-six feet in three jumps. As an encore he jumped on to a policeman's helmet and off again without damaging it.

The Aquarium specialised in hypnotists and phrenologists who claimed to tell character from the bumps on people's heads. On the night George went there he was intrigued by Professor T. Kennedy, the American mesmerist who put his subjects under a spell and made them do odd things. It was not so much Kennedy's act, efficient enough in its way, as the possibilities for himself that impressed George. After the show he went backstage and was introduced to the Professor, or 'Tom' as his friends in the business called him. Why should not Tom use him as a subject, he enquired?

'Indeed? Have you ever been mesmerised?' asked the Professor.

'No, and I don't want to be,' answered the volunteer, 'but, if you like, I'll sit in front and pretend you've mesmerised me. Then you can call me to the platform, apparently under your spell.'

The reason was that he had seen a chance of testing himself out 'cold' against a real audience in a real theatre. Tom agreed that next evening he would put him under a spell and that he would command him to sing. It was a way, George explained, of breaking himself in. But, he added as he shook hands on the bargain, there was to be no sticking of needles into him or drinking oil or eating pepper, which were favourite tricks used to prove how completely under the spell a 'subject' was.

The following night he took his seat in the stalls. Professor Kennedy fixed him with a piercing glare and rapidly fluttered his hands. Like a man in a dream, George stood up. His eyes glazed over, his face became vacant. In silence he groped his way to the stage. There were other 'subjects' up there, all old hands at the game, and they examined him with professional interest.

The Professor flapped his hands again in magical passes. 'Young man,' he declared, 'you are now under my power. You will do whatever I tell you. *You are a comic singer.*' George was commanded to imagine a piano near the footlights and a pianist awaiting his instructions. He moved, like an automaton, downstage and told the invisible executant what to play. Then he sang a ballad called 'A Little Peach in an Orchard Grew'. The audience liked it and encouraged him to go on into the second chorus. They were enjoying his performance and so was he.

At this point one of the 'subjects' lined up at the rear of the stage grew jealous. A vicious kick from behind suddenly took George off his guard and made him stagger forward. He sailed over the footlights and landed, still standing, on a seat in the third row. When he had disentangled himself from an elderly gentleman who was his involuntary and panic-stricken neighbour, he climbed back on the stage apparently still under the influence, and completed his song as if nothing had happened. The audience roared with delight. Afterwards, in a quiet corner, George had what he described as 'a private settlement' with the 'subject' who had sent him flying.

His association with Professor Kennedy flourished. Sometimes he would pretend to be immune from occult powers. Then the Professor would wave his hands, the diamond and gold rings flashing eerily, and draw him under protest up to the stage as the audience watched in fearful fascination. A kindly old lady sought to detain him. 'Young man,' she cried, 'I have watched you here more than once.' She indicated with a dramatic finger the mysterious Professor. 'That dreadful man has you in his power. I have seen his hold over you growing and growing. Don't deny it!

I am not going to let him ruin a young life like yours. I'm going to take you away!'

George winked at the Professor. His would-be saviour dragged him to the exit. 'He has never had me in his power – never, never!' shouted George. He swung round to meet the Professor's glittering eye. A quiver ran through his body, he trembled, seemed to lose control of his limbs. And then, erect, he marched stiffly towards him. His acting entirely convinced all who saw it.

Another time a group of doctors attended to investigate the scientific claims made by the Professor. Among them was one who recognised George. The medical man took off his tie-pin and jabbed it into George's cheek. The victim remained mute and impassive, despite the agony, and resolved, as the pain died away, to get his own back.

'Make me an acrobat!' he hissed at the Professor.

'You are an acrobat!' intoned his master. 'Do you hear? I said an acrobat!'

George spread his arms, balanced on one foot and then on the other. After a short run he turned a back somersault that projected him into the midst of the assembled doctors. The heel of his left foot struck the chin of his tormentor. Justice had been done.

His unofficial engagement as the Professor's stooge continued for several weeks and brought him valuable experience. 'It gave me my chance,' he said later. 'I was only a growing lad but I had begun the serious lifelong study of what made people laugh and, as certainly, how they got their fun out of life.' One evening the manager of the Aquarium looked in to see the mesmerist's act. He was interested by George and offered him the chance of singing professionally in the main hall. The young man went home in a state of exaltation.

'George,' said his mother, 'has something happened?'

'It has!' he replied, and he told Mr and Mrs Wade of the engagement.

They were not overjoyed to know that their clever son proposed to desert engineering and become a public entertainer.

'Wait and see,' he observed confidently.

Mr Wade Senior, still puzzled, enquired, 'But what can they want with comic songs in an Aquarium?'

'Peradventure, sir, to mitigate the damp'

George disarmed his anxious parents with a sample of the humorous orotundity which was to become his trademark. 'Peradventure, sir,' he answered, 'to mitigate the damp.'

[ii]

'Then he drives like hell to the Paragon'

On the bill in the main hall Robey appeared among a non-stop variety of turns that included a 'flying man-serpent', a puppet show, an acrobatic monkey, a ballet and a troupe of performing reptiles. The pace was fast and the work exhausting. He needed to project far out into the cavernous building and to make himself heard above the constant chatter of an audience whose attention was fickle. His voice was strong and he quickly learned how to dominate the buzz of talk and the clink of beer glasses. Mere volume of sound, though, was not enough. He perfected the craft of timing, of pointing a line, of judging the length of a pause. Consonants and vowels were given their full value and exploded with clarity at the back of the hall. He worked on his diction and made it crisp and lucid. Every audience was different and he soon found out how to gauge its mood and react accordingly, how to capture its attention, hold it and win it over. This duel with an audience was something he relished, and each performance offered a new challenge. He revelled in it.

His aim, now, was to break into what he looked on as the real music-hall, for the Aquarium, though a useful training ground, did not have the cachet of places like the Oxford, the Tivoli or the Alhambra. It happened that Charlie Brighten, then manager of the Oxford music-hall, dropped in and heard him sing. Brighten came round afterwards and spoke to him as, exultant from his latest battle with an audience, he washed off the sweat and greasepaint. 'Would you like to come and try your luck as an extra turn at the Oxford on Saturday afternoon?' Brighten enquired. 'You never know,' he added, 'it might lead to something.'

The Oxford was an important and well-known hall. It stood in Oxford Street near that point where the Charing Cross Road meets the Tottenham Court Road. The site was originally occupied by a wayside tavern of stagecoach days called the Boar and Castle. In 1861 the inn was demolished and replaced with a music-hall. A few years later the new hall, a palace of ornate chandeliers and sparkling mirrors, went up in smoke. So, not long afterwards, did its successor. The third Oxford music-hall that followed survived, with alterations, until 1927 when it vanished to make way for a Lyons Corner House. Parts of the latter still survive in the dingy white-tiled façade that may be glimpsed towering above a cinema and a gramophone record store. The originator of the Oxford was Charles Morton, a figure reverently described as 'the father of the music-hall' and one who casts a long shadow over the history of an institution which gradually evolved out of the 'coal-holes', 'caves of harmony', 'free and easies', sing-songs and smoking concerts that preceded it. In the middle of the nineteenth century he ran the Canterbury Arms in Lambeth, a tavern where a parlour was devoted to 'harmonic meetings'. He built a hall on a former skittle alley and, a revolutionary move, invited ladies to attend what up to then had been an all-male resort.

At these musical entertainments, where an audience of fifteen hundred could be accommodated, glees and madrigals were heard and even operatic extracts from Gounod's *Faust*. Admission fees of threepence provided what was known as 'dry money', although, of course, the bulk of the revenue came from 'wet money', that is, the bar takings. Later Morton turned the foyer of his handsome establishment into an art gallery displaying work by fashionable artists. He also, on the side, prospered as a bookmaker. Yet his private life was impeccably chaste. He rarely drank, hardly ever smoked and seldom ate meat. His favourite luxury was a trip to Ascot and, in the evening at half past nine, a cup of tea and a small biscuit at the back of the stalls.

After the success of the Canterbury he decided that the really big money lay across the water. He moved from Lambeth and travelled west to found the Oxford music-hall. It cost him what was then the vast sum of thirty-five thousand pounds and could seat over eighteen hundred people. Huge Corinthian columns supported the ornate ceiling. Down each side of the hall ran bars smothered in flowers and glittering with mirrors. The barmaids were chosen for their beauty and their business ability. Upstairs, until one o'clock in the morning, a supper room offered de luxe meals for bookmakers, dandies, mashers and swells. Morton was as shrewd in his engagement of entertainers as he was in his catering arrangements. One of his stars was George Leybourne whom he paid a generous thirty pounds a week to sing 'Champagne Charlie is my Name', though not for long: the *lion comique* died prematurely from drinking too much of the wine he praised in song. Another attraction was 'The Great Vance' who answered his rival Leybourne with the song 'Clicqot! Clicquot! That's the Wine for Me!' before dropping dead at the age of fifty on the stage of a Knightsbridge music-hall. At the same time Morton kept on his operations at the Canterbury and retained three broughams to whisk his performers from engagements in Lambeth to the Oxford and back again. By the 1890s he had matured into a venerable figure, the incarnation of music-hall. His aspect was Gladstonian, his side-whiskers had a pure silvery hue, and he wore a high collar to his old-fashioned dress-suit. At the age of eighty-three, still spry, he could run up and down stairs to the top-floor dressing-rooms two or three times a night.

Every night was Saturday night at the Oxford. The manager wore tails and so did the conductor of the orchestra. The air was thickly blue with smoke from cigars, cigarettes and pipes. Beer flowed and soda syphons hissed. The conductor tapped with his baton and, at each side of the proscenium, a small frame lit up the number of the act that was to begin while a brief and brassy overture crashed out over the murmur of the audience. The opening turn, always difficult for the performer charged with it, since he went on cold and had to warm up the house, might be a comedian or a comic vocalist. He would be followed by gymnasts, acrobats, a soloist on the cornet, a ventriloquist, a juggler, more funny men, a violin player, a singer of patriotic songs, with, perhaps, a troupe of performing dogs or a school of learned seals. Each act was strictly timed, and any performer who overran by so much as a minute displeased the stage-manager severely. Where a programme was done twice nightly it was essential to get through the bill on time so that the house could be cleared and a new audience installed without delay.

Robey made his debut at an Oxford Saturday matinée in July

1891. The audience, as usual in the afternoon, was a quiet one and he did not really know whether he had pleased or not. As he came off Brighten walked over and he waited to learn what he feared would be the worst. Instead of which, to his elation, the manager said, 'Would you like to have another go tonight before the Saturday night crowd and see how you get on?'

Robey nodded.

'They're a bit critical,' Brighten went on, 'and rather demonstrative.'

'I'll do my best.'

That night the auditorium was crowded and noisy. Wearing his unbuttoned cassock and wig suggesting baldness, he gave them a number of songs including a fatuous piece called 'The Simple Pimple' about a girl who, in various escapades, can never avoid recognition because of the pimple on her nose. This was one of the very few occasions when he was nervous – so nervous that he could not detect what sort of reaction he had evoked. Panting and perspiring afterwards in the wings, he trepidantly awaited Brighten's verdict. The manager appeared and offered to sign him up for a twelve-month engagement. As Robey went home on the tram, a contract in his pocket, he looked up, so he later said, at the stars in heaven, and spoke aloud: 'Good evening, gentlemen! Permit me to remark I am one of *you* now! – or will be one day!'

His 'bill matter', as the trade called those captions under the names of turns on programmes, described him as 'GEORGE ROBEY, the coming man'. At the Oxford he was billed next to such established favourites as Vesta Tilley. She was famous for a speciality which, today, has faintly repellent undertones, that of male impersonator. As Burlington Bertie in full evening dress, glossy topper and dazzling white shirt-front, she brandished a cigar and charmed the audience with impressions of a man-about-town. Accoutred in a soldier's garb and lacking only a moustache, she belted out 'Jolly Good Luck to the Girl who Loves a Soldier'. She was the Piccadilly Johnny, the masher and the recruiting sergeant. It must be admitted that she chose her songs well, swaggering up and down the stage and swishing her little cane with a virile air as she carolled 'Following in Father's Footsteps' or 'After the Ball'. Sometimes she attained a degree of pathos, as when the audience joined in her song about the bitter-sweet joys of a seaside flirtation:

> From the sad sea waves back to business in the morning,
> From the sad sea waves to his fifteen bob a week,
> Into a cook shop he goes dashing,
> Who should bring his plate of 'hash' in,
> But the girl he had been mashing
> By the sad sea waves.

Her career lasted a very long time, for she made her stage debut at the age of three in a hall reeking of tobacco smoke and the fumes of beer. 'Don't be frightened,' her father advised her as she straightened out her little skirts before going on. 'Sing as if you meant it. Don't cough, and speak clearly.' When she was thirteen she played the first of many principal boys in pantomime, all flashy tights and feathers. She was eighty-eight when she died after a lengthy and dignified retirement as the wife of a theatrical knight, Sir Walter de Frece, music-hall impresario and later Member of Parliament.

After his Oxford beginnings in the company of stars like Vesta Tilley Robey encountered a setback to what had been an unusually smooth upward progress. His contract allowed him to take outside engagements from time to time, and he accepted an offer to play the Star music-hall in Bermondsey at three pounds a week. It began on a Bank Holiday Monday when the audience in those parts was traditionally drunk and riotous. Whatever the quality of the individual turns, Bermondsey convention demanded that each be catcalled and made the target of rotten fruit. With a sinking heart Robey saw his number go up. The band played his introductory music and he bounced on with a ready smile. The smile froze when he received a barrage of shouts and foul invective, as if, he later recalled, a whole zoo had broken loose. Somehow he bludgeoned his way through the first song, and then a second, though no one could have heard either him or the orchestra. When he came off and listened to the cacophony that swamped his successor, he regretted the order and decency of his Oxford audiences. 'Never again, George Robey,' he muttered to himself, 'never again.' It struck him that three pounds a week equalled ten shillings a night. This, he decided, would be not only his first but also his last appearance in Bermondsey. So he borrowed ten shillings from the manager, treated his fellow performers to a drink and swore he would never set foot in the place again. It was a resolution he had no difficulty in keeping.

Another East End music-hall provided a more disagreeable experience, though this time for a quite different reason. He took with him a song that had gone down well at the Oxford, chiefly because of its catchy rhythm and an absurd chorus:

> My hat's a brown 'un,
>   A brown 'un, a brown 'un,
> My hat's a brown 'un –
>   And don't I look a toff!

As he sang it the first time his audience glowered in baleful silence. When, however, he invited them to join in, they did so with unexpected vigour and in tones to awaken the dead. He came to his second number and again gestured for them to sing the chorus with him. They did – but insisted on chanting 'My hat's a brown 'un', once more. The words rolled round the hall and thundered out with the crash of a storm at sea. Even as he made his exit they were still bellowing the lines. What is more, the unfortunate turns who followed him and who asked them to sing their choruses were obliged to have 'My hat's a brown 'un' thrown lustily in their face. Well, thought Robey, he was famous now and perhaps he would be offered a fat contract.

Next evening the manager approached him in ireful mood. 'Gawd!' he exclaimed, 'so here you are again!'

'Yes,' answered Robey, smiling pleasantly, 'here I am.'

'Get out!' said the exasperated manager.

'I beg your pardon?'

'Get out!' he thundered. 'You and your brown hat ruined the show last night, and I'm damned if you're going to ruin it again! All my artists are complaining that you've simply made their work impossible. The kids in the street are all singing "My hat's a brown 'un", and the audience here are only waiting for you and your infernal drivel! So get out, and be sharp about it!'

'Peradventure, sir, to mitigate the damp'

Robey went home on the tram meditating the paradox that success, in the theatre, could also mean failure. The song was too obvious, the rhythm too effective in its banality. He wrote later in his autobiography that he thought, as he fell asleep, he should be more subtle in future.

One of his happier engagements occurred in Chatham at Barnard's music-hall. This was one of the few places to retain the custom of the 'Chairman', a dignitary who, florid, heavily diamond-pinned, wearing an evening suit maculate with beer stains and cigar ash, sat at his own table and introduced the turns. These he announced by rapping with a wooden hammer and launching into an address extolling the brilliance, the overwhelming talent, nay, the sheer genius of what the audience was about to hear. Then he returned to the large glass of brandy and water ever at his side. The more he drank the more his dignity grew and his magniloquence flowered, the only physical effect being that his face became redder and shaded imperceptibly into a violent shade of purple. Robey, presented by the Chairman in tones of monumental stateliness, gave his audience a song about how he had left his wife at home and taken a girl to the theatre. During the interval, he related, they bumped, of all people, into his wife and their lodger:

> Staring me in the face!
> Staring me in the face!
> There was she and that lodger of ours
> Staring me in the face.

There's a nice thing, he went on in his patter, there's an unpardonable liberty! 'How dare my wife go out with another man? I'll teach her!'

Suddenly a woman started up from the audience, her face red with anger, an accusing finger pointed in his direction. 'Well!' she screeched. 'But you was there yerself with another woman. Serves yer right!' Having paid unexpected tribute to the veracity of his performance, she sat down amid bellows of laughter.

Apart from his minor contretemps in the East End, Robey's ascension to star billing was remarkably quick. Soon, like all the other popular entertainers, he was playing as many as four or five different halls a night. Since each bill consisted of independent acts and had no continuity, an artist could be slotted in at his accustomed place following a schedule minutely calculated to give him just enough time for travelling between halls. As Bessie Bellwood, who knew the routine well, used to sing:

> First he's at the Tivoli,
> Then he's at the Pav,
> Then comes out and begins to shout,
> Fifteen minutes you have,
> Then he drives like hell to the Paragon.

(Bessie Bellwood had been a rabbit skinner in the New Cut and never forgot the vigorous customs of her youth. Once, believing herself to have been insulted by a member of the audience, she grabbed his head between her brawny arms and bit his ear until the blood cascaded down. Her command of invective was Homeric and she could outswear any man imprudent enough to take her on. 'Wot cheer, 'Ria' was her most famous song, and she was overshadowed only by Marie Lloyd. She died at the age of thirty-six, much lamented.)

On a typical Saturday night Robey would arrive in his brougham at the Metropolitan, Edgware Road. His trunk would be hurriedly shot through the stage door and a call-boy would rush up to carry away the band parts. There was no time to look for a dressing-room: Robey made up in a corner of the wings and quickly rehearsed to himself the words of his songs. His number clicked up on the board and he bounded into the white-hot glare of the footlights. Back he ran into the wings for a quick change, then sauntered on again. Saturday night audiences were always difficult, even in the politest halls. You had, he found, 'to keep hitting them in the eye to hold them'. His song went well, though not, perhaps, quite so well as at the more sophisticated Oxford. The final chords banged out, and, keeping on his make-up for the rest of the evening, pausing only to throw on an overcoat, he rattled through the streets, his dresser perched on the box of the brougham, to Collins's music-hall in Islington.

At nine forty-five, having deftly evaded a gang of trick cyclists who were just coming off, he did his turn on Collins's stage.

From Islington he whirled off through the thickening traffic to the Oxford, where, by half past ten, he was waiting for 'Mademoiselle Diane de Fontenoy' to complete her 'art-statuary' act. That lady having gracefully shimmered off, he was in front of the audience again, one eye on their reaction and the other on the clock. 'We're late!' whispered his dresser. They stumbled into the brougham, galloped down the Charing Cross Road and along Shaftesbury Avenue for Piccadilly Circus and the Pavilion. It was ten to eleven when they arrived at the stage door. His dresser was right: they had missed their turn and were obliged to loiter until the singer currently occupying the stage had finished. As he came off he passed them in the wings and told them it was his eighth performance that day. He'd lost his voice, he said, and was dead beat. 'How do *you* feel?' he asked.

'Fit to do all my shows over again!' answered Robey, a picture of health and confidence. 'Just warming to the work! I am never nervous and never tired.'

'What! Never?'

'Well, hardly ever,' said Robey, prancing with eagerness to get back on the stage.

A sign of how far, and how quickly, he had risen in the profession was his friendship with Marie Lloyd. As early as 1891, the year of his debut at the Oxford, he was going to parties at her home and had become a member of her circle. She was then at the peak of her success, the most popular and the most widely loved of all women music-hall stars. Born Matilda Wood, in Hoxton, she took her name from *Lloyd's Weekly News*, a scandal sheet of the time. Within a year she was famous and had acquired a repertory of songs whose titles have passed into the language. 'A Little of What You Fancy Does You Good' advised that 'I always hold in having it if you fancy it. If you fancy it, that's understood! But if that's your blooming game, I shall want to do the same, 'cos a little of what you fancy does you good!' In 'Don't Dilly Dally on the Way' she immortalised an episode that many of her audience knew from grim experience: a moonlight 'flit' to avoid paying the rent. 'Oh! Mr Porter', the epic of a girl who took the wrong train and ended up in the arms of a 'kindly' old gentleman, was full of the same cheerful innuendo that flavoured her other songs about the lass who'd never had her ticket punched before, or the little sister who was given half a crown to go away and leave the parlour to a courting couple. She was improper, she was vulgar, but she was never lewd. An official committee formed to 'clean up' the music-hall summoned her to appear before them. She performed all her most risqué songs with a blandness, a propriety that would not have offended the strictest censor. Then, her eye glinting, she sang them the blameless 'Come Into the Garden, Maud', and gave it a wealth of suggestiveness that made everyone blush. As she used to remark in one of her songs, 'Every little movement has a meaning of its own, every little story tells a tale.'

Marie Lloyd was not pretty. She was pert and inclined to dumpiness. Her face was round and her teeth were disproportionately big, 'like those of a jovial horse', remarked an admirer. The few gramophone records she made are disappointing in their scratchiness and the hollow squawk that emerges from them. Yet those who saw her were captivated by the charm she projected to the back of the hall, the saucy look, the neat little hands and feet she used with cunning skill, and the illusion of beauty she was able to create. Her voice, which had nothing remarkable about it, was saved by what Max Beerbohm called her 'exquisitely sensitive ear for phrasing and timing'. Sometimes, in her later years, she could be very moving, especially when she sang 'The Boy I Love Is Up in the Gallery', a sweet little tune which she imbued with an endearing poignance. Moving, too, though in a different way, was 'It's a Bit of a Ruin That Cromwell Knocked About a Bit'. The raucous measures are sung by a drunken old woman staggering beside a pub called the Cromwell Arms – 'Outside the Oliver Cromwell last Saturday night, I was one of the ruins that Cromwell knocked about a bit.' It was the song she sang at her last appearance. Worn out, unsteady, fuddled on whisky, she careered drunkenly around the stage while the audience, not knowing she was mortally ill, roared hilariously at her lifelike antics. Three days later she died at the age of fifty-two.

Twice married, twice divorced and mother of a daughter by her first husband, she had, like Edith Piaf, a deplorable taste in men. At the age of forty she fell in love with an Irish jockey eighteen years her junior. He was a drunkard and a parasite who regularly beat her up and once favoured her aged father with the same treatment. Yet still she loved him, flattered by the attention of a younger man and enchanted by his virility. Only towards the end, when, in the words of her own song, she had become 'a thing of the past, old dear', was she disillusioned. Is her lover coming to the show that night? someone asked. 'No, the bastard isn't,' she grunted wearily. Again like Edith Piaf, she threw away the large amount she earned, two hundred thousand pounds, it was said, on a retinue of sycophants and spongers, for she was kind-hearted, liked to help people in misfortune and enjoyed seeing her friends have a good time.

She was forthright and detested sanctimoniousness. A singer whose primness vexed her was lunching one day with a well-known impresario in a famous restaurant. As Marie walked past her table she called out gaily, 'That's a nice bit of cock you've got there.' She spoke the same language to her audiences. On a bad night in Sheffield the first house gave her a poor reception. 'You don't like me,' she told them. 'Well, I don't like you. And you know what you can do with your stainless knives and your scissors and your circular saws – you can stick 'em up your arse.' She refused to appear at the second house.

A tactful manager came to her dressing-room and said the audience had asked him to apologise.

She remained obstinate.

'They'll do what you say with the knives and scissors,' he continued, 'but can they be spared the circular saws?'

She burst into laughter. 'All right, then,' she answered, 'play "God Save the Queen" and tell 'em she's here.'

Vulgarity alone would not have won 'Our Marie' the great following she enjoyed. 'Miss Marie Lloyd,' said Bernard Shaw, 'like all the brightest stars of the music-hall, has an exceptionally quick ear for both pitch and rhythm. Her intonation and the lilt of her songs are alike perfect. Her step-dancing is pretty; and her command of coster-girls' patois is complete.' James Agate observed: 'She depicted the delight of humble life, the infinite joy of mean streets . . . Marie's "dial", as the Cockney would put it, was the most expressive on the halls. She had beautiful hands and feet. She knew every board on the stage and every inch of every board. In short, she knew her business.' And Robey marvelled at her 'brimming vivacity'. For him, she was 'a generous, lovable woman, a good mother, a good friend, and in her way an incomparable artist'. She was to repay the compliment. There were, she said, only two other performers with whom she would be prepared to share top billing: one was Little Tich and the other was George Robey.

[iii]

'I look upon you as my beanyfactor'

By 1900 there were forty or so music-halls in London and the suburbs. Within the next few years the number verged on seventy, to which may be added a couple of hundred and more scattered through the provinces. This relatively new industry reposed upon a complicated sub-structure of organisations. Among them was the Music-Hall Artistes' Railway Association, founded in 1897, which arranged a twenty-five per cent discount on railway and steamboat journeys. Since touring the provincial halls was now an important activity, the Association quickly gained adherents. There were benevolent societies like the Music-Hall Sick Fund, the Music-Hall Ladies' Guild of which Marie Lloyd was President, the Music-Hall Home in Camberwell which looked after aged and infirm members of the profession, the Variety Artists' Benevolent Fund, and the Grand Order of Water Rats, 'a more or less exclusive association of music-hall artists whose proceedings are to a great extent conducted privately under the aegis of a "King Rat" and a "Prince Rat",' as that body so described itself. Newspapers like the *Era*, the *Stage* and the *Performer* chronicled news of the profession. There also came into existence a body of men who were much abused and even detested. They called themselves agents.

Agents were operating as far back as the 1850s when managers at a loss to fill an urgent and unexpected vacancy would call on them as a last resort. Many of them worked from a public house on the corner of York and Waterloo Roads in Lambeth which became known as 'Poverty Corner'. Later they moved to the Charing Cross Road and transacted business in the shadow of what was then the London Hippodrome. On Monday mornings they interviewed luckless performers who had been unable to find an engagement. The average wage amounted to a couple of pounds a week less ten per cent for the agent, a drink for the manager, a cigar for the conductor, and tips for the stage-manager and the limelight man. Theatrical lodgings, three to a room, cost thirty-five pence and included a morning cup of tea and fish and chips at night. This was the lot reserved for the majority of performers. A few, a very few, emerged from the grinding obscurity, and they were people such as Marie Lloyd, Bessie Bellwood, Harry Champion and Charlie Chaplin.

As the music-halls developed so did the agents. Some of them travelled abroad in search of talent, others stayed at home and built up promising locals. With their intimate knowledge of halls up and down the country, their contacts with managers and their keen eye for business, they were much better equipped than the average 'artiste' to find out opportunities. One of them for years even supplied the complete weekly bill at the Bedford music-hall and thereby saved the manager a great deal of expense and trouble. Perhaps the most successful was Hugh Jay Didcott. He had tried his luck as a Shakespearean actor in *Macbeth* and as a comic singer on the halls. In neither branch of the theatre did he shine so he became an agent, a very rich and powerful one on his ten per cent, though he modestly referred to himself as 'your old father'. No one ever knew his real name. He was a Russian Jew, and, happening to pass one day in a railway train through the Berkshire town of Didcot, he adopted the name to which he added a final 't'. One of his rivals was unique in that he only took five per cent commission from clients. He flourished just as mightily as Didcott. To emphasise the point he built himself a grand house at Kew and baptised it 'Five Per Cent Villa'.

Robey was lucky enough to avoid the humiliations undergone by the majority of his colleagues in their quest for work at the hands of agents whom they despised but were obliged to court. He dealt direct with managers who booked him for months ahead without a break. From his base at the Oxford he travelled the London halls and came to know them well, adjusting his act continually and shaping it to suit the personality of each audience. The halls around Leicester Square were the best conducted and most civilised. Then came those on the periphery of the West End, smaller and not so smart. The suburban halls were at once gaudier and dingier, bedizened with crimson and gilt and off-white plaster. At the bottom came the halls in the slum districts. Typical was Sebright's in Hackney, where the seats were rough benches and the shirt-sleeved occupants of the gallery munched, throughout the performance, nuts, whelks and shrimps, and spat the shells and other debris on those below. At the Workman's Hall, Stratford, a hulking attendant stood in the wings and, if the audience booed a mediocre performer, would, at a sign from the manager, shamble on stage and drag the offender off by his collar. Among the worst halls in London was the Hoxton Palace of Varieties. It had the nickname, for reasons not hard to guess, of the 'Sod's Opera'.

Such horrors were not to come Robey's way. In 1892, at the age of twenty-three, he was playing what later became known as the Holborn Empire. It had been built by one of Charles Morton's competitors and survived until 1940 when it was gutted by a German bomb one evening soon after the curtain fell on the second house. With Robey on the bill was Eugène Stratton, 'The Idol of the Halls', although today his 'black-up' turn would repel, despite the charm of his soft-shoe shuffle to 'The Lily of Laguna' and 'Little Dolly Daydream'.

A more robust turn was Charles Coborn who sang 'The Man Who Broke the Bank at Monte Carlo'. He took his name from a street in the East End and began life as a music-hall Chairman at twenty pence a week. The writer of Coborn's most famous song happened to see a newspaper poster that read 'Man Who Broke the Bank at Monte Carlo' and immediately said to himself, 'There's rhythm there.'* He worked at the song all night and all day, but, when he'd completed it, found no one to take it. After initially refusing, Coborn changed his mind and paid him five pounds for the rights to 'The Man Who Broke the Bank at Monte Carlo'. From this small investment he made thousands. When he introduced the song at the Oxford his audience showed little enthusiasm. Determined to convert them he sang the last chorus ten times over

---

* The man to whom the newspaper headline referred was a swindler called Wells. He broke the bank six times, turning four hundred pounds into forty thousand pounds within three days. Unfortunately, the publicity he won enabled the police to find him and bring him back to England where he stood trial and was sentenced to penal servitude for his confidence tricks.

until they were finally dragooned into taking it up as well. Thus he became the first song-plugger in history. The other gilt-edged item in his repertory was 'Two Lovely Black Eyes', a parody of the sentimental ballad 'My Nelly's Blue Eyes'. So popular did it become that the Salvation Army, determined the devil should not have all the good tunes, produced its own version as 'My Jesus Has Died'. Thanks to 'The Man Who Broke the Bank at Monte Carlo' and 'Two Lovely Black Eyes', which are among the music-hall's legendary numbers, Coborn enjoyed a career lasting over sixty years until his death at the age of ninety-three in 1945.

Another of Robey's fellow stars at the Holborn was Albert Chevalier. Although he came of a loftier background than most performers, having been born and bred at Notting Hill, he specialised in studies of Cockney costermongers whom he portrayed from the viewpoint of an outsider looking in. Chevalier depicted them as lovable old things in pearly jackets and flat caps. The words and music he often wrote himself, as he did for 'Knocked 'Em in the Old Kent Road', an irresistibly perky song about a character who receives an unexpected legacy – something his audiences, too, always dreamed about. More often, though, he mined with depressing persistence a vein of cloying sentimentality. 'My Old Dutch' was played against the backdrop of a workhouse. In a preliminary dumb show accompanied by tremulous violins, an ancient couple arrive and are devastated to learn that, according to the regulations, they must take up separate quarters. Whereupon the husband totters up to the footlights and quavers, 'We've been together now for forty years, and it don't seem a day too much – An' there ain't a lady living in the land as I'd swap for my dear old Dutch! . . . etc. etc. etc.' Despite the treacly nature of his wares he was much admired by Max Beerbohm, who described him as '. . . small and electric . . . Chevalier's songs always had a clear form. They were well constructed. I knew them all by heart once.' Max even wrote a song for him, a deft little pastiche entitled 'But 'E'll Never Be the Man 'Is Father Woz', which he, Max, would sing in private to his friends. He never offered it to Chevalier. 'Nothing so irks a creative artist as to be offered an idea, good or bad,' he explained. 'And I did not irk Chevalier.'

Of his companions on the Holborn bill, Robey found Charles Coborn perhaps the most congenial. Another of Coborn's popular songs was 'Come Where the Booze is Cheaper' ('Come where the pot holds more, Come where the landlord's a bit of a sport, Come to the pub next door'), the subject of a favourite anecdote which Robey often told with glee. A regimental band once played it at Windsor Castle while Queen Victoria was in residence. She liked the stirring melody and summoned the conductor. He arrived nervous and ill at ease. What, she asked, was the number?

A little song, he stammered with embarrassment, 'rather popular just now in some of the variety houses'.

'Indeed! And what is it about?'

Deeply troubled, the conductor replied, 'Well, Your Majesty, it's a kind of an argument recommending places of refreshment where the charges are, so to speak, reasonable.'

'Dear me! And what is it called?'

The conductor faltered, after a long pause, 'Please, Your Majesty, it's a little thing called "Come Where the Booze is Cheaper".'

A few years later Robey was billed equally with Dan Leno at the top of the Oxford programme. 'Even in those days,' Robey recalled, 'he was tearing from hall to hall, night after night. One would see him coming in from his brougham, still dripping with perspiration and looking so tired! Then the moment he stepped on the stage and heard the audience cheer, all his weariness would seem to vanish, and he would sing and dance and crack his jokes like a two-year-old!' The little man with the saddest face you ever saw would rush on stage and shout, 'Don't look so stupid!' at an audience whom he already held in his hand, such was the magnetism he exerted on them.

None of the songs Leno sang are remembered now, for he was an actor rather than a singer. Acting in the music-hall was more difficult than anywhere else because the performer had to make an instant impression, helped only by elementary props and without the aid of other people on stage. As a shop assistant, as a landlady, as a lodger, as a pantomime dame, Leno transmuted squalor into radiance, hardship into comedy, and the desperation of Cockney life into laughter. When a child of four he danced in public houses to earn a few coppers. Later he toured the provinces as a champion clog dancer. Eventually, after years of experiment, he perfected a technique that enabled him to persuade his audience that the imaginary people he talked to actually existed, that he himself, as an aristocratic rider to hounds or as a Cockney newly-wed, was larger than life. Every gesture, every grimace, every inflection of the voice was subtly and economically disciplined to create the precise illusion he aimed at. For Max Beerbohm he was a great artist, the greatest of them all. At the age of forty-three his mind gave way and he conceived mad delusions of playing Hamlet. Only a few months after he appeared with Robey at the Oxford he was dead. 'So little and frail a lantern could not long harbour so big a flame,' lamented Max Beerbohm. 'Dan Leno was more a spirit than a man.'

Robey, on the other hand, was at the start of his joyous career, resilient and greedy for new audiences to conquer. Not content with playing the best halls in London, he resolved to put on a show of his own. He booked the Gresham Hall in Brixton and issued posters advertising 'Mr George Robey's One Hundred and Third Annual Performance'. A prominent notice added: 'Ladies Invited'. This was a novel stroke, since at the time very few respectable women attended music-halls. Even at the Oxford Saturday afternoon matinée, which ended by the sober hour of five o'clock, not many of them appeared in the audience, and those who did, a trifle nervously, were accompanied by a male escort. There was nothing in 'Mr George Robey's One Hundred and Third Annual Concert' to upset them. Thirty or so friends joined him on the programme, and, with contributions ranging from 'The Lost Chord' to 'Come Into the Garden, Maud', the entertainment proved as harmless as a Temperance Penny Reading.

At the end of 1892, some eighteen months after his professional debut, he launched into another sphere that was to bring him as much fame as the music-halls. The 1880s had seen the growth of modern pantomime out of the old-style harlequinade which often featured at the end of theatrical performances as a sort of *bonne-bouche* to send the audience home in a jolly frame of mind. The harlequinade itself emerged from the sixteenth-century Italian *commedia dell'arte* with its traditional characters of quick-witted Arlecchino, pretty heroine Colombina and foolish old Pantalone. Augustus Harris, later Sir Augustus, was the impresario who created what today is known as pantomime. Nick-named 'Druriolanus' on account of the glamorous productions he mounted at Drury Lane Theatre, he was particularly noted for the splendour of his Christmas offerings. These were based on well-known fairy tales and included as hero a principal boy, who was always a beautiful woman, and a comic dame who was invariably a man. As historians point out, men have been dressing up as women for fun ever since the Bacchanalian revels of the Roman age, and even today the tradition persists in the classic drama of China and Japan. The villain was often a demon king, horned, tailed, clad in red robes and shooting up amid smoke and flames through a trap-door. Or he might have been a terrifying giant (*Jack and the Beanstalk*), or an evil magician (*Aladdin*), or a wicked uncle (*Cinderella*). A host of quaint characters became familiar to generations of pantomime-goers, among them the Ugly Sisters, Dandini, Dick Whittington's Cat, Buttons, Puss-in-Boots and Baron Hardup. The more excruciating the rhyme the greater the fun, as in this exchange from *Jack and the Beanstalk*:

FAIRY QUEEN: Well, give the calf!
JACK: I do!
FAIRY QUEEN: The beans are thine.
JACK: Though this transaction bears a strange character
               I look upon you as my beanyfactor.

At the end there was always a transformation scene where gorgeous palaces and cloud-capped towers loomed out of the haze, golden vistas unrolled into the distance, glittering canopies and lace-like gauze receded to show woods and foaming seas, and spangled nymphs darted and sparkled beneath triumphant archways. Harris knew all about spectacle, as he did about comedy. It was his idea to import music-hall comedians into pantomimes. Pantomime was 'respectable', the music-hall not, with the result that those who would never have seen Dan Leno in his natural setting only became aware of him when he starred as Dame Tickle at Christmas. Pantomime was a flexible genre which could accommodate all sorts of interpretations. The basic script followed a traditional story line on to which were grafted individual acts who made their own contribution. Double acts would play the brokers' men, jugglers would perform a crockery-smashing sequence in Dame Trot's kitchen, and comedians had a wealth of opportunity as comic policemen or stupid page-boys or daft servants. Blanks were left in the script which they filled with their own business.

'Peradventure, sir, to mitigate the damp'

In December 1892 Robey went down to Brighton where he had been engaged to play in *Whittington-Up-To-Date, or Harlequin Bow Bells and the Good Old Times.* The theatre was the Alhambra, then a well-established music-hall on the sea-front. The manager of the Alhambra was a tall and handsome personage wearing impeccable evening dress. He had been an actor in youth and was given to larding his everyday conversation with bits and pieces remembered from the lofty speeches he once delivered on stage. One evening Robey bade him goodnight with the words, 'Bye-bye, Charlie; be good! Walk ever in the path of virtue!'

Perfectly on cue, the manager grasped his hand and orated gravely, 'My dear George, I have trodden in that path so consistently that at last it has become a *rut* across the face of the universe, out of which I could not escape even if I would!'

As Idle Jack in *Whittington-Up-To-Date*, Robey won praise from the *Era* for what it called 'his merry antics, grotesque by-play and amusing costumes'. The *Stage* remarked that 'Mr George Robey alone is quaint and funny enough to make any pantomime and ere many days are past will undoubtedly be the central figure of the show.' Among his 'merry antics' was the performance of a song, very popular with audiences in Brighton and later all over England, entitled, 'Clarence, the Last of the Dandies'. For this he put on a black moustache, dilapidated evening dress and a shabby top-hat. His patter included a description of how, at a dance, his baggy trousers had lost a button and fallen down while all those around had sung, to the tune of 'Jerusalem! Jerusalem!' from the famous ballad 'The Holy City', 'He's losing 'em! He's losing 'em!' Then he went on to talk about his fashionable acquaintances: 'You wouldn't know my friend Cholmondely.* You're not in his set. He's in the Guards. He loves the dear old Flag! He has two – a red one and a green one! [*Whistle.*] Right away!' At which point the audience became helpless with laughter. In print the effect is not all that amusing. A hundred years ago, aided by Robey's glistening eye and his mercurial gestures, it was very funny indeed.

---

* Each syllable, of course, given equal stress and pronounced exactly as written.

CHAPTER II

A VILLA OF MACHICOLATED STUCCO

[i]

'Let there be merriment by all means'

'As Mr Robey enters from the wings his eyes command the house like the blazing headlights of a car rounding the corner of a night-dark road,' observed a critic. This was typical of Robey's lightning attack. It was the custom in those days for a solo artist to come on at stage left, walk across to the centre and then turn, face the audience and go up to the footlights before starting his number. Robey ignored the ritual. Like Dan Leno, he bustled on in a tremendous hurry. He would suddenly halt and look in astonishment at the audience, as if amazed to find them there. Without a word he slowly advanced on them, brows raised, eyes twinkling, his mouth creased interrogatively. Before very long someone would break the silence with a laugh. Others would join in. Raising an admonitory finger, Robey would point at them and rap: 'Out! Out!' They laughed still more. 'Desist!' he commanded. Fresh laughter ensued. Before he said a word of patter he had the audience completely under control.

His method of entry was, in fact, a very old one and dated back to the Elizabethan comedian Richard Tarleton who specialised in the sudden appearance. Dan Leno's entrance has been described as 'a quick run down to the footlights, a roll like a drum with his feet, his leg raised, and brought down with a loud clap from the foot'.

His golden rule, Robey said, was 'Sing to the last man in the gallery!' If he could hear you, then everyone else could. Should an audience want to laugh, you must let them do so. He found that when he raised his hand and intoned 'Desist!' firmly, seriously, they laughed for a moment even louder. When he kept his hand aloft and intensified the serious look they gradually settled down. Then he had them where he wanted them.

Quite early on his costume had evolved into the familiar shapeless *soutane* without a collar. In his hand he carried a short flexible cane useful for emphasising points. A small flat bowler someone had once plonked on his head as a dressing-room joke completed the ensemble. Such an outfit had advantages. Being plain and black it did not distract attention from his facial expressions. There was also the convenience that, since it identified him with a trade mark, he did not need to change while travelling around five or six halls a night. His make-up was topped by a bald-fronted wig. 'I decided that as nature had endowed me with a somewhat comic face,' he said, 'all that was necessary was to emphasise the various lines and features that nature had supplied. Consequently I emphasised the arch of my eyebrows which I inherited from my parents, my nose, and the lines around my mouth.' The nose was painted red and the eyebrows were heavily blacked.

So equipped he would shoot on stage, bowler at a precipitous angle, cane whirling. The welcoming applause made him stop in apparent surprise. His dignity was affronted, his notion of good behaviour offended. As the applause faded he said something which, innocent though it might seem, was capable of a dubious interpretation. (If, for example, he was doing a female impersonation, it might be: 'Sorry I'm late. I got blocked in the passage.') Someone with an impure mind laughed. 'Desist!' he admonished the others who joined in. 'Really! I meantersay!' The laughter flowed. Regretful, surprised, the hand was raised again: 'Let there be merriment by all means,' said the black-clad figure in tones that could be heard in every corner of the theatre. 'Let there be merriment, but let it be tempered with dignity and the reserve which is compatible with the obvious refinement of our environment.'

Once order was restored he went into his patter and sang his songs. They were about henpecked husbands, awkward neighbours, bullying wives, nosy landlords and interfering relatives. When he had wrought up the audience to a pitch of delirious laughter, the hand rose again, gravity cast its shadow, and he said, 'Kindly temper your hilarity with a modicum of reserve.'

They giggled all the more. It was what might be called the ratchet effect, whereby the laughter level was cunningly hitched up by subtle degrees.

His delivery was staccato, each plosive, each vowel being clearly heard by 'the last man in the gallery'. Just as his deportment was a glorious example of absurd solemnity, his material relied on Dickensian incongruity, on the contrast between the pompous and the slangy. In a song describing how he sought permission to marry the heiress daughter of a rich father he rattled off:

> He told me my society was superfluous,
> That my presence I might well eradicate.
> From his baronial mansion he bade me exit
> And said I might expeditiously migrate.
> In other words, 'Buzz off!'

At the end of each line he fixed the audience with a glare, knowing he could depend on a burst of laughter. They never disappointed him. Every line made its point, helped sometimes by a squeak or a sudden intake of breath. In another song he told of how he had been an inmate at Holloway prison:

> The villa was machicolated stucco,
> The waiters' coats broad arrows all displayed.
> The table was anaemically liberal
> And the temperature was ninety in the shade.
> My apartment was mephitic and octagonal,
> The air non-ozonically fugged.
> The attendance inattentive and discourteous –
> To put it mildly – I was jugged.

All this was punctuated by an occasional rise of the eloquent eyebrows and by exquisite timing of movement. Surviving films of him bear witness to the clarity of his enunciation and the beautiful economy of his gestures.

The performer's act is a fugitive one. Having had his moment on the stage he vanishes and leaves his audience with no more than a memory. It is, therefore, impossible wholly to recreate the flavour of Robey's performances. The critic C. E. Montague made a brave attempt when he wrote:

A Villa of Machicolated Stucco

Last night he came on the stage first as that veteran theme of
the halls, the middle-aged toper in black, frock-coated, tieless
and collarless, leering with imbecile knowingness, Stiggins and
Bardolph and Ally Sloper in one, his face 'all bubukles and
whelks and flames of fire'. He ended as the equally familiar
old woman of the same repertory, also of bibulous aspect,
also half-knowing and half-crazy, a scold, farcical with relics
of variety, ugly as a gargoyle. Nothing could be staler than
the subjects, nothing more fresh or fuller of gusto than their
treatment. What he sang was nothing, you might have left it
out without much lessening of the fun . . . Mr Robey's patter is
everything now and yet he says, altogether, wonderfully little;
just a word, and then he seems to detect some misplaced laugh
in the audience, checks, bridles up, passes in pantomime from
tantrum to tantrum, the gusts and squalls outworn and trivial,
the mere words insignificant, the humour metallic, rasping or
worse, but the art within its limits, is not to be surpassed in its
gleaming, elliptical terseness, the volumes it says in an instant,
its suddenness, fire and zest.

Robey himself would not have agreed with Montague that his
songs were dispensable. He believed them to be an essential part of
his act and chose them with the greatest possible care. Music-hall
performers were in the habit of buying their songs outright from
the composers and using them as their exclusive property. (Marie
Lloyd once breached professional etiquette by stealing 'The Boy
I Love Sits Up in the Gallery' from the woman who introduced
it – but then 'Our Marie' could get away with anything.) Robey
found that the money spent on buying a song could be a valuable
capital investment. If the song caught on, then he was able to keep
it in his repertory, it became identified with him and no one else
could detract from his glory by singing it. The money he paid
was, indeed, little enough. An army of hungry songwriters stood
by ready to sell individual numbers for no more than a pound
or two.
   'George,' one of them would say as he came out of the stage
door, 'I've got a good title for a song.'
   'All right! Go away and write it.'
   That night the writer would come back with the words and

music complete. If they were any good, the conductor would provide an orchestration and the song would be tried out at Robey's next performance. More often than not it failed to make a stir. This did not worry Robey. He knew that, once in a while, he would come across a hit that made it worth his while to buy four or five songs a week. Over the years he bought hundreds which he never sang, hoping to turn up among the dross an occasional nugget. In any case, he found it difficult to resist the pathetic appeal of the fellow who came up to him on a Saturday night and muttered, 'George, I'm broke for the Duke.* Will you buy a song?'

Some of his better songs came from the man who later, under the pen name of 'Sax Rohmer', created those best-selling adventures of the sinister Dr Fu Manchu. 'And Very Nice Too', one of Robey's famous numbers, was provided by another character, Joe Tabrar. Joe toured as a boy with the family troupe, and then, when his voice broke, turned his hand to plumbing and bell-hanging. He discovered a gift for creating songs and, in the course of sixty years, claimed to have written up to ten thousand songs. 'Wagner!' he would snort. 'I could put him to bed, an' he wouldn't know he'd been alive!' His earliest success was 'Ting, Ting, That's How the Bell Goes', though his best-known was certainly 'Daddy Wouldn't Buy Me a Bow-Wow'. For a time he published his songs from a shop near 'Poverty Corner' in the York Road, but then, careless and easy-going, reverted to his old habit of selling a number outright for a guinea or a couple of pints. 'Arthur Sullivan?' he used to say. 'I can do all that he could, an' more, while you wait – on the bit of old paper the trotters are wrapped in!' It is easy to forgive Joe his bragging since he could neither read nor could he write. His son, Fred Earle, also a songwriter, was a chip off the old block and noted for the verse:

> Where did you get that boko, Uncle,
> Is it your nose or a big carbuncle?
> Hide it under your handkerchief, or cover it with your hat.
> The driver will take it for a danger signal,
> Don't stick it out like that.

* 'Duke of Kent' = rent.

A Villa of Machicolated Stucco

It was not so much a tune Robey looked for as an idea that could be worked up and developed into a sketch. Although he began as a singer of comic songs he had also developed into an actor with a repertory of sketches as distinct from simple patter. 'Clarence, the Last of the Dandies' was one early example of these. Others included 'Prehistoric Man' which he owed to his photographic hobby. One morning, in the mood for a lark, he stripped to the waist, donned wig and whiskers, and asked a friend to take a snap of him – you never knew, the make-up might come in handy some time or other. When the print was developed he showed it to one of his songwriters. 'You look like a prehistoric man,' said the latter. 'I'll write a song on that!' With a doormat slung over his torso, a flaming auburn wig like a rising sun around his face, eyes gleaming ferociously, Prehistoric Man tramped over the stage whirling an immense club. He loved a sweet maiden called 'She of the Tireless Tongue' and did battle with his rival 'He of the Knotted Knees' whom he eventually clubbed and threw into the sea. As a scientific archaeologist, said that learned journal the *Pink 'Un*, Mr Robey knocked Huxley and Darwin into a cocked hat.

Other historical characters followed. William Shakespeare was given an immensely broad and towering forehead which improved on Droeshout. 'You people sometimes complain of a headache,' he observed. 'Marry come up, look at me, and conceive what I suffer when I get one!' Oliver Cromwell revealed that he had once been a brewer and was nicknamed 'Sweet Noll of Old Brewery'. 'Take away that bauble,' he ordered. 'Take it away and see how much you can get on it.' Richard the Lionheart, Queen Elizabeth, Sir Walter Raleigh and Guy Fawkes were to join him in Robey's historic portrait gallery. The most boisterous of the lot was Henry VIII who made his entry dressed in a perfect Holbein costume and bearing an umbrella. 'Have after me, wenches, I have a groat in my pouch!' he brayed. His matrimonial problems, he explained, arose purely out of the need for self-defence. Had not one of his wives been guilty of eating biscuits in bed? His brow darkened as the audience laughed. His beard bristled. 'Let there be mirth,' he said, raising a beringed hand, 'but let it be mirth *tempered with reserve*.'

More modern impressions were the theatrical landlady, a subject on which Robey was perforce an expert, and Daisy Dillwater the district nurse, a manic figure in voluminous black cape perched on an absurdly high bicycle. From time to time they were accompanied by the Chinese laundryman, the lost luggage man and the Mayor of Mudcumdyke. The Mayor, in top-hat, granny glasses and full ceremonial robes, was the sort of windbag who, in his welcome to a distinguished visitor, prosed on and on until the assembly wilted in tedium. 'You have no idea of the famous people who call upon me at the Town Hall,' he babbled. 'Only the other day Count Hong Kong called. I am also honoured with *repeated* visits from a Count Rendered.'

Robey's German music professor was a plump pedant with thick horn-rimmed glasses and a beetling moustache. His hair flowed down over the back of his collar, his cheeks were red and puffed up, a vast Lavallière cravat flopped over his chest. He came on to a stage littered with musical instruments of every description. Gruff, thick-voiced, he began a learned discourse inflected with a precise German accent. As he wandered around the stage he halted in front of the more unusual specimens and seemed about to play them. Expectation grew. Then he changed his mind and strolled on to another, even more complicated set of instruments. Again he paused while the audience looked on in anticipation. And again he moved off without making music. Finally he stopped in front of a humble triangle, gave it a few timid taps . . . and the act was over. The idea was not a new one. For years it had formed the staple of the clown Grock's famous number. Robey's achievement lay in the delicate humour, the kindly satire, the pathos, even, of his acting. As James Agate commented: 'It is often said that we have no great actors left. This is to overlook Mr Robey who is of the great order of laughter-makers who are immortal.'

In time he evolved a unique assembly of characters, many of them with a Dickensian flavour. Drawing on his observation of people seen in the streets, in buses, on trams, in shops, in theatres, he created the Caretaker, the Barrister (with many puns on the word 'bar'), the Lady Dresser, the Blacksmith, and a Lion Tamer who, despite his belligerent moustache and haughty stance, was terrified of animals, wild or otherwise. From an earlier age came the Roman Gladiator, or 'Frantic the Fearless'. Robey played these sketches at halls in London and at many others throughout the country. Unlike the modern television performer who is obliged to offer something new at every appearance in a voracious medium, Robey used the same basic material over weeks, months and years. Each word, each gesture was tested out against a wide variety of audiences. Why did a joke that brought laughter in Halifax fall flat in Exeter? Why did a phrase that Edinburgh heard in silence provoke hysteria at the New Cross Empire? He cut and trimmed accordingly, furbishing up his act until pauses were timed to the last second and nuances were exquisitely in place. For many months of the year he toured extensively, from Exeter to Glasgow, from Edinburgh to Southend. His sketch, 'The Theatrical Landlady', was based on close experience of the type. Sunday would find him arriving, fortified by the discount on his ticket from the Music-Hall Artists' Railway Association, at the provincial town where he was to play the following week. His first call, after depositing props at the theatre, would be on one of the landladies who took in 'theatricals'. They were a variable race. Some were motherly souls, other hardbitten tyrants.

'What will you have for breakfast?' a Brighton landlady once asked him.

'Can I have a little porridge, some scrambled eggs, a kidney or so, and a rasher or two of bacon?' he innocently enquired.

'No, you cannot,' she firmly replied. 'The only thing in the house is a kipper, and you can have that. This isn't the bloody Metropole!'

Certain landladies were much given to relating at great length the sorrows and disasters of their unhappy lives. Robey's technique in handling them was direct and effective. 'Mrs Plinge,'* he would say, 'I can see you have had better days. Now, sit down in that chair and tell me all about it. I am going to give you half an hour. In that half-hour you shall tell me everything and then – not another word for the remainder of the week.' Thus he ensured that he would be able to eat his dinner every night in peace.

The landladies who tested his ingenuity most were those who showed few scruples in their stewardship of guests' belongings.

* 'Walter Plinge' was the name traditionally given in the cast list when an actor doubled a part. The name and the custom are said to have originated in Sir Frank Benson's company. A charming examination of the legend is given by J. C. Trewin in his *Benson and the Bensonians*, Barrie and Rockliff, 1960.

One of them explained that he could safely store his 'little dainties' on the top shelf of a cupboard to which she gave him a private key. 'But mind,' she warned, 'there's some valuable old china of mine on that shelf, so please be careful.' Yet despite these precautions, over the week that followed certain items disappeared. On Monday morning a pot of strawberry jam was found to have vanished. Next day a tin of corned beef unaccountably went. Were there spirits in the house? On Saturday evening Robey tied up the 'valuable china' with skeins of white silk and fastened the ends to the lock so that if the cupboard were opened the landlady's heirlooms would be pulled down. He went to bed and sat up listening. At half past one in the morning he heard a sudden and terrible crash of broken china. Someone obviously possessed a duplicate key. Next day 'Ma' did not appear and sent her daughter in with the bill. There was no charge for 'breakages'.

The 'nosey-parker' Ma was another threat to quiet enjoyment of theatrical 'digs'. Robey learned how to circumvent her from a trick passed on to him by an old pro versed in the habits of landladies. He would unpack from his luggage six tins labelled mustard, pepper, salt, sugar, coffee and tea. These he put in a row on the table with lids off. Then he swooped madly around the room catching flies. Into each tin a live fly was deposited and the lid deftly clapped on. After arranging the tins ostentatiously he went out for a walk. On his return he would know instantly whether Ma was the nosey-parker type by checking the tins to see if any of the flies had been released.

One type of landlady defeated Robey, however, and she was the secret drinker. He noticed that the level in his bottle of whisky fell each day rather more quickly than could be explained. He marked it. Suspicion pointed to Ma. Having emptied the bottle, he duly filled it with what nurses would call a sample of his water. Even so, day by day, the level went on sinking. At the end of the week he was determined not to let the villainess get away with her larceny, and when she presented her bill he held up the bottle and remarked pleasantly, 'Oh, Ma, I've noticed that day by day my whisky seems to have been going.'

'Oh yes,' said she, 'of course, I've always been meaning to mention it. You see, I've been putting a couple of tablespoonfuls in your soup every day.'

A Villa of Machicolated Stucco

Many landladies kept a Visitors' Book wherein guests were invited to record their parting remarks. This was an opportunity for compliments that were, at the very least, double-edged. In one Visitors' Book he was about to sign Robey saw the verse:

> Friends may come and friends may go,
> And friendships often sever,
> But the soup Ma makes with a pennorth bones,
> Goes on for ever and ever!

Ma was puzzled. 'It doesn't seem very complimentary,' she remarked in her simple fashion. After turning over a few pages she came across an even more enigmatic inscription. Next to the date of her guest's departure was written the phrase: 'Quoth the Raven – '. Again she was perplexed. 'What does that mean?'

Like everyone else, Robey had no wish to hurt her feelings and murmured vaguely, 'It looks like a bit of a quotation.'

She shook her head. 'Nobody seems to understand it. And he was such a nice young man who wrote it!'

After spending a flea-infested night in a theatrical lodging the comedian Fred Leslie told his landlady what he thought of her, paid his bill and prepared to leave.

'Good heavens!' she said, 'I've never had any complaints before. Why, there isn't a single flea in the house.'

'No, you're quite right,' Leslie answered. 'They're all married with large families.' The same story is also attributed to H. J. Byron, the Victorian dramatist.

Yet although, in his long years of touring, Robey was to have more than his share of beds tenanted by fleas, of scrawny mutton, of gritty coffee and of tepid tea, on the whole he had affection for the theatrical landladies with whom he stayed. After all, he said, some of the guests they took in would have been enough to drive anyone crazy. Landladies had to put up with moonlight flits, tiresome eccentricities and frequently plain drunkenness. In the face of it all they were, he concluded, most often motherly souls and good friends. His attitude towards them was revealed when a friend of his gave a Manchester Ma tickets for his current show. 'Stalls? *Stalls?*' she said. '*Mr Robey* always gives me a box!'

Having set up in his 'diggings' he would, on Monday morning, go to the theatre for a band call. This was a rehearsal when he and other acts in the programme briefed the conductor on the necessary cues and went through their numbers with the band. The players had to be good sight-readers and able to tackle whatever was put before them. Some, especially in the Hippodromes and other big theatres, were very skilled. Others, in more remote places, were not, and the first house on Monday evening was awaited in some apprehension. The audience was often small and frequently made up of theatrical landladies and their families admitted on a free pass. Sometimes the manager would need to 'paper' the house by giving away tickets to people in the street. The second house on Monday was livelier since by then the audience had had the time to enjoy a few drinks. Each house, in fact, was different, and it was by adjusting to them throughout the week, by shaping material instantly to fit in with audience reaction, that Robey and his fellow performers learned how to perfect their act. And then, on the following Sunday, it was time for the train again. For some arcane reason there was nearly always a change at Crewe, a lugubrious outpost where it became a custom for members of the theatrical profession to meet and talk shop. Such was the origin, inspired by the freight handled at Crewe station on a Sunday morning, of the phrase 'Actors and fish'.

Appearances in London and extensive provincial tours were varied by pantomime at Christmas. Robey's Brighton debut marked the beginning of a long career in pantomime throughout the country. At a music-hall in Rochdale he was introduced to an impresario called Pitt Hardacre. 'I was anxious to meet the young man who had been described to me as "the finest singer of comic songs alive"', Hardacre recalled. 'So introductions followed and I said, without any preliminary chat, "Are you engaged for pantomime?"'

Robey said he was not.

'What are your terms – twelve shows a week, mind?'

'Twenty-five pounds a week,' replied the finest singer of comic songs alive.

'Done,' said Hardacre, scribbling the agreement on a visiting card and handing it over to him.

The pantomime was *Jack and Jill* at the Manchester Comedy Theatre in 1894. Robey made his appearance in the third act as a stowaway on board ship. 'Bring him out!' ordered the captain. Sailors carried in a bundle of rags, threw it on the stage and departed. A pause followed. Then, from out of the rags peered a face, mouth quizzical, eyebrows raised in thick dismay. It was Robey. 'The effect was electrical!' said Hardacre. 'You can't imagine how it brought the house down and from that moment George Robey became *the* pantomime which went on its successful run for thirteen weeks, twice daily – almost a record.'

Already engaged for pantomimes over the next two years in Birmingham and Liverpool, Robey was not available for another until 1896. Hardacre insisted on engaging him. Terms were mentioned.

'I'll sign the contract now,' said Robey. 'Put down any figure you like and I'll sign it.'

Hardacre noted sixty-five pounds a week.

'Oh, guv'nor, I don't want all that,' objected the modest comedian.

'Look here, George,' replied Hardacre, 'by that time you'll have got on and you'll be worth it. I don't want you to come to me as a friend for less money than you could get elsewhere, and I certainly don't want you to be disappointed at having refused better offers than mine.'

Hardacre was right. Before the end of the century Robey's fee as a pantomime dame had risen to a hundred pounds a week, a figure more than a hundred times greater than the then average wage.

[ii]

'Go on and say something'

Women liked Robey. Off stage, when not disfigured by grotesque make-up, his features were dignified and pleasant. Beneath the thick brows the eyes looked out direct and clear. The full-lipped mouth, which might have been austere, was relieved by the suspicion of a quirky smile. Though not tall, he had presence and a confident mien. He was brisk in dealing with men and

45

protective in his attitude towards women. They were impressed by his self-assurance and his positive manner. He had, besides, an air of success and fame that created an irresistible aura. Women enjoyed his company because he treated them with a courtesy not often seen in the rough-and-tumble world of the music-hall and because, most important of all, he made them laugh. Another recommendation was that he did not always try to seduce them. A chorus girl down on her luck would find herself taken out and ordered to buy a new dress at his expense for no other reason than that he wanted to cheer her up. One of his leading ladies treated herself to a diamond ring. She was told he did not like her in diamonds. They were too cold, he added, too cold. Next evening in the wings, about to go on, he gave her a small package. When she made her exit she opened the wrapping and found inside a set of brooch, earrings and necklace. The gift was inspired simply by his desire to see her in something 'warmer' than diamonds. They weren't 'you' he told her.

The girls who passed through his existence left few traces. He did not talk about them and kept his private life to himself. If an enquirer probed further he would advise him to go out front – a seat in the stalls would, he said, tell him all there was to know about George Robey. One girl did, however, make a profound impression on him. She was Ethel Haydon, an Australian actress from Melbourne who had made her first London appearance in 1895. Now, three years later, at the age of twenty-one, she was playing in *The Circus Girl* at the Gaiety, a theatre noted for musical comedy and beautiful women. Her features were neat, small, a shade wistful, and she had a pretty voice. Robey married her on 29th April, 1898, at the church of St Clement Danes in the Strand. His best man was Pitt Hardacre and the congregation included numerous music-hall friends, among them Alec Hurley, Marie Lloyd's lover and, briefly, her husband. The organ was played by Leslie Stuart, perhaps the most accomplished of light music composers at the time. He had, in fact, begun his career as a church organist, and a glance at the polished harmonies of 'Little Dolly Daydream' or 'The Lily of Laguna' show that he benefited from a more solid technical training than most composers for the music-hall. *Floradora* and 'The Soldiers of the Queen' confirmed his mastery, and when he played for Robey's wedding he had reached the peak of his fame. Twenty years later, having spent, with the aid of hangers-on, all the money his lovely music brought in, he was destitute.

There followed a wedding reception at the Hotel Cecil. A honeymoon on the Continent was announced. It did not take place. That night, wedded even more indissolubly to his profession, Robey made his scheduled appearance at the Canterbury music-hall. So, from the very start, Mrs Robey learned that his career was really the most important thing in his life. After his turn at the Canterbury some admirers, having heard of his marriage, presented him with a cradle containing a doll. He withdrew, embarrassed, but the audience insisted on recalling him until he came on stage again bearing the doll, reluctantly, in his arms.

Mrs Robey, née Haydon, completed her engagement at the Gaiety and for a short while featured with her husband on music-hall programmes and in pantomime. Two years later, in 1900, a son was born. He was christened Edward George after his father. A few years later he was joined by a sister, Eileen. At the time the Robeys were living in St John's Wood at Circus Road. They soon afterwards moved to a bigger house at 83 Finchley Road, where the children lived in a nursery on the top floor and, as was the custom then, were brought out and displayed to their parents on formal occasions. The boy Edward, even at an early age, showed that he had inherited his father's mouth and eyebrows. Robey liked to take him round to the first houses of the music-halls where he was appearing. They went in a hired car driven by a chauffeur, the boy upright and solemn, Robey wearing heavy overcoat and full make-up. On Guy Fawkes day the adoring father mounted spectacular firework displays and entertained his son's schoolmates to a lavish tea.

Although the stage ruled his existence he was, in some ways, unusually domesticated. He enjoyed slicing up beans, a chore he carried out with impressive accuracy, and peeling and cutting oranges for marmalade. Carpentry had always attracted him, and now that he had a household of his own he liked to potter about knocking up shelves and tables. He was not, on the face of it, a difficult man to live with, so long as his little peculiarities were respected. The doors of the room in which he sat always had to be open. In the evening he kept every light throughout the house burning brightly. Yet he hated wasting matches and was shocked if more than one were used to light two cigarettes. On the other hand he was negligent over money, would leave clothes stuffed with notes in his dressing-room, and sometimes forgot to cash cheques until it was almost too late. Like Queen Mary, he loathed the telephone. If anyone rang him up he would ask his wife or an assistant to speak on his behalf.

Domesticity, pleasant though he found it, provided no more than brief interludes in a life almost wholly devoted to the theatre. The only night when he could expect to be at home was on Sunday, and even then he was often away on tour, journeying from one provincial date to another. His bookings extended four or five years into the future, and managers knew they could rely on him. 'I consider you a very steady young man,' wrote one of them. In a profession not noted for sobriety or punctiliousness, Robey made it a point of honour to fulfil each engagement scrupulously.

The scope for his activities widened considerably in the early 1900s. This was an era when the large music-hall circuits were being constructed by a handful of shrewd entrepreneurs. From Scotland came Edward Moss, who, at the age of seventeen, had toured a diorama of the Franco-Prussian War. As manager, stage director and accompanist, he handled it so well that the profits enabled him to open a variety theatre in Greenock. He travelled south and opened up a string of Empire Theatres which became, as he proudly put it, 'features of importance in nearly all the cities of Great Britain'. In London he founded, with a capital of two million pounds, the organisation he christened Moss Empires. A site in Cranbourn Street was prepared and on it rose the flamboyant structure of the London Hippodrome. As a precaution he also included in the complex a number of flats, offices and shops to provide revenue should the theatre takings be sluggish. They never were. With its vast stage, a tank capable of holding a hundred thousand gallons of water, and an immense gleaming cage that rose from the depths to display lions and tigers, the Hippodrome entertained six thousand people each day and contributed largely to the twelve and a half per cent dividend paid on Moss Empire shares. Moss was a smooth, exquisitely dressed figure with a compelling eye and a heavy moustache of the sort Lord Kitchener wore. Substantial contributions to charity bought him respectability and the inevitable knighthood. A brief biography of him noted that

> privately, his ambition has been in the direction of leading the life of a country gentleman; bought an estate marching with the Dalmeny property of Lord Rosebery . . . his charities and public spirit are well-nigh boundless, and when in 1905 he received the honour of knighthood from His Majesty, it was felt that the distinction was well and worthily bestowed; is a Justice of the Peace and Deputy Lieutenant for Midlothian.

We may rely upon the authenticity of this statement since it was written by Sir Edward himself.

One of his partners was Richard Thornton, a rough gruff diamond who played the violin. Moss played the piano, and the two men soon found that their musical talents were complemented by a money-making flair. Thornton usually got what he wanted, even in private life. Fascinated by the wooden houses he saw on a holiday in Norway, he had one built in his garden, moved into it and rented out his house to a tenant. When neighbours objected that he was violating their privacy he bought the freehold of all the houses that made up the terrace, evicted those who had protested, and lived on tranquilly in his back garden.

Another partner with Moss and Thornton was, for a time, Oswald Stoll. At the age of fourteen he had helped his mother run a theatre in Liverpool. He was, as he described himself in the third person, 'always a very studious boy, and devoted himself principally to the clerical side of the business . . . Many curious anecdotes are told of his experiences in those early days, when he more than once offered artistes £3 or £4 a week in place of the £20 or £25 usually commanded by them . . .' The 'artistes' who, in later years, suffered from the impresario's steely bargaining powers, must have smiled ruefully if they ever read those bland words. Moss Empires quickly proved too small to accommodate Stoll's vaulting ambition, and he set up on his own a chain of theatres that included the London Alhambra and the Hippodromes in Manchester and Bristol. As time went on he added, by way of insurance, what then were known as 'picture theatres'.

His greatest achievement was the Coliseum which he opened

in 1904. To do this he cleared, at enormous expense, what had once been a Dickensian slum and put in its place a mammoth building with a triple stage that revolved at twenty miles an hour and a foyer that welcomed patrons amid a profusion of marble pillars and glossy mosaics. A bust of his adored mother glowered over the main entrance. When the theatre was shut the bust was veiled by a curtain which, at opening time, duly parted to reveal the features of the woman who aroused the warmest human feeling Stoll is ever known to have exhibited. There were large refreshment rooms and orchestras and lifts to take people up to the grand tier and the balcony. You could send telegrams from the Coliseum, dictate messages, buy sweets and stamps, ring up for a District Messenger, and even post letters in a special pillar-box. Stoll was very proud of the royal box and a carriage on rails which he had installed to convey Their Majesties from the royal entrance and spare them the fatigue of walking. At its inauguration King Edward VII stepped into the luxuriously upholstered cabin and deposited himself among its plush coverings. The electric button was pressed. Nothing happened. The button was pressed again, still without avail. A gentle heave was essayed. The carriage remained implacably motionless. Stoll squirmed in horror. The King, beaming, got out and quoted a current Marie Lloyd song, 'What, What, What?' Then, declaring that he might as well walk, he stepped forward manfully.

Stoll introduced the régime of four performances daily at twelve o'clock, three, six and nine, as well as the idea of booking seats in advance. He used the revolving stage to show the Derby and Roman chariot races. His programmes bore the proud device: '*Pro bono publico*'. When these spectacular productions failed to draw, he caused a sensation by inviting people like Sarah Bernhardt and Ellen Terry to play one-act pieces between jugglers and comedians on the same bill. Although Stoll learned from his mistakes, he did not like other people to mention them. An employee once dared draw his attention to an error he had made. 'As long as you continue to work for me,' Stoll answered, 'don't ever tell me I am wrong. You can go now, but if you offend again, you will be dismissed.' Some time later the employee was obliged to tell Stoll that he had committed yet another oversight. 'I warned you before not to dispute my orders,' came the reply.

'Go down to the cashier and draw three months' salary in lieu of notice.'

In his top-hat and black frock-coat Stoll looked like a bank manager, an undertaker, anything rather than a music-hall tycoon. His humourless eye glittered coldly behind pince-nez, and his face resembled that of an expressionless pug. He did not smoke or drink, and would patiently sit through auditions and first nights, blank-faced, unsmiling, while everyone around him roared with laughter at the antics of the comedians. His all-devouring preoccupation was balance sheets, ledgers, figures. There is a story that he once came across a beggar selling matches in the gutter.

'Buy a box of matches, guv,' said the beggar.

'Why?' enquired Stoll icily.

'Well, I've only taken fourpence all day.'

'Really,' answered Stoll, beginning to show interest. 'Tell me, how does that compare with the corresponding week last year?'

From the lofty tower of the Coliseum in St Martin's Lane there flashed a revolving globe that lit up the night sky as a symbol of Stoll's achievement. He regarded his creation not as a mere music-hall but as a temple of art, a place where the values of hearth and home were to be celebrated with wholesome entertainment for all the family. 'COARSENESS, VULGARITY, ETC, IS NOT ALLOWED' threatened a warning line to be found prominently displayed among instructions to performers about band-parts, bill matter and the fireproofing of props. In the dressing-rooms were hung notices which read: 'Please do not use any strong language here. Coarseness and vulgarity are not allowed in the Coliseum. Gentlemen of the chorus are not allowed to take their whips to the dressing-room.' Stoll himself was ever-present, alert to every detail in the running of what he called his 'colossal palace of amusement, the Coliseum'. Should anyone dare to throw the butt-end of a cigar or cigarette on to the carpet, he would bend down and pick it up, frigidly enquiring at the same time whether the culprit would have done such a thing in his own home.

Despite his austerity, however, he once wrote a song for Vesta Tilley called 'Mary and John' which became one of her most popular items. Shakespearean scholarship attracted him, too, and at one time he planned to found a Shakespearean theatre. He also published books of much complexity on financial matters and once bought up a newspaper to propagate his views about economic affairs. Another of his interests was philosophy. As he pointed out in an autobiographical entry he supplied for a book of reference: 'Mr Stoll is an earnest student of Herbert Spencer, and the author of a book, *The Grand Survival*, in which he argues that immortality may ultimately be obtained on earth, through enlightened direction and a wider application of the principle of heredity, in short, by due regard to natural law.'

Heredity fascinated him. An associate complained of gout and said that it seemed unjust since he was a teetotaller.

'Oh,' said Stoll. 'That was the sins of the fathers. Your ancestors were probably four-bottle men. It's atavism. Do you know what that is?'

The other confessed that he did not.

'Atavism,' Stoll went on, 'and that is the true explanation of the Virgin Birth.'

Startled, the sufferer from gout was anxious to learn precisely why. But more urgent matters supervened, and he never heard from Stoll the reason for this unnerving theory.

Stoll and Moss between them controlled some forty theatres in London and the provinces. The existence of these large circuits, together with smaller ones, meant that performers enjoyed the convenience of booking for weeks ahead instead of taking single dates, and could rely on continuous work over long periods. Rivalry between the various organisations also ensured that salaries were competitive. In the early 1900s Robey was earning at least a hundred and fifty pounds a week. He had equal billing with Dan Leno and was signing contracts for engagements that lasted as long as three months at a time. In Manchester, in Liverpool, in Birmingham, in Edinburgh, he would dash on stage and rebuke the audience with a gorgon-like glare: 'Desist! I am not here as a source of public flippancy. I am surprised at *you*, Ager-ness!' The laughter pealed and rolled as, with reproving aspect, he cunningly timed and manipulated it. Max Beerbohm never forgot that air of comic outrage and loved to imitate it. His biographer recalled:

He began to sing from the repertory of one of the favourite music-hall comedians of his youth, George Robey. When

A Villa of Machicolated Stucco

Max sang, he leaned far forward in his chair, his expression immensely solemn. Assuming an air of honest indignation and injured innocence, he sang, in full Cockney but with unimpaired diction. Max's eyebrows became very active; they twitched in Pecksniffian outrage. The burden of the song was that Robey had been accused by malevolent spirits of playing Peeping Tom at the bathing machines at Brighton. When Max came to the end of the song, his voice and eyebrows cried out in gruesomely lascivious protest:

> Did I go near the bathing machine?
> *Naow!*

Max had adored Robey. He smiled as he spoke of Robey's impersonation, in a sketch, of Queen Berengaria; evidently she was putting on the royal raiment in a bathing machine, and the sudden startled expression, half reluctant, half experimental, indicated that the Queen was herself suspicious that George Robey was lurking somewhere in the vicinity.

Another critic, W. A. Darlington, paid Robey an even greater tribute. He saw him first at Manchester Hippodrome immediately after a painful encounter with the dentist. No anaesthetist was available and an abscessed root had been extracted without gas. Darlington joined a family party at the Hippodrome in such agony that he could barely see the stage. Robey came on last. At the end of the turn, twenty minutes later, Darlington had long since forgotten his aching gum. The pain was completely gone. Some time later he told Robey of his experience. It must have been the finest compliment the comedian ever received. 'I never saw a man more pleased,' commented Darlington afterwards.

It was in Manchester, too, that Robey confirmed his reputation as a pantomime dame. Neville Cardus judged him to be the greatest of all those English comic actors who created an unforgettable range of pantomime dames. After half a century he still remembered the scene in Mother Goose's cottage when the landlord arrived demanding rent that was three weeks overdue and threatening eviction. 'At this moment George Robey appeared, bland, with kindly recognition, wiping imaginary soapsuds from the hands on the apron. "Ah, there you are, landlord," said Mother

Goose in Robey's fruitiest voice, "*there* you are – such a lot wants doing in the house!" '

Later there was an interlude during which Robey held the stage alone for half an hour in front of a backdrop that sometimes bulged unexpectedly while, behind, an elaborate change of scenery was put together. For his purpose Robey created an imaginary next-door neighbour called Mrs Moggeridge who, like Sairy Gamp's Mrs Harris, was real though never seen.

Robey came on from the side of the stage in a condition of agitation, fingers twitching, nose sniffing. He cast glances to the direction whence he had entered; they were glances poignant with contumely and injured pride. Simmering a little, but still on the boil, he folded arms, gave another toss of his head sideways and said, simply but obliquely, 'Mrs Moggeridge!' Nothing more than her name to begin with, but the intonation, with a descent of pitch at 'ridge', was contemptuous. Then he bent to us over the footlights, and in a sudden hysteria of ridicule, stated (or rather he conveyed) this information: 'Fairy Queen in a Christmas pantomime!' After another snort and a pause he added, in a voice pitched to a deeper note of irony, 'Ha!'

Satisfaction and triumph here became evident in Robey's eyes and gestures; but suddenly he stiffened, and the neck was thrust again towards Mrs Moggeridge's garden wall, whence obviously some Parthian thrust had been aimed. 'And what of it?' asked Robey, the voice rising in mingled menace, disdain and clear conscience. 'What of it?' (Pronounced 'What arvert.')

Speculation sought in vain to deduce the nature of Mrs Moggeridge's innuendo that it should have compelled this final bridling and this unanswerable fiat. Enough to say that after the pronouncement of it Mrs Moggeridge was heard no more. It is hard to believe we did not actually hear her or see her; there wasn't never indeed 'no such a person'; it was a conjuration of comic art.

In other pantomimes as well he displayed his acting ability:

Robey was a master of tantrums, or in other circumstances, of spasms [wrote Cardus]. In *Jack and the Beanstalk*, when Jack returned home with beans for the sale of the cow, Robey as the Dame achieved an awe-inspiring expression of twitching incredulity, woe and mortification, all evenly blended. He (or she) hurled the beans through the window, and at once the stalk began to grow upward. Robey caught sight of it out of the corner of his eyes as he was suffering another wave of distress. And he began to giggle, to experience hysteria . . . but no words can describe this masterpiece of comic acting. It was done by imaginative absorption into a character and a scene; and here is the difference between the old great pantomime comedians of my youth and the comedians of today, who get their laughs by the things they say and are not funny in themselves, and are certainly not actors.

A scene in *Mother Goose* might show Robey as the dame, floating, for no good reason at all, with his son in a balloon over Manchester. Robey inspected the land below and pointed out Rumford Street, a place where actors used to rent 'digs' while in Manchester. 'And there's Rumford Street,' said Robey, 'looking more elegant than it really is. Well, we seem to have been floating about here for a considerable time without any tangible result.'

'Tangible, Mother, what's tangible?' asked the boy.

Robey snorted. 'Do you mean to tell me that you don't know what tangible is? I've sent you to Eton and Harrow, to Oxford and Cambridge, and you don't know what tangible is?'

'No, Mother.'

'Well, tangible is . . . why, those little oranges, of course.'

The joke is but a mild one. Robey's delivery of it, brows a-tremble, eyes blazing with helpful erudition, voice full of triumph, made it seem the wittiest of epigrams.

It all ended with the grandest of grand finales. As Cardus remembered:

The convention of pantomime persisted that the dame and her son should begin poor and end wealthy. All the good characters, in fact, shared ample fortune as a reward of virtue; and during the last scene they came before us most opulently garbed – Robey's magnificence was like a fantastic dream or apotheosis of a riotously lunatic Schiaparelli. The lesser male luminaries of the show, Idle Jack or Tinbad the Tailor, would wear terrific check suits with huge buttons of gold, and their choice in walking sticks was *rococo*. Nobody was harshly treated in this last of all the pantomime's consummations of glory and electricity; even the Demon King received a burst of applause when he appeared, apparently a reformed character, in morning-coat and grey topper. And the children crowed their delight as the Cat came on for his share of the general recognition and acclamation, wearing a fur coat most likely.

Then the final chorus and the last ruthless descent of the curtain. Nothing left but to return to the world, to find oneself again in the streets outside, where life had been going on just the same on a winter day; it was dark now, with the gas-lamps burning, and when we have entered in realms of gold it has been afternoon and broad daylight . . . I knew the pantomime word-and-music-perfect, with all the patter and action, so that on any afternoon or evening wherever I happened to be – probably walking the Manchester streets – I could follow any performance and live in it by proxy, so to say. As I mumbled to myself and imitated Robey's eyebrows and bulging cheeks, I was probably regarded by passers-by as an idiot boy.*

Robey only appeared once in a London pantomime. He spent his Christmases, up to forty of them, in big provincial cities where as Dame Trot, Widow Twankey or Mrs Crusoe, hair tied in a bun, feet jammed into elastic-sided boots, he ruled over a large following of enthusiastic admirers like the young Neville Cardus. Sometimes he shared his glory, as at Newcastle in 1907, when he was partnered by George Formby senior as Idle Jack. Formby's son was the toothy comedian with the ukulele who confirmed the family tradition and, thanks to the films he made, achieved a celebrity greater than his father's. Yet in his time Formby senior regularly played the top of the bill. He wore a too-small bowler, a jacket as shapeless as a sack and boots on the wrong feet. As a boy he worked in an iron foundry where the toxic fumes he inhaled damaged his lungs permanently to give him a chronic, racking cough. This he used with droll effect – 'coughing better tonight,' he would croak in

* As quoted in Benny Green, *The Last Empires* (see Bibliography).

an aside to the orchestra, 'coughing summat champion' – and his spluttering delivery as Idle Jack provided a raucous counterpoint to Robey's mellifluous tones. While the audience shrieked with laughter he would be struggling for breath in the wings. Some years later, still in pantomime, his cough became so violent that he burst a blood vessel and died at the age of forty-four.

Another father of a more famous son with whom Robey acted in pantomime was Fred Emney. The latter's progeny took the shape of that immensely fat comic actor with the beery voice, scarlet cheeks, monocle and cigar. Fred senior had a sketch called 'A Sister to Assist 'Er' which itself grew out of a pantomime number. Equally riotous were 'The Arrival of a Rival' and 'The Plumbers', in which latter Fred as a plumber and his mate called a fortnight after the event to repair a burst water pipe with tools designed for mending a gas leak. In an exchange of roles he played the dame in *Sinbad the Sailor* at Birmingham and Robey for once took the part of Sinbad's father. A critic wrote:

> Was there ever a finer combination than these two great comedians who always left me with the feeling that Herbert Tree ought to produce *Romeo and Juliet* with Emney as the Nurse and Robey as Peter? They had one scene, 'a domestic interior', when Robey was a huge collier in a hugger suit who sat still and silent for ten minutes while Emney as the wife nagged, nagged, nagged. George Robey said nothing, did nothing but look at his nails with murderous intensity as he clenched and unclenched his hands. Only that and nothing more. It was perfect, incomparable, as an exhibition of comedy.

Even the stage-hands crowded round to watch the scene each night. Not long afterwards, in *Cinderella*, poor Fred slipped on soapsuds left by a slapstick whitewashing episode and fell heavily. The audience laughed and applauded what seemed to be a very comic gag. He died, as a result of the injury, a week later. He was fifty-one.

Sometimes, in the days before they had a growing family, Robey's wife would appear with him. At Liverpool, in *Jack and the Beanstalk*, 'Miss Ethel Haydon makes a very pretty Princess,' observed the *Stage*. When he was Justus Badd in *Red Riding Hood* at the Manchester Comedy Theatre, she was playing the Spirit of Youth in *Babes in the Wood* at the Royal in the same city. Pantomime gave him the opportunity to develop not only his technique but also sketches that he later featured independently. As the Queen in *Queen of Hearts*, sitting by mistake on his crown and shouting, 'Assistance! Methinks I have sat upon a hedgehog', or declaring, 'Then there's Mrs Simkins, the swank! Many's the squeeze she's had of my blue bag on washing day,' he introduced an episode which later became a permanent item in his repertory.

The chief honours fall to Mr George Robey who has scarcely a rival in his own particular line [remarked the *Birmingham Post*]. Fun is fast and furious when he is on the stage and never more so than in the little scene when he has the stage to himself and gives a song sketch, 'The Dresser', in which he impersonates one of the humbler employees of the music-hall who has made up her mind to go on the stage herself. But there are very few scenes in which he is not about or is not one of the most prominent figures, and many of the scenes owe much of their go to his inimitable manner.

Pantomime taught him many things. One was how to deal with an emergency when, as inevitably happened, a technical hitch delayed the show. In Manchester one year the scenery became immovably stuck. The stage-hands pushed and sweated and cursed while the seconds turned into minutes and the drop curtain stared blankly at a restive audience. 'Go on and say something!' Robey was told. Wearing the rags of a stowaway in *Jack and Jill*, he went on 'trembling inwardly'. He paused and looked at the audience with a stern gaze while trying desperately to think of something to say. 'I have just been dining with the Lord Mayor!' he announced pompously, articulating the first remark that came into his head. The incongruity of the tatters he wore produced a big laugh which gave him time to think up more material. He went through the menu enumerating the *hors d'oeuvres*, pronounced 'horse dovers' because they came from Kent, and the *entrées*, so named, he explained, because they were served on trays. From time to time he threw anxious glances at the wings to check if the scenery had yet been heaved into place. When at last he saw that it was ready, he came off to warm applause. He knew now that henceforward he need have no fear of drying up and that, if he did, he would be able to improvise. On another occasion, in *Jack and the Beanstalk*, the magic seeds refused to grow and the canvas clouds remained immobile. An impatient audience began to sing 'Wait Till the Clouds Roll By'. Robey stepped into the breach. He brandished a long stick, and, in the manner of a magic lantern lecturer about to display his next picture, informed them: 'We have just reached Cairo.'

In Manchester one year he hired an elephant as publicity for himself and the pantomime. It called each day at his lodgings and bore him, at a majestic pace, to the theatre for the performance. As the hour of his departure approached a crowd of sightseers gathered to watch the elephant amble up to the house, lift her trunk and rap briskly on the front door. She was an amiable and intelligent animal. He became very fond of her, and she, he liked to think, of him. After a matinée one day he stopped at a public house and slid off for a drink. She guessed his intention and decided to get in first by going ahead and mounting the steps up to the entrance. Once there she stuck in the doorway. Those inside tried to push her out while those outside attempted to pull her back. Neither succeeded. A helpful passer-by suggested removing the door. Another proposed demolishing the hotel. Eventually, having inspected the bar in vain for signs of her favourite barley water drink, she solved the impasse and backed downwards into the street with a flick of her tail. There she waited peaceably, a living advertisement for her rider inside.

[iii]

Humpsti-Bumpsti by Royal Command

Robey lived in an age when social distinction was founded on what used to be known as gentle birth combined with money. Today, of course, money alone is quite enough, and it is even fashionable to mention, if not to boast of, lowly origins. In those days, however, the social classes were sharply defined. When the writer Thomas Hardy became famous he took care to draw a veil over the line of humble ancestors who preceded him. Robey had a deep respect for authority and for the established social order. He enjoyed invitations to the houses of the aristocracy and loved to be seen dining with millionaires. When he gave interviews early in his career he often dropped hints that his background had been somewhat grander than Kennington might have provided. One of his favourite fantasies was that he had received a university education, at, he suggested, Cambridge. The legend became so well rooted that Max Beerbohm, writing about the new generation of music-hall entertainers, could refer to 'The most gifted and popular of these younger men, Mr George Robey (who was educated at Cambridge and is, in my opinion, one of the few distinguished men produced by Cambridge within recent years) . . .' Max, of course, was an Oxford man and could not resist the temptation of a feline gibe.

For all his harmless snobbery it must be admitted that Robey cherished intellectual and artistic pursuits of a quality unusual in his profession. An entry he wrote for the 1908 edition of *The Green Room Book* details his career to date and adds that he is 'a talented painter, having exhibited at Royal Academy and Royal Institute of Painters in Water Colours; one of his hobbies is the study of ancient Egyptian history and antiquities; is also much interested in the geography and exploration of Africa.' While it might be possible to find another music-hall personality who executed watercolours in his spare time, one doubts if there were any, apart from the metaphysical Oswald Stoll, who devoted themselves to Egyptian antiquities. Robey also took up comparative religion.

> I think if I had to declare myself definitely attached to any religion I should say that the Parsee has got hold of the right idea. I think we are all idolaters. Every religion has an idol which it worships – an ideal expressed in some tangible form.
>
> My idol is the sun. That to me is the supreme symbol of creative intelligence. Look upon the sun and rejoice. That is my creed. Then sometimes, even when I am enjoying immense success, I wake up and find myself asking, 'What is it all for?' Most of us reach that stage. It is the starting point of all philosophy.

A Villa of Machicolated Stucco

> When I find myself throwing out that self-challenge I do not go to gay places and mix with frivolous people and try to escape the searching question. I go into the fields. I look at the flowers and then look up at the sun. And in that way I am reminded that we are little human beings, and our little conceits and worries do not matter much.*

This was the voice of the bright inquisitive pupil at the dame's school who asked his own questions and tried to supply his own answers.

If the Zoroastrian sun worshipper never succeeded in discovering the secret of life's mystery, he at least found a degree of satisfaction in beautiful objets d'art. As soon as he had money to spend he began indulging the love of antiques which his elderly aunt had inspired him with as a boy. By 1913 the inventory he kept recorded that he owned eight hundred and seventy-five items acquired for a total outlay of over nine thousand pounds. From childhood onwards he collected Zulu war weapons, assegais and knobkerries. 'I am an ardent collector of antiquities and have a pretty good collection of weapons of various descriptions,' he told an interviewer. Unable to resist a flight of fantasy, he added, tongue in cheek, 'I learnt to throw an assegai at a very early age, when we lived out in South Africa.'

His eye for old china was sharpened by years of prowling round junk shops in the provincial cities when he went on tour. In Glasgow near the theatre he happened to pass the shop-window of a painter and decorator. In it was displayed a small yellow bottle which had been put in to 'dress' the otherwise bare expanse. He recognised it immediately as a very fine piece of Chinese Imperial yellow. Later that evening he asked the stage carpenter if he knew the owner of the shop. 'Oh, yes, I know the bloke well,' came the answer. Robey, agog, told him about the bottle and asked him if he would try to buy it on his behalf. He added, confidentially, that he would go up to twenty pounds for it.

The following day his emissary handed over the bottle with a broad smile.

* A taxi-driver who found he had Bertrand Russell as a passenger turned to him and said, 'What's it all about, then, Earl Russell?' Recounting the story afterwards, the taxi-driver added, 'And do you know, he couldn't tell me!'

In a daze, Robey asked, 'How much did you give for it?'

The carpenter's grin widened still further. 'Half-a-crown!' he replied, 'and he stood me a drink with it.'

Robey gave him a handsome reward for his honesty.

Many of his choicest pieces were acquired like this through a combination of luck and alertness. He soon learned the ways of the auction room. Often he bought a 'lot' which, it would turn out, a dealer who arrived late had wanted. Often the dealer would buy it from him at much more than the price he had paid. The moral Robey drew was always to be punctual at auctions. He once picked up a lovely set of old Persian armour in excellent condition. It cost him two pounds. Afterwards a man came up to him and remarked sadly, 'I remember my father buying that set and how proud he was of it. He paid eighty pounds for it.' The lesson on this occasion, Robey decided, was that relatives should not go to the auctions of family belongings. The experience could be distressing.

Robey must have made his mistakes too, though with typical breeziness he did not mention them. In any case, he was more often right than wrong, and the evidence was shown by the hundreds of items that filled his drawing-rooms and gave them the appearance of a private museum. When he lived in Kensington, at a house in Victoria Road, he at last found a place big enough to honour his large collection. Two rooms were made into one by taking down a wall and replacing it with lofty pillars through which could be seen still more glass-fronted cabinets and display stands. Beside a tiger-skin carpet on the floor stood a netsuke table holding a massive oriental vase. On other tables and shelves were K'ang Hsi porcelain in blue and white, and whole sets of *famille rose* and *famille verte*. He was especially proud of half a dozen eighteenth-century Quan Yin pieces of porcelain. They represented the Goddess of Mercy:

> . . . with her wonderfully calm expression and her feet on the clouds and waves. The story is that she will not enter the celestial region so long as there is one sorrowful heart on earth [he wrote]. Poor dear! If the legend be true, she is in for a long stay here below. There is a look in her face that reminds one of certain portraits of Queen Victoria – a fact which the Chinese people

recognised, and which caused them to revere the Queen in quite a special way. But the lines and the whole composition of the figure and its draperies make it as lovely a work of oriental art as any I have ever seen.

The things he amassed over a period of forty years dedicated to collecting would have aroused the envy of the Goncourt brothers, those pioneers of the vogue for oriental art in Europe. Sets of Japanese armour stood next to Buddhistic horses and intricately chased spears. Here were swords and daggers glittering on the wall. There were Japanese bronzes, blue and white figurines in robes with dragons picked out in underglaze blue, and ivory bowls and sweetmeat dishes. One of his loveliest possessions was a series of miniature paintings which depicted the Shah Jehan and his favourite wife Mumtaz Mahal. They culminated in a picture of the Taj Mahal, the white marble tomb he built for her. As the collection grew so the demand for space became more and more imperious. With a certain feeling of relief he allowed the Birmingham Art Gallery to house two hundred of his pieces on loan for several years.

It was, perhaps, the Chinese element that gave him most pleasure. 'I find Chinese porcelain very restful and helpful to concentration,' he said. 'It never irritates. The French, even in their greatest period of art, imported Chinese porcelain and mounted it with ormolu, and they were good judges of beauty.' He took a friend to see the loan exhibition at the Birmingham Art Gallery. The friend said little until they parted. 'Well, old man,' he finally observed, 'that's a better way of spending money than backing horses.'

His collecting mania embraced postage stamps also. Over the years he put together an impressive general collection. But insurance was expensive, his son did not show much interest, and he sold the lot. To appease the collector's instinct that continued to nag him, he started specialising in Portuguese stamps. While he was playing a Birmingham pantomime a little boy called at the stage door and sent in a small collection asking if he would like to buy. At first it looked like any schoolboy's effort with all the stamps stuck down and not worth much more than half a crown. Suddenly, among the dross, Robey spotted a British Guiana stamp then worth the large sum of eight hundred pounds. He sent for the boy, told him he did not really want the book, but, if he liked, would offer him five pounds for it. This was intended as an opening move in bargaining. To his surprise the boy held out his hand for the book. 'If it's worth a fiver to you it's worth more than a fiver to me! Good afternoon!' Robey never saw him again. That boy, he thought to himself, had developed early.

Other items he collected more or less as a joke. One of them he claimed to pick up at a rate of between six and fourteen a week, although he never kept them.

> They are always charming to look at – very quiet while standing up, but disposed to be demonstrative when seated. When I hit upon a particularly fine one, I photograph it. One afternoon in Winnipeg I came across one which looked a quarter of a mile long – in a photograph I have it seems to stretch away with infinity. As a rule, however, I collect them without seeing them. The finest specimens I often miss altogether through having gone in by a back door.

The sought-after objects were theatre queues.

Collecting was equalled among Robey's lifelong passions only by sport. He was immensely proud of his constitution, of the perfect teeth he kept to the end of his life, of the strong chest and excellent breath control that enabled him night after night to dominate noisy audiences and be heard in the remotest corner of the theatre. This, he claimed, he owed to his good health and his love of athletics, of football, rugby, cricket, boxing, sprinting, tennis, even golf. During his early years in Birmingham he had been a member of the Handsworth Rugby Football Club. Cricket he had played ever since his return from Germany as a boy. Between afternoon matinées and evening performances as Dame Trot in pantomime at the Birmingham Prince of Wales Theatre, he succeeded in winning the hundred yards' race and the two hundred and twenty with no difficulty at all. Each day of his life he spent an hour or more in practice.

Often, unfortunately for him, spectators thought he was being funny, and his most elaborate manoeuvres were received as bids for laughter. Once he played soccer for Millwall and was disappointed to find his performance greeted humorously. 'Robey takes his

football seriously,' reported a journalist, 'but his professional reputation debars the public from regarding his efforts as any other than
farcical. That is the penalty he pays for his fame.' It was not always
Robey, however, who provided light relief. He remembered in
particular a match against Cambridge University:

> I dribbled half-way up the field and knocked the ball in under
> the goalkeeper's nose. He didn't seem to mind and threw the
> ball back into the centre of the field with an air of superiority
> that galled me. Later I said to him, 'It may be easy to throw
> the ball out of the goal but it's damned difficult to kick it in.'
>
> 'It's not,' he said as cool as a cucumber. 'I did it twice this
> week into my own goal!'

For years, with the aid of the Football Association, he organised
annually a charity cup match. In these an international team
was challenged by an eleven drawn from the town where he
was currently appearing. Receipts were boosted by autographed
pictures of himself which he sold to the fans. One afternoon his
sales reached four thousand. At the end he always presented a cup
to the winning side and, to the players, gold medals. While at the
Glasgow Empire he played a match in Ibrox Park. The goalkeeper,
reaching wildly for the ball, instead hit Robey and bowled him
over, much to the spectators' amusement. Despite intense pain
he finished the game and went on that night for his turn. A
medical student in the audience came round and examined him.
He diagnosed two broken ribs.

Once, as a cricketer, Robey played against W. G. Grace. He was
entertained, and impressed, by the cunning tricks the old hand used
to disconcert his opponents, and he thought he would follow his
example. Robey, as batsman, hit the ball with the very tip of the
bat and saw it fly up and up and up. The wicket-keeper lazily
prepared to catch this easy one. As the ball was about to drop into
his wide-open hands Robey shouted, 'My usual luck! Snapped at
the wicket again!' The wicket-keeper laughed and missed his catch.
Sometimes Robey was unintentionally funny. Elected a member
of the MCC in 1905, he arrived at the anniversary dinner wearing
a frock-coat instead of tails. His fellow members were too kind,
or polite, to mention this social gaffe.

In later life he took up golf. He did not play so much for the game as for the exercise. When he played football or rugby he was boldly competitive. Where golf was concerned he aimed only to keep moving. On arrival at the course with his partner he would summon the caddies and address them.

Before we start this game I wish you to understand that my friend and I are two elderly gentlemen who are here for exercise. There's to be no dawdling, and no looking for lost balls. If my friend hits one into a furze-bush, or I slice one into a ditch, you are to put down another at once, so that we can carry on without interruption. If at any time you observe anything wrong with my stance, please keep it to yourself. I'm not out for advice, I'm out for a quick walk, with club-strokes thrown in. I'm too old to learn anything about this game. You understand? No tuition. No looking for lost balls. Just a good quick round!

So he began, enjoyed himself thoroughly, and returned to the clubhouse feeling, as he put it, 'years younger'.

As dear to him as his antique collections was a cricket bat dating from 1902. It bore the signatures of close on two hundred celebrated players of the time and included those by members of the Australian eleven who came to England that year. Most of them he had bowled at in the nets at Lords – and hit their wickets, although, as he carefully added when making the boast, to hit the wicket of a great cricketer in the nets was something quite different from hitting it in the course of a proper match. Among the silver-framed photographs which famous personalities had signed and given him, the watercolours he had painted and the oil portraits of himself by leading artists, the 1902 bat held a place of honour.

Zoroastrian, collector of Chinese porcelain, connoisseur of Japanese antiquities, all-round sportsman, he did not fit into the traditional mould of red-nosed comic. This tended to disconcert others in the business, if not antagonise them. One north-country comedian expressed himself succinctly. 'Robey?' he said. 'A toffee-nosed twot if ever there was one.' In other ways, too, Robey stood slightly apart from his profession. Although privately a generous man, ever ready to help friends down on their luck, a giver of handsome tips and a strenuous worker on behalf of charity, he believed there was an irreducible minority of

Englishmen who did not deserve help because they disliked work and preferred to live on other people. The English attitude, he complained, looked on failure as being as praiseworthy as success. 'The man who gets to the top is regarded almost as a usurper,' he said. 'The man who gets kicked down is regarded almost as a saint. It is never suggested that both men are in places where they deserve to be. In other words, we are witnessing an elaborately organised deification of inefficiency.' Given these opinions, he could not be expected to support with zeal the trade union movement which had begun to flower in the music-hall.

The Variety Artists' Federation was born in 1906 out of meetings between the Music-Hall Artists Railway Association and benevolent organisations such as the Water Rats and the Terriers. Almost immediately it was plunged into dispute with managements over various practices which had for some time caused ill feeling. The chief issues involved the employers' insistence that matinées should be played without extra payment in addition to the normal two shows a night, and the habit, common among big circuits, of transferring performers at very short notice to halls often inconveniently far away. Early in 1907 the disagreement burst into war. Musicians, stage-hands and front-of-house staff came out on strike, as well as performers, and twenty-two London theatres were closed down as a result. A prominent leader of the strike was Marie Lloyd. As she explained, she was one of the stars and could dictate her own terms. 'We are fighting not for ourselves but for the poorer members of the profession, earning from thirty shillings to three pounds per week . . .' Managements retaliated at first by making up programmes of obscure, unsuccessful or retired artistes. At one theatre a troupe of performing elephants lumbered through the pickets and was greeted by 'Our Marie' with the cheerful cry of 'Blacklegs!' A not very good performer called Belle Elmore was held up by the pickets who roared 'Stop her!' 'Don't be daft,' shouted Marie Lloyd. 'Let her in and she'll empty the theatre.'*

---

* This was by no means the most unpleasant episode in the sad life of Belle Elmore. Her husband was Dr Crippen. In 1910 he disposed of her in a cellar and attended a Water Rats dinner dance with a younger woman decked out in Belle's jewellery.

Management was nonplussed. Oswald Stoll protested at what he called the irresponsibility of the performers. He hoped, he added venomously, that Marie Lloyd's statements were inspired more by her talent for dramatic effect than for the truth. However much he and other managers raged against the strike, they were for the time being powerless. Leaflets signed by Marie Lloyd and others carried a little verse:

Twinkle, twinkle, brilliant star!
Oh, I wonder where you are.
With the VAF so bright,
You will *not* show here tonight.

When managements of 'blacked' theatres asked leading stars to appear they were irritated still more by facetious excuses. 'I am learning a new cornet solo,' replied Little Tich, an enthusiastic member of the trade union. 'Cannot tear myself away.' Marie Lloyd sent the message: 'I am busy putting a few flounces on my dress so I cannot appear tonight.' By now representatives of theatrical employees and musicians had joined with the Variety Artists Federation to form the National Alliance of Music-Hall Artists. Exercising their right under the Trade Dispute Act passed by the newly elected Liberal government, two thousand five hundred pickets forced the closure of major halls. After some five weeks the managements agreed to the appointment of an official arbitrator. His findings, enshrined in the Music-Hall Award of 1907, generally favoured the employees and produced the basis of a standard contract to be used in future.

In all this excitement Robey held aloof. Only towards the end of the episode, when a settlement was about to be reached, did his name appear in newspaper accounts of the bargaining. His character was a paradoxical blend of independence and a deferential attitude to the hierarchy. While his stage persona exuded disrespect, anarchy even, he prided himself, as a professional, on always filling an engagement and on never disappointing the management who employed him. He needed no trade union to protect his interests and took little part in the activities of the Variety Artists Federation. While Marie Lloyd was directing strike pickets he busied himself organising a charity match for Chelsea Football Club to benefit the widow of a player who had just died. He himself played so well at the match that afterwards the team signed him on as an amateur. When, later, it reached the First Division, he would remark blandly in the course of his stage act: 'I just wanted to make sure that Chelsea stay in the First Division.'

Provincial tours carried him up and down the country, a new town each week involving what was known in the profession as 'a long jump' from, say, Blackpool to Exeter, from Glasgow to Brighton. Every Sunday between May and October he was shuttling along the main railway lines. As fresh at the end of a long journey as he had been at the start, he was never tired, never bored. His stamina was inexhaustible, uncanny. In Birmingham his annual pantomime appearances had made him a favourite. Despite his popularity there, however, he once offended the Watch Committee, a body run by the local council, where vigilance over questions of morality earned the place a nickname as 'the holy city'. Just before one of his visits a ballet company had disturbed the committee by showing too much bare leg and was ordered to cover up with tights. When Robey came on to play his act with, as usual, nothing more elaborate than a plain backdrop and a piano, the audience noticed something strange about the setting. Then they realised what it was. The legs of the piano were modestly swathed in football socks bearing Aston Villa colours. The Watch Committee summoned him to appear before them and imposed a fine as punishment for his contempt of the council.

Echoes of the music-hall strike in 1907 continued to resound as late as 1912 when the first Music-Hall Command Performance was given. The idea came originally from Edward Moss, who pointed out that royalty, in particular Edward VII, had often visited music-halls privately, and that artistes had played at functions held in royal homes. To date, however, no public recognition such as the 'legitimate' theatre already received had been accorded to the music-hall. The notion was approved in exalted circles and King George V prepared himself for another evening of dutiful boredom. The three men responsible for organising the event were Moss, Oswald Stoll and Walter de Frece who between them controlled a large part of the music-hall world. All of them had suffered annoyance during the strike three years ago. They were determined that those who crossed them on that occasion would suffer for their misdemeanours by exclusion from the list of performers. Many old scores were settled, many antagonisms aired and many jealousies ventilated. Stoll resolved that his enemy Marie Lloyd would be kept off the stage.

The venue chosen was the Palace Theatre, that rambling pile at Cambridge Circus built by Richard d'Oyly Carte in the vain hope of creating a home for English opera. It soon failed and was turned into a music-hall under the direction of old Charles Morton who made its revival the concluding achievement of his long and ingenious life. Here Pavlova danced and Bernhardt acted under a proscenium arch of Italian marble. A grand staircase columned with green marble and gilt capitals led up to the royal circle and provided a setting fit for King George V and his Queen. Morton's assistant was Alfred Butt, an accountant whom he recruited from Harrods. When Morton died Butt took over and, at the time of the Command Performance, ran not only the Palace but also a number of other big theatres and circuits. He, inevitably, was to join the band of impresario knights, in his case as a reward for having directed rationing at the Ministry of Food during the 1914–18 war. As Sir Alfred Butt he took up racing, shooting and country life pursuits appropriate to the Conservative Member of Parliament which he later became.

On the night of 1st July, 1912, the Palace auditorium bloomed with the scent of thousand upon thousands of red roses. Wisteria trailed over the electric lights. Baskets of carnations dangled from the royal box. The theatre, said Conan Doyle who happened to be there, was 'a floral fairyland'. All the gentlemen wore white tie and tails, and their ladies sparkled in diamond aigrettes. The King with a white flower in the buttonhole of his evening dress, the Queen wearing a new creation of pale lavender, advanced at the head of a numerous procession which included the royal family down to its remotest kin. Schleswig-Holsteins proliferated, Tecks teemed and Battenbergs abounded.

The bill put before them opened with 'Humpsti-Bumpsti' by the two eccentrics Pipifax and Hanlo. Things could only improve after this, which they did with the clamorous arrival of Harry Tate. In private life a thoughtful, even lugubrious man, on stage he created an atmosphere of joyous confusion and muddle. ('You realise Harry's only being himself?' his wife told a friend. 'At home, everything he does goes wrong! If he takes a photograph and he goes in the dark-room – something explodes!') He wore an immense property moustache which jumped, jiggled and shot up vertically in sympathy with action that grew more and more frantic.

In his 'Running An Office' sketch he made an alert irruption demanding, 'Any letters?'

'No, sir.'

'Then we must write some. Get some ink in the office – I can't keep writing with chalk, it's absurd.' Finding a parcel on the table he picked it up and demanded, 'What's this?'

'Don't know, sir,' replied the office-boy.

Harry banged it back on the table. 'Send it to Milan!'

In 'Fishing' he threw some ground bait by mistake at an innocent bystander, an individual with a red nose, drooping moustache and bowler hat several sizes too small for him. The man was furious. Tate said he'd mistaken him for a swan.

'Do I look like a swan?' enquired the man angrily.

'Not now you've turned around you don't,' bellowed Tate, eyes goggling with surprise.

Some of the catch-phrases he invented have become a part of the language. 'How's your father?' he would splutter when someone asked him a question to which he did not have the answer. 'I *don't* think!' was his way of expressing ironic disbelief. When, in 'Motoring', his car repeatedly failed to start up, he vociferated 'Good-by-ee!', a word that became the title of a popular song in the 1914–18 war. This was the sketch he presented at the Command Performance. Everything, of course, went wrong, bits fell off and the starter never worked. Exchanges were heard such as, 'Excuse me, could you tell me the way to Plymouth?'

'Plymouth? I don't know – I've never been abroad.'

The curtain went down on clouds of blue smoke and a machine roaring, panting but still not moving.

For the thirteenth of the twenty-five turns a blazing spotlight illuminated a tiny figure who pranced in wearing boots almost as long as he was tall. Little Tich, so named because as a baby he resembled the claimant in the famous Tichborne case, was only four and a half feet high. The sixteenth child of a seventy-seven-year-old father, he had five fingers and a thumb to each hand.

When his own son was born the doctor patted him on the shoulder and said, 'It's all right, my little man, you've got a baby brother.' All these disabilities he turned to brilliant artistic use. His dance wearing the inordinately long boots was a marvel of eccentricity. Sometimes he appeared to knock himself out with them. Then he would anchor the tips near the footlights and balance himself on them precariously, swaying back and forth with a beatific grin on his face. In Paris, where Toulouse Lautrec painted him and the government awarded him the Légion d'Honneur, he was even more popular than in London. At the Folies Bergère dressed as a lady, a Duchess at least, he would gargle in Franglais, '*Je m'appelle Clarice* – I'm an admiral's daughter – I've just come from the court ball – oh, my success! – what a *succès fou* – *beaucoup de succès* – very nice!'

But, this being a Command Performance, he avoided impersonations of grand ladies which might have offended a distinguished audience, and drew instead on his grotesque boot dance and a repertory of sketches, imbued with mercurial impishness, as waiter, gamekeeper, dandy, 'soldier bold' or 'bolger sold'.

> Would you like me to tell you the story, sir, of the
>   horribleness of war?
> Well, it was half-past six in the morning, sir,
>   when the clock struck five to four.
> There was something went wrong with the works, sir,
>   but the enemy wanted a fight.
> Why, they lay with our right on their left, sir,
>   and we lay with our left on their right.
> And I wanted a Turkish Bath, sir, but the Colonel
>   said, 'Lad, there's no hope,
> For the drummer boy's drunk all the water and the
>   bugler's swallowed the soap.'

As well as prefiguring surrealism in his act, Little Tich off stage was, like Robey, a painter in oils and watercolours, a photographer and a keen reader. 'A knowledge of the best in literature,' he said, 'can help even a comedian.' He was a waiter who could not balance a glass on a tray, a gamekeeper who failed appallingly to keep game, a dandy who persistently lost his hat, a soldier who never fought a war in his life, and a ballet dancer whose tumbles were far more breathtaking than the most elaborate pirouettes. His bill matter always included a line which was the inspiration of a Shakespearean-minded journalist: 'One Tich of Nature Makes the Whole World Grin.'

More comedy was offered by Wilkie Bard, a bald-headed loon with a black spot ornamenting each eyebrow. He, too, had a repertory of characters including a Turkish Bath attendant, a bookshop salesman, a night watchman and a park keeper. A favourite tongue-twister of his was 'She sells sea shells on the sea shore'. He was reported, also, to have invented the 'interrupted turn'. His finest creations were pantomime dames and a group of female impersonations that included both charwomen and Duchesses. At the Royal Command Performance he flounced on heavily bewigged, wearing a pinny and carrying a bucket of soapsuds. Kneeling down, he traced a circle on the stage with his wet cloth preliminary to cleaning the floor. Then suddenly, having risen again to his feet, he approached the footlights and delivered in a sweet contralto voice the waltz that had become his signature tune:

> I want to sing in opera, if I could have my choice,
> I want to sing in opera, I've got that kind of voice,
> Signor Caruso told me I ought to do so,
> So that's why I want to sing in opera,
> Sing-in-op-op-opera-a-a.

Glamour was represented by Vesta Tilley. Years ago, when she and Oswald Stoll were young, the cold-hearted impresario cherished an unlikely affection for her. In those days, when his writing paper bore the proud heading 'Oswald Stoll: Song Writer', he had written half a dozen songs for her. Then, to his annoyance, she married the rival impresario Walter de Frece. Still, he remained fond of her and insisted that she do her 'Algie, the Piccadilly Johnnie' at the Royal Command Performance. An amusing irony ruled that Stoll, the monument of respectability, the puritanical dictator, should have sponsored an act that offended Queen Mary. It was observed that, as Vesta Tilley swaggered around the stage twirling her gold-knobbed cane, both Queen Mary and the Grand

Duchess George of Russia studied their programmes intently to avoid looking at the stage. A newspaper reported '. . . there was an expression on Queen Mary's face that she does not approve of actresses appearing in masculine clothes.'

The grand finale was 'Variety's Garden Party' in which over a hundred performers appeared, including those for whom there had been no room on the main bill. They all joined in singing the National Anthem led by a burly baritone called Harry Claff who wore a suit of glittering armour in his persona as 'The White Knight'. Only Little Tich was absent, he having been overcome with a bad attack of nerves after contributing his turn. Robey did his Mayor of Mudcumdyke number clad in venerable top-hat, moth-eaten robes and granny glasses. Around his neck dangled what could only have been a convict's ball and chain, and from his hand there dropped a limp umbrella. He, of course, was not at all put off his stroke by the august presences before him and, if anything, tended to emphasise the vulgar familiarity of his act. This, at a time when the royal family, not yet a long-running soap opera, inspired exhibitions by their subjects of rank sycophancy, was thought incredibly daring by his fellow comedians. 'Some of them,' he wrote later, 'were apparently rather overwhelmed by the solemnity of the moment, and did not quite do themselves justice.' He added, diplomatically, 'Everybody, too, was sorry that two of the best artists of the day, Marie Lloyd and Albert Chevalier, were not in the bill.'

Chevalier was so annoyed by his exclusion that he took a whole-page advertisement in a trade paper to assuage his wounded feelings and quoted prominently a remark by the *Morning Post*: 'Historically as well as artistically his omission is a blunder of the first magnitude.' Marie Lloyd engineered a more effective riposte. Well aware of Stoll's animosity towards her, she irritated him by appearing at the London Pavilion on the night of the Royal Command Performance. There, only a few minutes' walk away down Shaftesbury Avenue, she delighted a full house packed with her loyal admirers. Large posters outside described her as 'The Queen of Comediennes'. And a further headline declared: 'Every Performance Given by Marie Lloyd is a Command Performance by order of the British Public.'

CHAPTER III

. . . THE ONLY GIRL IN THE WORLD

[i]

The Bing Boys Are Here

Historians of the music-hall tend to believe that its decline began
in 1912, the year when its stars paraded by command of George
V. Royal recognition implied, to a certain extent, respectability,
which was something music-hall had never known before. The
spirit of the street became dulled and the spontaneous expression of low life inhibited. Albert Chevalier and Pearly Queens
and Cockney costermongers took on a slightly out-of-date look.
Within two years a cataclysmic war changed the conditions that
gave birth to the music-hall and radically altered the society which
had encouraged its growth.

Already, too, unmistakable signs predicted the emergence of
rivals. As far back as 1896, tucked away in music-hall programmes
down among what were termed 'the wines and spirits' – the minor
turns, that is, jumbled between drink advertisements – were
references to a novelty variously termed the Bioscope, the Biograph,
the Animatograph or the Moving Pictures. In that year, at the
Alhambra, a film of the Derby showed the Prince of Wales's horse
Persimmon winning the race. It was made by R. W. Paul, an
electrical engineer whose experiments with Edison's Kinetoscope
enabled him to take films which could be shown on a screen
ten feet high. Without permission he stationed himself near the
Derby winning post and fervently cranked his machine as the
horses pounded by. At first he turned the handle at a rate of
twelve pictures a second. By the end he was taking over two
thousand a minute. The film was hastily developed and hung up

to dry in great loops. Next evening it was shown, all minute and three-quarters of it, at the Alhambra together with views of the Paris express arriving at Calais, the streets of Westminster, the swings and roundabouts of Hampstead Heath and 'A Rough Sea at Ramsgate'. It is pleasant to report that, unlike many other pioneers of science, Paul earned a material reward. When he died in 1940 he bequeathed two hundred thousand pounds to research.

An early witness of the New Biograph wrote:

> There's a rattling, and a shattering, and there are sparks, and there are showers of quivering snow-flakes always falling, and amid these appear children fighting in bed, a house on fire, with inmates saved by the arrival of fire-engines, which, at some interval, are followed by war-ships pitching about at sea, sailors running up riggings and disappearing into space, trains at full speed coming directly at you, and never getting there, but jumping out of the picture into outer darkness, where the audience is, and then, the trains having vanished, all the country takes it into its head to follow as hard as ever it can, rocks, mountains, trees, towns, gateways, castles, rivers, landscapes, bridges, platforms, telegraph poles, all whirling and squirling and racing against one another, as if to see which will get to the audience first, and then suddenly – all disappear into space!! Phew! we breathe again!! But, O, heads!, O, brandies and sodas!

So that everyone might see these wonders in full, a respectful notice advised: 'The Management politely request that where necessary ladies will remove their hats in order not to obstruct the view of those sitting behind.'

The first 'Animatograph' Robey saw was a film of traffic in Piccadilly viewed through a storm of white spots and wiggling gashes. It made his head ache, he said, for two days afterwards. He remembered another film about a trip to the moon where little pot-bellied Martians chased one another up and down mountains and then blew up. Things had improved by 1897 when he watched the Animatograph of Queen Victoria's Diamond Jubilee procession, a major production advertising no less than '22,000 pictures' of the event. In 1900 he made a film himself. It was called *The Rats* and has long since disappeared.

Given his interest in photography and his taste for innovation it was natural for him to be attracted by the new medium. Two short films he made in 1913 were entitled *And Very Nice Too* and *Good Queen Bess*. In the following year he shot *George Robey Turns Anarchist*, where, to judge from a still, the bald-headed, curate-like figure uses a soup tureen to conceal his bomb in a fashionable restaurant. He also, encouraged by Oswald Stoll who had already founded his Stoll Picture Corporation in a leafy corner of Cricklewood, experimented with an early sound system whereby the performer mimed his song on film to the accompaniment of a prerecorded wax disc. Yet conditions remained primitive. For a scene where Robey was supposed to jump on and off a bus the producer avoided the expense of renting a vehicle by obliging him to pounce on and dismount from whatever coach happened to drive along the street.

The content of the vanished films he made in those years may only be surmised. What, for example, was the story of *£66.13.4d for Every Man, Woman and Child*? All we know of *The Anti-Frivolity League* is that he played its flamboyant chairman. Even less familiar are *Blood Tells* and *George Robey's Day Off*. *Doing His Bit*, which dates from 1917, doubtless had some sort of patriotic flavour, and *One Arabian Night* was probably an excursion into fantasy. *The Rest Cure*, a major five-reel production by Stoll, is better documented since it was taken from a book by Robey. (Later we shall be looking at Robey's books, which included *My Rest Cure*.) It told how the comedian, exhausted by the effort of being funny, deserted London for the peace of a village deep in the country. There, however, his arrival was greeted by a brass band and the whole population turning out to greet him. More receptions followed, and parties and engagements. Goggled at by admirers while trying to dine quietly at the local inn, pursued even into his bedroom, he at last gave up his attempted rest cure and went back, thankfully, to the relative tranquillity of London. In *Widow Twankee*, another Stoll production, he played the title role. *Don Quixote* found him essaying the part of Sancho Panza. This would-be spectacular version of the classic story was filmed in the exotic surroundings of Keswick. While Robey sat waiting in a car for the pitiless rain to stop, a man was stationed on a hill nearby with instructions to wave a flag as soon as he spotted the patch of blue in the sky which might encourage a resumption of shooting. 'I seem to remember days, weeks, months, years spent in that motor car without a sign of the flag,' Robey commented bleakly. 'Nothing but rain and clouds.'

Other films he made, *The Barrister*, for example, and *Prehistoric Man*, were direct transpositions of his music-hall numbers. The camera was set up, he took his place, the film began running, and he went straight into his routine exactly as if he had been on the stage of the Alhambra. But there was no audience, no warmth of human reaction, and only the chill eye of the camera to watch him as he faithfully reproduced his act in the décor of a cold and unsympathetic studio. What had been conceived wholly in terms of one medium did not transfer happily into another. By contrast the American film industry, now a successful and dominant influence, had started from scratch, building up its technique as it went along and creating its own stars. No English film director really knew how to handle Robey for the best advantage in films. The easiest solution was to pay him the large fee of seven hundred pounds a week and to hope that his name on the posters would do the rest. It did not.

In the summer of 1914 he was sharing the top of the bill at the Palladium with Little Tich. The London Pavilion housed Marie Lloyd and Harry Tate, while at the Palace a new revue featured Elsie Janis. Mrs Patrick Campbell thrilled audiences with a shocked delight as she blurted out each evening the notorious swear word in *Pygmalion*. Oscar Asche and Lily Brayton starred in a gorgeous production of *Kismet*. An early play by Somerset Maugham, *The Land of Promise*, filled the Duke of York's, and at the St James's, Oscar Wilde having been respectably dead for a suitable period of years, *An Ideal Husband* was revived. Elsewhere Marie Tempest plied her gossamer craft in another of her airy trifles and Charles Hawtrey ambled his polished way through an elegant comedy. During that last London summer before the war an income tax collector drowned himself in the Thames. 'It was remorse,' commented a journalist. 'He realised at last that it was a shame to take the money.'

When Robey cleaned off his make-up and came out of the Palladium on the evening of Tuesday, 4th August, he felt too restless to go home immediately. At midnight, when England's ultimatum to

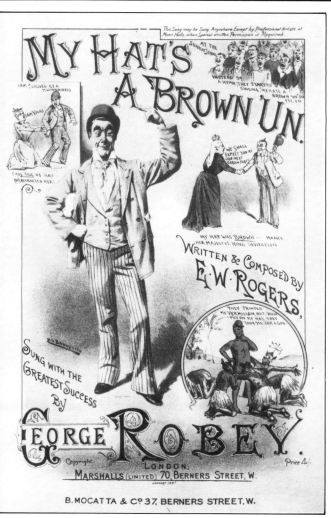

Robey's earliest hit, 'My Hat's A Brown 'Un' (left), was too successful - the riotous East End audience drowned out all the other acts with their noisy singing of the chorus. Robey (bottom left) and his first wife, the Australian actress Ethel Haydon, around 1908, with daughter Eileen and son Edward, later a prosecuting counsel with seventy-four death sentences to his credit and subsequently a well-known Stipendiary Magistrate at Marlborough Street police court. Robey in 1906 (bottom right), the top hat soon to be replaced with the battered bowler someone stuck on his head as a dressing-room joke.

Robey as pantomime dame in 1909 (above left) and as
Queen of Hearts (bottom left): 'Assistance! Methinks I
have sat on a hedgehog.' Robey's Shakespeare (above
right) disclosed that *Measure for Measure* and *As You Like
It* took their titles from two favourite pubs. 'Spoof'
caricatures Robey (bottom right) in 1906.

Over the years Robey bought hundreds of songs outright for a pound or less apiece, few of them as successful as 'The Simple Pimple' (left). He was always ready to give his fans a self-caricature which he drew on the spot (bottom left). As the German Music Professor (bottom right), he blended comedy with pathos.

Although aloof and self-contained off-stage, Robey had many friends among his fellow performers. Wilkie Bard (far left) portrayed a gallery of eccentric females, among them the would-be prima donna: 'I want to sing in op-op-opera-a-a'. Billy Bennett (left) was the essence of surreal bawdiness, billed as 'Almost A Gentleman'. Dan Leno (bottom left), who died insane at the age of forty-three, was the greatest of all pantomime dames, here as Mother Goose. Marie Lloyd (bottom right), pert and diminutive, said there were only two stars she would share top billing with: Little Tich and George Robey. Vesta Tilley (top right) specialised in male impersonations as Burlington Bertie and Piccadilly Johnnie. Little Tich (bottom right), who danced in boots almost as long as he was tall, was painted by Toulouse-Lautrec and awarded the Légion d'Honneur in France, where he was even more popular than in England.

Robey as Lucifer Bing in the long-running 1916 hit *The Bing Boys Are Here* (left), which featured 'If You Were The Only Girl in The World', and with his co-star Violet Loraine (bottom right). As Bold Ben Blister intent on his embroidery with Charlotte Leigh in *Jolly Roger*, 1933 (bottom left). Low comedians traditionally aspire to play Shakespeare — so did Robey, and he achieved his ambition as a memorable Falstaff in 1935 (right).

HIS MAJESTY'S

THEATRE, HAYMARKET, S.W. 1

Proprietor . JOSEPH BENSON

TELEPHONE. WHITEHALL 6606

Licensed by the Lord Chamberlain to THOMAS H. BOSTOCK

Evenings at 8.15   Matinees Wednesday, Thursday & Saturday at 2.30

"THE PERFECT FALSTAFF."—Daily Sketch.

STAGE PHOTO CO.

GEORGE ROBEY

IN

KING HENRY IV. Part I.

"THE MERRIEST JEST IN LONDON."— Daily Mail.

J. MILES & CO., LTD., Printers. 68-70, Wardour Street. W

Robey kept on working until the end, still touring valiantly in his seventies as the bill (right) testifies. How did he keep going so long? 'Early piety!' he once quipped. The true reason was a strong constitution, all-round sportsmanship and a fierce determination to stay on top.

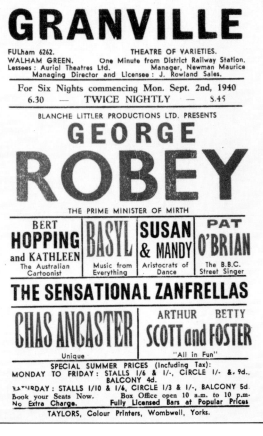

GRANVILLE

THEATRE OF VARIETIES.
FULham 6262.
WALHAM GREEN. One Minute from District Railway Station.
Lessees : Auriol Theatres Ltd. Manager, Newman Maurice
Managing Director and Licensee : J. Rowland Sales.

For Six Nights commencing Mon. Sept. 2nd, 1940
6.30 — TWICE NIGHTLY — 8.45

BLANCHE LITTLER PRODUCTIONS LTD. PRESENTS

GEORGE
ROBEY
THE PRIME MINISTER OF MIRTH

| BERT HOPPING and KATHLEEN The Australian Cartoonist | BASYL Music from Everything | SUSAN & MANDY Aristocrats of Dance | PAT O'BRIAN The B.B.C. Street Singer |

THE SENSATIONAL ZANFRELLAS

| CHAS ANCASTER Unique | ARTHUR BETTY SCOTT and FOSTER "All in Fun" |

SPECIAL SUMMER PRICES (Including Tax):
MONDAY TO FRIDAY : STALLS 1/6 & 1/-, CIRCLE 1/- & 9d., BALCONY 4d.
SATURDAY : STALLS 1/10 & 1/6, CIRCLE 1/3 & 1/-, BALCONY 5d.
Book your Seats Now. Box Office open 10 a.m. to 10 p.m.
No Extra Charge. Fully Licensed Bars at Popular Prices.

TAYLORS, Colour Printers, Wombwell, Yorks.

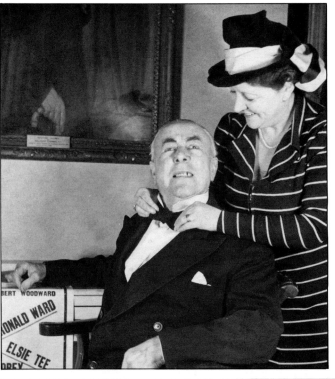

At the age of eighty-four, 'Sir' George, he gladly submits to being tidied up by his second wife Blanche Littler (left). She was his manager, secretary, accountant, nurse and most fervent admirer. One day, passing a statue of Queen Victoria, Blanche protested; "*She* shouldn't be up there, that's where my George ought to be. He was more popular than she was!"

Germany expired, he strolled down Whitehall. Government offices were lit up and crowds cheered and waved flags. He went up the Mall and saw, on the balcony of Buckingham Palace, the King and Queen in evening dress. The crowd serenaded them with the National Anthem. Volleys of raucous cheers broke out and hats were flung into the air. Did all those exuberant young people really believe, Robey thought to himself, that within a week or two Berlin would have fallen to the Allies? At the age of forty-five he himself was too old for active service. He did his best. To a recruiting officer he declared; 'If I swear I am only twenty-five, and if I show that I can run round the parade-ground four times at racing speed, will you take me?'

'No,' came the answer.

The Special Constabulary were willing to have him though, and he was issued with a badge, a whistle, a baton and a sentry box. After playing his music-hall engagements he would report for duty at two o'clock in the morning and sign off at six, more than ready for bed. His job was to track down suspicious lights and help out during air-raids. Once a zeppelin dropped bombs around Lincoln's Inn and a crowd gathered to view the damage. One of the spectators, a respectable but incautious little man, exclaimed in anguish, 'Ach! Dat is not de vay to vin this var!' A policeman emerged and led him away to internment.

Special Constable Robey later joined the Volunteer Motor Transport Corps and became an honorary lieutenant. At the main London railway stations he would welcome trainloads of soldiers going out to the Front or returning from the hell of Mons and Passchendaele. He also met and helped the women – mothers, sisters, wives – who accompanied wounded and dying men. 'They are among the countless memories,' he later said, 'that make me want to kill a man who gasses in a general way about the splendid thing war is.'

When the all-night buffet at Waterloo began to run out of money for its charitable work he promised to raise five thousand pounds. Next day he asked Oswald Stoll for the loan of the Coliseum so that he could organise a concert. 'Certainly!' said Stoll. 'Get it up at once! The theatre's yours for Sunday week: tack an auction on to the concert, get the interest of all the friends you can, and good luck to you.' At this, the first of many charitable functions he sponsored, money rolled in. Well-wishers would buy something and then put it back into the auction again. A popular lot was a bulldog called Peggie, mascot of HMS *Iron Duke*. She was put up for sale, sold, returned, and re-sold again and again before going home to her battleship. Even so, there were those who doubted Robey's patriotism. Among them was one of those women who went about proffering a white feather to men they deemed cowards for not having joined the army. In Regent Street on his way to the Alhambra, he was confronted by a virago who, pushing the white feather into his buttonhole, demanded, 'Young man, why are you not at the Front?'

Robey seized her, cried out loudly and attracted a crowd who recognised him. A policeman arrived who also found his face familiar. 'Officer,' Robey declaimed with mock heroics, 'long ago my mother made me promise that I would never speak to a woman who accosted me in Regent Street. This woman has accosted me. Officer, do your duty!'

Blind soldiers, sick children, shipwrecked sailors, the limbless, were just a few of the people for whom Robey raised many thousands of pounds. His skill was praised by James Barrie in an essay he entitled 'Mr Robey, auctioneer'. Those who had already come under his spell, wrote Barrie,

> mutter plaintively, 'All purses abandon, ye who enter here' . . . In the play he oozes across the footlights till he fills the house, but as an auctioneer he at once takes grip of you and shakes you till the cheque-book falls out . . . He indicates with a nod that you have just saved yourself, and immediately fixes some other bidder, and in a very short time (but it seems a long time to you) that other bidder adds another fifty. You sit back in your seat feeling that all is well with the world, when you suddenly discover that Mr Robey is looking in your direction again, with his hand to his ear. He evidently thinks you said something. You feel that he is mistaken, but he is so nice about it that a desire to make conversation overcomes you . . . The upshot is that, let us say, a five-pound note is knocked down to you for two hundred and fifty pounds.

The ruthless auctioneer then sold off Barrie's manuscript itself at the high figure of six hundred and fifty pounds. The bidder handed it back and Robey sold it again and again until it raised a total of eight thousand pounds. When he wanted to use it as a preface to his autobiography he had to rely on a copy – though he was repaid by a gilt-edged Barrie anecdote involving the actor Dennis Eadie at rehearsal. 'Eadie,' the dramatist is supposed to have said, 'I want you to indicate by your expression that you have a younger brother who was born in Shropshire.'

One of Robey's more terrifying wartime duties was to escort Sarah Bernhardt on her appearances at the Coliseum. When Oswald Stoll first invited her there in 1910, she, fearful of being exposed in the company of clowns and seals playing trumpets, is said to have telegraphed the brusque reply, 'After monkeys not.' He reassured her that she would not be sandwiched between comedians and performing dogs. Moreover, he offered her the vast fee of a thousand pounds a week under a contract by which she received equal instalments each night, before curtain-rise, in gold. By 1916 the indomitable woman was in her seventies and had only one leg, so she played her patriotic sketches sitting in a chair. Madame Bernhardt on the music-hall stage was no less electrifying than Madame Bernhardt in the theatre, and Stoll congratulated himself on the piece of showmanship that had filled his large auditorium. Each evening Robey hovered in the wings to take her back to the best dressing-room which had been lavishly redecorated for her exclusive use. A solemn procession marched in her train as, accompanied by Robey and her manager, Madame Bernhardt regained the dressing-room. Once she passed two chorus girls who had just come off and were chattering together. '*Bonsoir, Mesdemoiselles,*' said she graciously. '*Comment ça va?*' Rather taken aback, they rallied and chirruped, 'Rumbo! And you?' A rich red Turkey carpet was always laid down for her along the eighty feet that lay between the stage and her dressing-room door. Somebody once asked the manager of the Coliseum if this was done because the stage was dirty. Outraged, he insisted that it was immaculate. The carpet had been laid, he protested, 'so that the feet of the tragedienne should not touch the boards which possibly performing elephants had previously trodden'.

Despite the onset of war theatres and music-halls remained open. Most affected were the touring companies when the army requisitioned all their trains. Those which had begun their tour on the August Bank Holiday were stranded without carriages for actors or trucks for scenery. Gradually they reorganised and, in London at least, Stoll and his fellow impresarios decided that business must go on as usual. 'To the task before it,' intoned *The Stage Year Book*, 'our stage in all its branches applied itself with an energy and in a spirit of both self-preservation and self-denial that the historian will not fail to record.' This was an exalted way of saying that performers lucky enough to avoid the army had to take severe cuts in their earnings. 'In such anxious days,' continued the *Year Book*, 'it was for the stage to play a tonic part – to help and divert, cheer, and brace the minds and hearts of the people.' Patriotic songs multiplied. 'It's a Long Way to Tipperary', having languished for some years unknown, suddenly shot into immense popularity. Few music-hall evenings were complete without Paul Rubens's ditty:

> Oh! We don't want to lose you but we think you ought
> > to go
> For your King and your Country both need you so;
> We shall want you and miss you but with all our might
> > and main
> We shall cheer you, thank you, kiss you, when you come
> > back again;

or the jaunty measures of the girl recruiting sergeant:

> But on Saturday I'm willing if you'll only take the
> > shilling,
> To make a man of any one of you;

or

> Sister Susie's sewing shirts for soldiers
> Such skill at sewing shirts our shy young sister shows!
> Sometimes soldiers send epistles, say they'd sooner sleep
> > in thistles
> Than the saucy, soft, short shirts for soldiers sister Susie
> > sews.

Even Barrie wrote a war sketch called *Der Tag* which had been charmed out of him by Stoll in yet another stroke of showmanship for the Coliseum. Despite the presence of a famous actress it did not succeed. A commentator wrote severely: 'We have no need of or patience with ultra-resourceful heroes and heroines who outwit Hunnish adversaries upon a stage and in the limelight, for we know that our brave fellows are doing the real work on the rough roads of Flanders and in out-of-the-way places of the world.'

Robey went on raising large sums for charity. At an 'All-Woman' matinée in the Haymarket Theatre he queened it in petticoat and flounces on behalf of convalescent homes for French soldiers. At open-air rallies he clambered up on tanks, bowler and stick whirling madly, to make people laugh on a grey, misty morning and to sell National War Bonds. He gave concerts in Bristol, Liverpool, Brighton and other towns. In hospitals for the wounded he created light and laughter. Often, while singing, he would notice that, under cover of the laughter, screens were being hastily put round a bed where a man lay dying.

In 1916 Oswald Stoll approached him with another of his unusual ideas. This was for a revue at the Alhambra, and he wanted Robey to star in it. The notion at first seemed daunting. Robey's experience of long-running shows was confined to provincial pantomimes and he did not know how he would react to an extended performance in the West End. Even more important, he was conditioned to half-hour turns in the music-hall. Could he adapt to a whole evening's entertainment with several matinées each week? Would he be able to remember his lines over such a long period? Stoll offered him five hundred pounds a week, the largest salary he had ever earned on the stage. He thought of the figure. He thought of Stoll's undoubted flair. He accepted.

The revue was called *The Bing Boys Are Here* and sub-titled *A picture of London life in a prologue and six panels.* It had been adapted from a French piece by the writer famous as 'Rip', a sullen alcoholic who, despite his notorious bad temper, wrote many brilliantly satiric revues. The Bing boys were two contrasting brothers, the mischievous and daring Lucifer, and the shy with-drawn Oliver. They come up from their native rural Binghampton and visit London as a pair of yokels eager for adventure. They are accompanied by a lady's maid called Emma for whom Lucifer cherishes an inconstant passion. Equipped with grotesque suits too large and too small for them respectively, they undergo adventures in night-clubs, grand hotels, theatres and the zoo. While the brothers enjoy themselves Emma becomes a famous theatre star and marries a Duke, so enabling Lucifer to forget a duty that had become somewhat onerous and to cast his net elsewhere.

The first revue on the London stage is generally thought to have been *Under the Clock* which the versatile Seymour Hicks directed in 1893. Since then the genre had gained popularity and, in the hands of men like Cochran, Charlot and de Courville assumed a distinctive form. While *The Bing Boys Are Here* lacked the topical satire which had come to be associated with it, there were humour, colour, variety and scenes short enough not to bore wartime audiences anxious for distraction. Once again Stoll's instinctive grasp of what the public wanted proved correct. He had taken over the Alhambra at a low point in its fortunes and resolved that *The Bing Boys Are Here* should rescue it. The site of the theatre had originally been occupied by the Royal Panopticon, an institution designed to promote education and culture. At the ceremonial opening in 1854 the Bishop of London offered up a prayer, which, alas, does not seem to have been efficacious, for, within several years, the establishment went bankrupt and had to be revived with music-hall turns and tightrope walkers. It burnt down in 1882 and a building in the Moorish style took its place, all domes and pointed windows and gilt crescent moons. The Alhambra survived until 1936 when it gave way to the Lubianka-like building of the Odeon Cinema. It had several large bars and a promenade notorious for dalliance. Behind the stage was a dubious little bar, not much more than a brothel, where gentlemen entertained chorus girls. The oriental motifs of the façade were perpetuated in the auditorium. The designer, impressed by the aesthetic exuberance of Arabic letters, had even used them to embellish the walls. It seems there was no one available who could read *Jawi* and who could have told him that they proclaimed, with signal inappropriateness, 'There is no God but Allah.'

Stoll, of course, the apostle of purity and family entertainment, swept away the seedy bars and put a stop to the furtive transactions which, in the absence of successful programmes, had for some years kept the Alhambra in business. His policy was justified on that April night in 1916 when *The Bing Boys Are Here* made its triumphant debut. After the curtain calls Robey went back to his dressing-room. He could hear the distant applause of the audience, but no one came near him and he wondered what sort of impression he made in the daring experiment he had undertaken. Only now did he fully appreciate the risk. Accustomed to being in complete control of the audience, performing routines that were his and his alone, he had to take direction from others, to merge his personality with a group, to act as part of a team. Still he wondered. There was a knock at the door. In came an old friend whose judgment he trusted. 'Excuse me,' whispered the visitor raising his hand melodramatically, 'excuse me, but you have made the greatest hit that has been made in London for years!' He turned and, as melodramatically, vanished. He was right. *The Bing Boys Are Here* ran for three hundred and seventy-eight performances over a period of nine months and was seen by more than six hundred thousand people.

With Robey, pert and irrepressible as Lucifer, was Alfred Lester as his humorous brother Oliver. Lester was a gaunt and handsome beanpole of a man with a permanently lugubrious expression. He made his first appearance on the stage as a baby playing the part of Little Willy in *East Lynne*. His earliest success was in *The Arcadians* when he sang:

> I've gotta motter,
> Always merry and bright,
> Look around and you will find
> Every cloud is silver lined,

the humour of the situation springing from the contrast between the optimistic verse and his woebegone look. The role was not difficult for him since in private life he had a notably downcast nature.* One of his famous sketches was 'The Scene-Shifter's Lament', in which, as a melancholy stage-hand, he proposed ideas for brightening up *Hamlet*. In *The Bing Boys Are Here* he stopped the show with a robustly cynical counter-blast to all the recruiting

---

* The comedian Horace Kenney used a similar technique. He would shuffle on stage looking desperately miserable. In tones of the utmost depression, after gazing hopelessly at the audience, he quavered, "Ere we are again, always merry and bright.'

songs everyone sang at the time. It ran, 'Send out my brother, my sister and my mother, but for Gawd's sake don't send me.'

The part of Emma was taken by Violet Loraine. She was a trim, pretty girl who in her time decorated many a pantomime as principal boy and Gaiety productions like *The Spring Chicken* and *The Girls of Gottenburg*. Soon after the war she retired from the stage to marry Edward Raylton Joicey MC and lived in grandeur at Blenkinsopp Castle near Haltwhistle. Before that, however, she ensured a certain immortality for herself by singing a duet with Robey in *The Bing Boys Are Here*. It was, perhaps, the greatest moment of the evening and one that the audience always looked forward to with excitement. The two performers, alone on stage, sang:

> If you were the only girl in the world
> And I were the only boy,
> Nothing else would matter in the world today,
> We could go on loving in the same old way.
> A garden of Eden just made for two,
> With nothing to mar our joy;
> I would say such wonderful things to you,
> There would be such marvellous things to do,
> If I were the only girl in the world
> And you were the only boy.

The melody has a poignance that never loses its freshness and exquisitely matches the tender sentiment. In a moment of genius Robey decided to sing it absolutely straight, with no grimaces or comic business. More than any of his other songs or catch-phrases, 'If You Were the Only Girl in the World' became his personal property, a refrain that instantly identified him and evoked affectionate reminiscence in the minds of those who heard it. Inevitably it inspired a parody: 'If you were the only Boche in the trench/And I had the only bomb,/Nothing else would matter in the world that day,/I would blow you up into eternity . . .'

The music had been written by Nat D. Ayer who also provided the other songs in *The Bing Boys Are Here*. He was a young American settled for the time being in London where he contributed numbers to various revues and actually appeared in several of Cochran's productions, showing himself as talented a performer as he was composer. One of the best-known songs he wrote during his brief career was 'Oh! You Beautiful Doll'. His score for *The Bing Boys Are Here* included 'Another Little Drink Wouldn't Do Us Any Harm', a comic trio sung with mischievous point by Robey, Violet Loraine and Alf Lester. One day, at rehearsals, Robey heard Ayer playing over a tune at the piano which caught his fancy.

'What's that?' Robey asked.

'Only a little thing I've made up.' It was called 'I Stopped, I Looked, and I Listened'.

Robey said, 'I'd like to sing it.'

'You wouldn't!' said Ayer incredulously.

But he did, and the humorous number about an involuntary Peeping Tom became one of the most applauded items in the production and a permanent feature of the comedian's repertory. It was also, needless to say, banned by the Watch Committee in Birmingham.

In a similar way and at about the same time he acquired another of his characteristic songs. 'In Other Words' had been going the rounds for some time and had already been sung by various people but without the exquisite timing and finely graded emphasis which only he could give it. Such lines as:

> A lady of unlimited allurement,
> A proclivity for passion she displays.
> A desire for osculation she evinces,
> She's amorous and yielding in her ways,

might have been tailor-made for his plummy delivery and lubricious look.

The long run of *The Bing Boys Are Here* was, said Robey, 'a wonderful time'. There had earlier, it is true, been awkward moments with the American producer Gus Sohlke, a peremptory disciplinarian. He once caught Robey joking in the wings at rehearsal with the chorus girls and, in a voice of thunder that silenced the traffic of the stage, rebuked him majestically. Robey stepped forward and replied with equal firmness, 'Mr Sohlke, I am not accustomed to being spoken to in that way. I may have been wrong, but I won't be corrected in that fashion. If it happens again I shall not fight – I shall take other measures!' And he rambled on in a serio-comic digression about fixing mistletoe to his coat-tail and sweeping out of the theatre. What those mysterious 'other measures' were no one ever knew, and he was heard in puzzled silence. Then somebody laughed. Others joined in and, amid the hilarity, Mr Sohlke made amends to his star comedian. Robey, though, could not resist whole-hearted amusement at a later incident involving Sohlke. A new lighting board was installed at the Alhambra, a maze of switches and cables and bars wired up to deliver thousands of volts. An inaugural ceremony was conducted by Sohlke who bent over the safety rail to inspect it. Suddenly his heavy gold cigarette case fell out of a pocket and hit one of the current bars. An eerie flash sizzled over the stage and all the lights fused. The valuable cigarette case was instantly reduced to a molten lump.

'On the stage we were a real happy family,' Robey later said. He admired Vi Loraine for her versatility as singer, dancer and actress, and, an old hand himself, praised her ability to carry the audience with her. Alf Lester, he thought, never really had the confidence in himself which his talent deserved. At rehearsal he was acutely nervous and went through tortures of doubt. A deeply rooted natural pessimism left him no grounds for satisfaction with his own performance, and the gift which made him so effective a comedian seems to have conspired with a sort of death wish to carry him off at the age of fifty-three. Robey suffered from no such brain-sickliness. Warmed by regular applause, cheered by the mob of admirers who nightly crowded round him, he put up on the door of his dressing-room the notice 'GHQ' and delighted there to entertain soldiers on leave who came to say their goodbyes before rejoining their battalion in France. His cupboards brimmed over with the wartime souvenirs they bought him and his whisky bill rose vertiginously. 'If You Were the Only Girl in the World' was sung, hummed and whistled everywhere throughout the trenches. Leave in London was not thought complete without at least one visit to *The Bing Boys Are Here*. Even zeppelin raids were unable to spoil the audiences's enjoyment. After one unpleasantly large bomb had fallen nearby with an explosion that rocked the theatre, people were reassured by the sight of Robey's beaming, moon-like

face which popped round the side of the proscenium. 'Shurrup!'
it said.

The only tiresome feature of *The Bing Boys* for Robey was caused
by the long waits in his dressing-room between appearances on
stage. As a music-hall performer covering four or five places in
an evening he was used to being active all the time. The periods
of idleness bored him and he cast around for something to do.
'Why not,' suggested a musical friend, 'be a Stradivarius and
make fiddles?' Being already a carpenter he thought there might
be an idea here, although the challenge was a big one. He bought
manuals and textbooks and read up the subject industriously. On
visits to the workshops of violin-makers he learned the tricks of the
trade and familiarised himself with different woods. There were
tools to be acquired, varieties of polish to be studied and grains
to be appreciated. Gradually he worked up his skill and began to
enter into the mystique of the art. Visitors to his dressing-room
now included other makers of the instrument, connoisseurs and
players. It was all, he thought, very romantic. Eventually he was
able to turn out an instrument that real artists could use in public
and even taught himself to play after a fashion. His scrapings were
not always enjoyed by the neighbours of his dressing-room. One
evening, during an interval, some very beautiful sounds were heard
coming from it. A member of the company who up to then had
always protested bitterly at his playing tapped at the door and
said, 'My dear fellow, I want to congratulate you. At last you
have learned to play. I heard you in the interval and I listened
with delight. Now, my dear man, so far as I am concerned,
you may play as much as you like. Never again shall I wish to
destroy you!'

With mock emotion, Robey got up and replied, 'Thank you for
your comforting words. Never shall I forget them.' He went on
to point out that the lovely music was played by the great Belgian
virtuoso Eugene Ysaÿe engaged in trying out a violin he had just
finished making.

Part of his dressing-room was converted into a workshop where
the whiff of glue and shavings flavoured the reek of make-up.
Here, while the muffled sound of music and dialogue from the
stage provided a distant accompaniment, he toiled patiently over
his violins, devoting many hours to the delicate intricacies of a

bridge and applying often as many as forty coats of varnish to the gleaming body. He was modest about his work. 'I shall never make a Strad,' he confessed, 'I haven't the soul.' Yet Ysaÿe was not the only celebrated virtuoso to approve the instruments he made. Fritz Kreisler played one and so did Jascha Heifetz and Mischa Elman. Each of them wrote his signature on the instrument he tried out, as did other violinists who were at first amused by the novelty of a comedian turned craftsman and then impressed by the quality of the sound and the elegant appearance of the highly polished artifacts. The tone, though not brilliant, was warm and resonant, and the finish very professional.

Although Robey never played one of the classic violin concertos in public he did put on quite a distinguished show in another branch of music, that of conducting. At a Queen's Hall concert in aid of the Red Cross he appeared on the same programme as Henry Wood, Landon Ronald and Elgar. The item he conducted with a full orchestra was the 'Pizzicato' from Delibes's *Sylvia*. Each entry was immaculately cued, each variation of nuance eloquently indicated, and his timing was as perfect as if he had been delivering 'In Other Words'. After the concert an amazed acquaintance said, 'Is there anything you can't do?'

'Not that I know of,' answered Robey solemnly.

The secret, of course, was that he had spent a whole afternoon 'conducting' a gramophone record of the piece and rehearsing each flourish of his baton in time with the music.

Another novelty to which *The Bing Boys Are Here* introduced him was the custom of the understudy. When he did his turn on the halls he was unique and irreplaceable, and if, for any reason, he could not appear his slot on the bill would have either been filled by a different comedian or shared out among the others. In fact, up to then he was never known to have missed an entry and he took pride in his record. The 'legitimate' theatre was different. In *The Bing Boys* he was, although a star, part of a team effort, and the management insisted on his having an understudy. He did not welcome the idea and felt that it somehow implied doubt about his reliability. Only with reluctance did he accept the innovation, and throughout his long career he was to regard understudies with dislike and suspicion. The actor who performed that function for him in *The Bing Boys* was the twenty-nine-year-old Gillie Potter, a comedian whom Stoll had spotted in the provinces. Much later Potter became a well-known monologuist as 'The Squire of Hogsnorton'. He wore a Harrovian straw hat and Oxford bags, a club blazer and rimless glasses. On the radio he would, in a voice pedantic and prim, open his remarks with the salutation: 'Good evening, England, this is Gillie Potter speaking to you in English.' At the time of *The Bing Boys* he had enlisted as a cadet in the St John's Wood Artillery School. Robey lived nearby and made a point each evening of giving him a lift home in his taxi, often turning down flattering invitations from important people with the reply, 'No, thank you very much, I have to take this soldier boy back to barracks.'

Robey's taxi-driver, his regular, the one he always engaged, took them by an invariable route up Regent Street into Portland Place and along the Marylebone Road. When they reached Clarence Gate Robey had unwound from the tension of the evening performance and was ready to talk, which he did with humour and dash, fascinating Potter with gossip about the politicians and generals who confided in him. On the night before Potter, now a fully trained soldier, was due to go to France, he took his farewell of Robey. Next morning, very early as usual, Robey came to Waterloo Station and saw him off along with all the others. He held up Potter's tiny son to wave his father goodbye. It was a memory Potter never forgot. He was also the only understudy Robey ever treated with kindness.

Despite his exhausting routine at the Alhambra Robey continued with his charity work. At concerts where he entertained the war-wounded there were soldiers so horribly disfigured that they sat behind curtains or at the back of a box in order not to be seen. One of them had already gone through thirty operations to rebuild his face. Only his eyes were spared, and Robey, with his jokes about 'Merry Eyes', helped to give him back something of his humour. On another occasion he sang a comic song called 'The Little Pigs' to startling effect. In the front row there sat a man who had long since been struck dumb by shell-shock. Robey, snorting, grimacing, grunting, played straight at him. The man looked on stupefied. Suddenly he burst into loud laughter. Robey had cured him, as he cured W. A. Darlington of toothache.

Occasionally soldiers off to the Front asked him for a mascot or charm to take with them. Among his mementoes was a signed photograph of himself, a bullet hole through the top of it and bloodstains all round. It had been carried by one of his admirers who survived and handed it back to him. Robey's doctor, whose son had been called up, was offered a Japanese porcelain charm for the boy. 'Give him that,' said Robey. 'It will take up no room in one of his pockets, and tell him my wish is that the worst that may happen to him is the loss of a finger on his left hand!' Some time later the anxious father returned with news that his son had been listed among the casualties. Robey tried to cheer him up. Better news arrived. 'It's not so bad,' reported the father. 'He has lost a finger on his left hand!' Another Japanese charm for another father's son saved another life. The boy's company were ordered to evacuate their gun position because the enemy had located it. After they all left he remembered he had left the bit of Japanese porcelain behind and ran back to rescue it. While he was away a bomb fell and killed every man in the company.

Robey's charitable work made him notorious beyond the bounds of the music-hall and theatre. It resulted in a vast postbag. A plumber's wife wrote in tones of sad indignation to point out that his jokes about plumbers were very hurtful – after all, plumbers were 'very necessary people'. A grocer fallen on hard times asked for a loan and proposed to assign his business over to him until the debt was discharged. Others anxious to acquire a motor-bicycle or a house or a gift of a thousand pounds approached him with requests. Hundreds, if not thousands, of aspiring authors bombarded him with mediocre ideas for songs and sketches and revues. The most poignant in their naïveté were letters of this sort:

> Dear Sir, i am writing to ask if you would use your influence on behalf of my sone he has a double voice and can whistle like a Bird forgive the liberty.

As soon as the long run of *The Bing Boys Are Here* ended Robey was engaged for another revue, this time at the Hippodrome. The impresario was Albert de Courville, who, like his rival André Charlot, was of French extraction. He had been educated in Lausanne and began his career as a journalist, quickly finding his vocation as assistant to the managing director of the Hippodrome where he inaugurated, with *Hullo Ragtime!* in 1912, a series of revues that are said to have equalled in colour and vivacity those mounted by such experts as Charlot and Charles B. Cochran. After launching money-spinners like *Flirts and Skirts* and *Passions of 1926* he settled down to 'straight' plays and, in 1940, emigrated to New York and began all over again. *Zig-Zag*, in which Robey appeared, had been largely written by de Courville himself, who, as a former journalist, was a prolific contributor of revue material. At the time he was married, briefly, to the female star of *Zig-Zag*, a lady called Shirley Kellogg. Her hit number, which she belted out with elemental force, was the rousing 'Over There!' Another success of the production was Robey's music-hall number 'Prehistoric Man' which he built up into a full-length sketch, he playing Mr Umph with a cast that included Mrs Umph, a policesaurus and various cavemen. His contribution is immortalised in the famous wartime play *Journey's End*. The young officers in the trenches are talking nostalgically of home and mention *Zig-Zag*. 'George Robey's in it,' says one. Another remarks, 'Harper saw it on leave. Says it's damned good. George Robey's pricelessly funny.'

Among the charms of the Hippodrome which appealed to Robey as a collector of human curiosities was its manager Fred Trussell. Always in impeccable evening dress, a flower blooming from his buttonhole, he patrolled the foyer with affable grandeur and exacted a reverential salute from his staff as he swept by. On holidays in Sussex he organised cricket matches where he appeared wearing a multi-coloured silk belt with a scarlet silk handkerchief flaming in the pocket of his flannel shirt. At the Hippodrome he greeted customers as if they were old and valued friends and persuaded them, with many a courtly phrase, that the seats they had were really quite the best in the house. If, however, a crisis arose, or some complicated problem that could not immediately be solved, he retreated to bed with a supposed attack of gout. Trussell had fluent French and German, languages into which he translated a patriotic song he wrote at the time of Victoria's Diamond Jubilee year entitled 'The Queen, God Bless Her!' It became very popular, and when Edward VII ascended the throne Trussell ensured a future stream of royalties by changing the title to 'The King, God Bless Him!'

After the run of *Zig-Zag* ended Robey went back to the Alhambra for *The Bing Boys on Broadway*, a sequel that Stoll shrewdly timed to benefit from America's recent entry into the war. There had already been a successor of a kind which featured Vi Loraine and was called *The Bing Girls Are There*. *The Bing Boys on Broadway* outdid both this and the original. Having opened in February 1918, it played 562 performances and went on long after the war had ended. While the music, again by Nat D. Ayer, had nothing to offer that was comparable with 'If You Were the Only Girl in the World', it did include another attractive duet for Robey and Vi Loraine. 'First Love' had a wistful tune in minor key that echoed the words:

> The first love is the best love
> And it's the best love of all.

In the new show Robey as Lucifer accompanied his one-time love Emma, now the Dowager Duchess of Dullwater, on a trip to New York. The plot took them around Broadway, a Chinese opium den, a Ford car factory and Hollywood. One extravagant episode presented warring Indians and Mexican bandits. Robey's squaw, Laughing Cheese, was Vi Loraine, and he, as U-ke-lip-tus the tribal chief, wore a plumed head-dress with feathers that rose and wiggled in delight as he sampled the white man's whisky. At the first night, an occasion of intense excitement and of one particularly loud bomb, Robey was greeted with a huge ovation. He made his entry coming off a ship at New York dock. A customs officer descended on him with a predatory look. 'Anything to declare?' he snarled.

'Yes,' beamed Robey. 'No trumps!'

The evening performance on 11th November was riotous, for that day the Armistice had been declared. Through streets crowded with people dancing and cheering Robey struggled to the Criterion restaurant for lunch. There he was seized, urged on to a table and asked for a speech. All he could remember of his discourse was the remark: 'We have achieved our object, but – *at what a sacrifice!*' That evening, dining at a restaurant in Leicester Square, he was called upon for another speech. Afterwards, in the theatre, the atmosphere bubbled as hectically as outside. None of the cast took their work seriously and they all interpolated gags and extra business which under normal circumstances would never have been allowed. The audience, restless and feverish, kept on the move from auditorium to bar and back again. At midnight Robey walked home surrounded by a massed throng of Londoners noisily celebrating the end of the war. After years of night-time darkness windows blazed with light again and lampposts threw a sudden gleam once more. He was thankful it all had ended. And yet, he said, 'I could not help thinking of all the dear lads I had come to know and whom I should never see again, and, upon my honour, I felt more like crying than singing. Nor could I help thinking of the millions of people who, at that moment, behind windows closed and curtained, were thinking of the Dead.'

[ii]

Tremenjus! Tremenjus! . . . and the shade of Fu Manchu

Early in 1919, while preparing *Joy Bells*, an Albert de Courville revue which followed *The Bing Boys on Broadway*, Robey asked if he might be excused one of the rehearsals.

'On what ground?' enquired de Courville a trifle pettishly.

'Buckingham Palace!' answered Robey with grandeur.

He had been appointed CBE in the New Year Honours and was to attend the ceremonial levée that day. The award acknowledged his charitable work which had raised the then enormous amount of over half a million pounds. At a gala luncheon in the Criterion restaurant an assembly of lords and ladies and tycoons and industrialists presented him with a sparkling silver tea and coffee service bearing an inscription which recorded his 'generous, effective and very distinguished work for the benefit of war charities'. He had also raised fourteen thousand pounds for the French Red Cross. One day, accompanied by the Lord Mayor of London, he went to the French Embassy. It was the Lord Mayor who handed over the cheque, who received the ribbon of the Légion d'Honneur and who suffered, on both cheeks, a resonant Gallic kiss from the Ambassador. For Robey there was no more than a polite 'thank you'. 'Well,' he observed under his breath when it was all over, 'I meantersay . . .'

Yet although the war had finished, his charitable efforts were needed more than ever, for the blind and the wounded remained. His famous auctions continued. At one of them he sold at a high figure a manuscript by the self-regarding novelist Hall Caine. Cloak and whiskers flying, Caine rushed up to the organiser and jubilated: 'Did you see what my address brought in?'

'Yes, splendid,' was the reply. 'But there, Robey, of course, can sell anything.'

Despite the heavy commitment of twelve performances a week Robey went on touring hospitals between matinées and evening shows. He rarely had a Sunday to himself. On one of his hospital visits a man who had lost both his legs asked for Robey to speak with him.

'Hello, I remember you,' lied Robey as he came to the wheel-chair.

'Do 'ee?' said the man. 'Remember the old days in Cardiff? *Some* days, George!'

'Of course I do,' answered Robey. 'Let's see, what were you then?'

'I were swimming champion, I were.'

Robey froze. For a moment he was speechless. Then he quickly pulled himself together. He reached forward and touched one of the man's stumps. 'Can't swim so much now, can you?' he joked.

'No-a, George,' replied the invalid, a broad grin decorating his face, 'but I can float fine!'

By the end of the war Robey, at the age of fifty, had become as much a public figure as an entertainer. The music-hall which bred him was fading away, and although he and other stars continued to shine it had quietly changed into something called 'variety' which was to linger on until the 1950s. In the gloomy post-war years of unemployment and recession there was a need for entertainment. Not yet seriously rivalled by films or radio, variety could provide cheap and popular escapism. Unlike the music-hall, which drew its wry inspiration from the hardships of real life, variety depended on the fantastic and the grotesque rather than on realism. The public had supped its fill of horror during the war. People wanted humour and diversion.

These were provided abundantly by over sixty halls in London and six hundred more in the provinces. The major circuits, as always, dominated the business, the greatest of them being Moss Empires. Next came Oswald Stoll who controlled seventeen halls. His beloved Coliseum, the jewel in the crown, was not doing well. The vast building, so cavernous that a piece of paper bearing the legend 'Work to that' was pinned up at the back and centre of the circle to help new performers, looked like becoming a white elephant. While Stoll experimented successfully elsewhere with revue and was able to fill his other theatres, the Coliseum had entered the doldrums. Not until the 1930s, when he at last discovered a workable formula in spectacular musical shows like *White Horse Inn*, did he begin to solve, temporarily, the problem. Meanwhile he tried to draw the public with entertainment that certainly deserved the name variety: cricket matches, rodeos, racing cars on the Wall of Death, playlets by J. M. Barrie, and programmes which juxtaposed the Diaghilev ballet with Nervo and Knox who were later to be ornaments of the Crazy Gang. One of his calculations which deserved to have succeeded went badly wrong. He engaged the Marx Brothers (they were a quartet then) for two weeks in June. Their Coliseum appearance was disastrous. Before long derisive whistling was heard, and then the cruel, the unmistakable sound of pennies being thrown on to the stage. Groucho, however, did manage to retrieve something from the débâcle. 'Friends,' he announced, raising his hand and walking up to the footlights, 'we have come a long way. The trip's been expensive. Would you mind throwing a little silver?'

Variety was organised even more elaborately than had been the music-hall. Bookings for Moss Empires were handled by Cissie Williams, a tough and daunting female of a type not at all uncommon in that area of the business. Her days were taken up with planning the eternal jigsaw of engagements, her nights with visiting the halls in search of new talent. Detailed records were kept of each performer including theatres worked and eye-witness reports sent in by managers. A complicated system of card indexes ensured that no turn went on too often at any one hall or in places near to each other. The bill was made up with thoughtful attention to contrast. After a brief musical or tap-dance number a second-spot comic played before a front cloth. He was followed, after his difficult assignment was over, by an acrobat, and then by a comedian. The last act before the interval would be perhaps an 'adagio' turn mingling ballet with acrobatics. A ten-minute interval for the rush to the bar preceded the reappearance of the unfortunate musical act which earlier had opened the bill and now performed to the clatter of people returning from the bar and slumping into their seats. A specialist act took over, perhaps a weight-lifter or a paper tearer or a 'lightning' artist, and afterwards there was a comic. The latter made way for the star, top of the bill and therefore granted more time, usually as much as twenty minutes. The 'closer' after the top of the bill, acrobat or juggler, had an unenviable job since his task was really to stop people leaving early while the star was on. Each act, as in the old music-hall, was timed ruthlessly to allow for clearing the house between twice-nightly performances. Anyone who overran was duly reported to the formidable Cissie Williams or her counterpart on the other circuits. The hierarchy of billing was immutably established and rigorously observed as on the posters, where each performer insisted jealously on the exact size of the letters which spelt his name. Intense were the arguments that centred on a matter of quarter inches, and bitter were the disagreements over whether a name should appear on the right, the left or at the bottom of the sheet. Robey, of course, never needed to dispute the space or the extent of his billing. Everyone knew that he automatically came at the top over his bill matter 'The Prime Minister of Mirth', and even Miss Williams would not have demurred.

He was more than equal to the challenge of variety, as he had been to that of music-hall. Indeed, he found variety less exacting, for whereas in the old days he might play four or five halls a night, now he was only called on to appear twice at most. He had, in any case, moved away from his origins. During the 1920s and early 1930s he was to be found more often playing in revue than on the halls. There were, it is true, special occasions when he went back to form. One such was the 1919 Royal Command Performance 'in celebration of peace'. Here he sang with Violet Loraine 'If You Were the Only Girl in the World' on a bill which also included Harry Tate and the clown Grock. This was the second, and last, genuine performance 'by royal command', all subsequent ones being simply 'royal' and not commanded by anyone except, perhaps, by a variety profession anxious for *réclame* and charitable works. It also indicated a further step towards respectability: was not the concluding 'Pageant of Peace' conducted by the eminent Sir Edward Elgar, soon to be Master of The King's Musick?

Another wartime-inspired function in which Robey took part during 1919 comprised a 'Warriors' Night' at the Hippodrome. This was organised by Bransby Williams, a larger-than-life trouper best known for his Dickens impersonations. Alone on stage, a master of the quick change, he became in speedy succession, a roseate Mr Pickwick, a snarling Scrooge, a ghastly Fagin, a murderous Bill Sykes, a hopeful Micawber, a debonair Jingle. About the only Dickensian character he seems to have overlooked was Little Nell. In his time he had done everything in the theatre, from blacking up as a Moore and Burgess minstrel to running his own company as actor-manager. It is often forgotten that he sometimes played a quite creditable Hamlet, a role to which his fine, square, handsome features were particularly suited. While giving solo recitations from that play at an Oxford matinée he was puzzled, when he came to the speech 'Angels and ministers of grace defend us', by the roar of laughter that greeted him. He turned round to see Robey behind him rigged up like the ghost, a spectral expression on his face and a white towel wrapped round his head. On tour together they often played a favourite trick which ensured they had a railway carriage compartment to themselves. One of them would stick winkle tops on his face, drape himself in a towel and, with the aid of sherbet, foam at the mouth. No traveller dared disturb them.

Williams devised 'Warriors' Night' in memory of his dearly loved son and of all other young soldiers who had been killed during the war. He obtained the patronage of the Prince of Wales and the assistance of friends in the profession like Robey, Harry Tate, Lupino Lane and Harry Lauder. On the night the audience suddenly recognised Lloyd George sitting in a box opposite the Prince of Wales. The Prime Minister walked over to the royal box and, taking off his make-up, revealed himself as Bransby Williams who went on to announce 'The Prime Minister of Mirth'. This was only one of the gags in a brilliantly staged spectacle. At the end of it all, exhausted by playing fourteen characters in an evening and by the strain of putting the show together, Williams sat alone in his dressing-room. Out front he could hear laughter and the tinkle of glasses. No one came to thank him or to congratulate him on his effort. He thought of his dead son, wearily crossed the empty stage and drove himself home.

'Warriors' Night' and the Royal Command Performance represented time off for Robey from his main commitment which, at that moment, was the revue *Joy Bells*. Among his fellow players was the Australian Leon Errol who, very shortly, emigrated to Hollywood and filmed scores of two-reel comedies in which he appeared as a henpecked drunk or an irascible next-door neighbour. He was completely bald, piggy-eyed and moved about on quavering legs that seemed to be made of rubber. In later years he served as an excellent spluttering foil to the passionate Lupe Velez, otherwise known as 'The Mexican Spitfire'. Another member of the cast was Rupert Hazell, author of material for Robey and, when not writing, an accomplished actor. Much less agreeable to Robey was the presence of the Original Dixieland Jazz Band. These white American players were largely responsible for the jazz craze then sweeping the country. Whether or not he knew that the word 'jazz' was an obscene slang expression, Robey disapproved intensely of music which he considered to be ugly and degenerate. More dangerous still, the great success of the Jazz Band threatened to shadow his glory as the sole star of *Joy Bells*. He went to the producer de Courville and insisted that they be taken off. De Courville, faced with the anger of his crowd-pulling big name, had no alternative but to do as he asked.

Robey's feeling of outrage was soothed by a tribute from an Italian writer which appeared in the Rome newspaper *La Tribuna*:

> Robey, just by being Robey, makes us laugh until we weep. We do not want to see either Figaro or Othello; it is quite enough for Robey to appear in travelling costume and to turn his eyes in crab-like fashion from one side of the auditorium to another . . . Robey's aspect in dealing with his audience is paternal and, one might almost say, apostolic. There are times when he appears to communicate to them in a gentle and almost affectionate manner.

Robey sent a copy of the translation to de Courville with a gleeful note suggesting that he deserved a salary increase. This time de

Courville was equal to him. He replied that he would pay Robey's salary in Italian lire rather than English pounds sterling. 'This,' he added, 'will correspond with your English value.'

To the violin-making which helped fill the backstage hours during *Joy Bells* Robey now added another pursuit that gave him quite as much enjoyment. He had already, in 1911, brought out a bland autobiography entitled *My Life Up Till Now*. This gave him a taste for writing and he soon afterwards published little collections of anecdotes of which *Jokes, Jibes and Jingles* is a typical example. In 1919, the year of *Joy Bells*, he issued *My Rest Cure*, the book on which one of his early films was based. In the following year he published *After-Dinner Stories*, which, like other books, included items he had written for papers such as *Tit-Bits* and *Cassell's Story Teller*, names with an unmistakable flavour of the period. Over the next decade he became a prolific writer and often produced a book each year. 'Entirely delicious,' said the *Referee*. 'One is kept in a continuous chuckle from first to last. It is real humour.' The *Manchester Guardian* observed: 'George Robey, our acknowledged greatest comedian, altogether excels himself in sheer delightful humour, and there is sure to be a tremendous run on the book.' Another comment, from *Truth*, was nearer the mark: 'A fine handbook for comic reciters.' The stories he tells are those which, declaimed by amateur monologuists in the parlours of the 1920s, would have delighted admiring families. Today they do not seem quite as funny.

Often told in the first person, the anecdotes evoke *The Diary of a Nobody* with, from time to time, an echo of W. W. Jacobs. They are usually domestic and have for subject troubles with servants, the problems of engaging a suitable cook, the horrors of amateur theatricals, unsuccessful attempts to sweep the chimney, holidays that go wrong, and adventures with a defective motor-bike. There is one about an amateur detective who tracks a suspect only to find that he is the highly respectable Mayor of a northern city. In another the detective unearths what he thinks is a corpse – but discovers it is nothing more than a decaying kipper. When a story begins: '"Far be it from me to cross your slightest wish, my dear," I remarked, addressing my wife; "and since you have set your heart on Margate, to Margate we will go. And what is more, we will enjoy all the fresh air we can and go by water,"' you know that the trip will end in disaster. Similarly, it is obvious that there will be a bungled rescue attempt if the opening paragraph reads: ' "You mean to say, George, you really consider yourself qualified to save a man from drowning?" It was my friend Billie Anchor who asked the question. He spoke with the faintly incredulous intonation which, on occasion, I find a little irritating.'

Other tales relate to his professional life and are based on experience. 'The Pro's Landlady' from *Bits and Pieces* recounts the incident, mentioned earlier in this book, of the landlady whom he suspected of sampling his whisky, although the liquid with which he doctored the bottle is referred to, for decency's sake, as 'a yellow chemical of unpleasant flavour'.

A story about dinner with a knight of the shires and his grand family contains an opinion Robey must often have heard expressed. The knight remarks it is a very lucky thing that Robey does not have to work for a living.

'I beg your pardon,' replies the comedian, 'I *do* have to work, and pretty hard, too! I practically live in the theatre.'

The knight is unimpressed: 'If you call *that* work! I have only seen you once, Mr Robey, and if my memory serves me, I found your antics most diverting, and I must own I laughed immoderately.' Why did he go on the stage? they ask him.

'Because I felt I must, I felt I *had to.*'

'I understand,' says the knight's lady. 'Everything else had failed you, so you had to. Rahly. It must be terrible for you.'

'Terrible?'

'For a man to have to paint his face and let people laugh at him, and have no redress whatever.'

The knight of the shires and his lady were not, and are not, alone in their naïf views of the theatre.

The titles of Robey's books pitter-pattered forth over the years with easy regularity. 'First appearance in volume form,' claimed *Family Affairs. Thereby Hangs a Tale* was followed by *The Lady in Question* and *An Honest Living*. Bringing up the rear came *Mental Fireworks* and *Don'ts*. As the 1920s dissolved into the 1930s he used one of his own catch-phrases to baptise a collection: *In Other Words*. He wrote, unstoppably, about 'The Young Person in Puce', 'My Piscatorial Boarders', 'On the Immortality of Nursery Rhymes', 'My Hyde Park Oration', 'I Dye Hard', 'Sports I Have Met', and 'By Char-à-Banc at Whitsuntide'. He was inexhaustible on 'My Wireless Concert', 'My Subconscious Aunt', 'My Burglary', 'My Morning Dip', and 'The Mudcumdyke Minstrels'. His books appeared in the company of John Long's select Half-Crown Library which offered the latest 'Copyright Novels' by Pett Ridge and Maurice Hewlett, writers now so long extinct that their works cannot today be found even in the darkest corners of remote country bookshops. The final touch of period flavour is to be found in the illustrations. These were sometimes drawn by Robey himself, who, as a paid-up member of the Royal Institute of Painters in Water Colours, could dash off neat and graphic sketches. Others were usually provided by E. P. Kinsella, a dextrous black and white artist in the line of Phil May and gifted with a touch often as light and subtle as that of Will Owen, the inspired illustrator of W. W. Jacobs.

The run of *Joy Bells* gave Robey plenty of time for writing in his dressing-room since the revue lasted over seven hundred performances. Even before it ended Oswald Stoll had invited him to appear at the Alhambra in another revue to be called *Johnny Jones* and subtitled *A Robey Salad with Musical Dressing, or, The Adventures of a Naughty Boy*. He opened in February 1920, at a salary of six hundred pounds a week. It was one of those revues in which the setting was more substantial than the script. One scene, the palace of Haroun Al Raschid in Baghdad, glittered with such magnificence that it had a round of applause to itself. 'One almost expected it to step forward and bow its acknowledgments,' said Robey. Others showed the lagoons of Venice and the royal gardens of Versailles. In the last act he came on as an Italian musician accompanied by a mischievous monkey that stole the show. This evoked a pleading letter from a mother in the audience. Her daughter, she wrote, was going to school in Switzerland and felt she could stand the homesickness better if she could take the monkey with her. Would Mr Robey consider selling it to her? Mr Robey gallantly offered it to the juvenile admirer and found a substitute to take its place, rather hoping that this time the animal chosen would not upstage him quite so expertly.

The music for *Johnny Jones (and his Sister Sue)* was supplied by the French composer Charles Cuvillier. His *Lilac Domino*, with its haunting waltz, had been a triumph in London and he for a time became much in demand there for revues and musical comedies. His contribution to *Johnny Jones*, including a duet for Robey and Ivy St Helier called 'A Little House, a Little Home', was as always fluent and graceful. Yet the script and story line were mediocre. As a critic wrote:

> Mr Robey appears in every scene except one and shows the extraordinary effect of personality. To do him real justice he should act on alternate evenings and allow the audience to see the feebleness of the words when he is absent. For there is very little wit or fun in the piece except what he puts into it. When he is off the stage interest flags. When he is on the whole revue seems to be a totally different affair. Such is the effect of personality.

Robey thus earned every penny of his high salary. The criticism, though, seems a little unjust towards a cast which also featured Lupino Lane and Eric Blore. The latter, with his bulging fish eyes, worried pout and genteel diction, soon afterwards decamped to Hollywood where he became the personification of the English butler in musical films with Fred Astaire and Ginger Rogers. He excelled in the expression of feigned surprise and wary unctuousness. That he could play something else beside butlers was proved when he appeared as an artful beachcomber in the film of Somerset Maugham's *The Moon and Sixpence*.

Having kept *Johnny Jones* alive for eight months by the glamour of his personality alone Robey went straight into the next Alhambra production, *Robey en Casserole*, in March 1921. It is an indication of his star quality that by now he could be relied upon to carry the whole weight of a revue on his own shoulders. One of his best gags was a scene when he impersonated the curly-headed boy in Millais's famous picture *Bubbles*, which Pears' Soap used as an advertisement. Whereas Millais's little fellow in the Fauntleroy suit had been blowing bubbles through a dainty tube, Robey brandished a villainous old clay pipe. He also led a policemen's ballet in which the 'constables' wore uniform from the waist up, and, from the waist down, fairy-like saucer skirts.

Robey en Casserole, or the *Kaleidoscopic Invention* as it was subtitled, faded away by Christmas to give him the opportunity of making his only London appearance in pantomime. Over the past twenty-five years his pantomime work had been restricted to the provinces. It was there that he had perfected his craft in the genre and there that he built up his reputation as the true successor of Dan Leno. As Arthur Askey, himself an adroit pantomime artist has pointed out, the whole *raison d'être* of a dame is that the character is a woman being played by a man. The audience should never be allowed to forget that beneath the skirts there is a pair of trousers. Despite the fluting gestures of the hands, the simpering expressions of the face, the arch wriggling of the eyebrows and the airy pirouettes which are to be seen in an old film clip of Robey, no one could mistake him for anything but a particularly virile man. In *Jack and the Beanstalk* at the Hippodrome during the 1921–2 season his Dame Trot showed London a touch of the magic that had built up his enthusiastic provincial following. One of his best numbers in earlier Manchester productions had been 'Archibald, Certainly Not!' In this he was supposed to be the wife of an unfortunate, henpecked wretch called Archibald whose every wish was snubbed by his imperious consort. 'Archibald, certainly not!' became another of Robey's well-known catch-phrases and was always eagerly expected when he put on dame's clothing.

His son Edward remembered his father in this Hippodrome production as 'a pretty unattractive, middle-aged dame'. King Gerald XXX was played by Tom Walls, soon to be, with Ralph Lynne and Robertson Hare, a star of Ben Travers's Aldwych farces. Tom was not always word-perfect and, it must be said, was more inclined to be thinking about what had won the three thirty at Lincoln than about his lines. One wonders how he handled this snatch of nonsensical dialogue which remained for no good reason in Edward Robey's memory:

TILLY: When did you first bogin to love me, Kingy?
KING: I haven't bogun yet, Tilly.

Jack, the principal boy, was played by Clarice Mayne. She, like Robey, came from the music-hall where she was billed as 'Clarice Mayne and That' – 'That' being her husband J. W. Tate, who accompanied her at the piano in songs he had written like 'Put On Your Ta-Ta Little Girlie' and 'Joshua'. With her long elegant legs and willowy figure she was all that a pantomime principal boy should be. She also gave a piquant example of how in-bred music-hall families could be. Tate's first wife had been Lottie Collins, virtuoso of 'Ta-ra-ra-boom-de-ay!', and this made him stepfather to Josie Collins, star of *The Maid of the Mountains* for which he wrote some of the music. When he died Clarice married Teddie Knox, partner in Nervo and Knox of the Crazy Gang, and so remained within the charmed circle.

Jack and the Beanstalk was produced by Julian Wylie who had just taken over management of the Hippodrome. He was a large and enthusiastic north-countryman from Southport where he had been born Julian Ulrich Mettenberg Samuelson. As a child he sat on the lap of Phineas T. Barnum who fired his mind with tales of showmanship. One of his brothers dabbled in a bewildering range of business activities which covered motor transport, cheap lending libraries, films and bright ideas for marketing fish and chips. The other, whom Julian wished to emulate, went into the theatre where he acted and wrote books of musical comedies. Julian's talent lay in management, and his accountancy training had perfected an already lightning grasp of figures and balance sheets. He married a woman much older than himself with a small son – he delighted, when introducing her to embarrassed friends, in asking them to guess her age – both of whom he adored single-mindedly until the end of his life. She lent him the only capital she possessed, one pound, and with it he launched himself on London. He first established himself as manager to the magician David Devant. Soon he was able to repay his wife's loan with interest.

'Tremenjus! tremenjus!' was his favourite expression of approval. It is what he said when he saw Clarice Mayne do her act with J. W. Tate, announcing the title of her song, 'Sung by this' (pointing to herself) 'and composed by that', indicating her plump beaming husband. He went into a business partnership with Tate and began to specialise in pantomime. Ever since childhood he had been fascinated by the theatre and there was nothing he did not know about the technical side. Rehearsals were the joy of his life and he was always sad when they ended. Lighting in particular absorbed him, and he always wrote out the lighting plot himself with meticulous attention. Once, at a lighting rehearsal, things went badly wrong. He shouted through his megaphone at the electrician way up in the roof. Did not the man have his immaculate lighting plot?

Yes, came the muffled reply.

Couldn't he get it right?

A grunt no one understood was the answer.

'What's the matter with you?' Wylie bellowed at the end of his tether, 'can't you read?'

'No!' shouted the terrified electrician.

Wylie's rages were titanic. If the slightest hitch occurred he would hide his face in his hands and moan that he was ruined. Then the problem came right, his smile returned and all was 'tremenjus!' again. His storms of anger masked the very nervous personality that lay behind them and that expressed itself in perpetual movements of the hands, fiddling with a pencil, rolling up paper, brushing away cigar ash from the lapel of his coat. His hands, incidentally, were very shapely and contributed to his acknowledged skill as a conjurer. He became known as the King of Pantomime and revelled in the technical problems of transformation scenes and flying fairies and demon kings that vanished in a puff of smoke. It hurt him, a little, that people in the theatre tended to regard him as an unsophisticated northerner on the West End scene, for no one could rival him as a master of production. Still, he loved pantomime and by the end of his career had produced over a hundred gorgeous examples of it. Perhaps the reason for his success was that he had a brain of commercial shrewdness and the heart of a child. When, in times of crisis, other men would have taken to drink, Wylie took to ice-cream, buckets of it, which he regarded as the perfect conclusion to a meal of steak and onions at three in the morning after a long and difficult rehearsal. During the interval of an especially trying first night he would eat half a dozen cartons of gooey vanilla. He also had a passion for butterdrops, and, if he showed signs of losing his temper, an assistant would prudently feed him with them, knowing that the thick glutinous toffee filled his mouth and stopped him vociferating. Once, on the pier at Blackpool, he proffered a vast bag of jelly-babies to the actress Binnie Hale. 'I love these,' he said. 'Guess what I do with them first?' She did not know the answer. 'I bite the heads off them!' he went on greedily.

The sudden death of his partner J. W. Tate during the run of *Jack and the Beanstalk* saddened him deeply. The two men had been very different in character. Tate's bland and genial personality enabled him to mix smoothly with everyone he met. Wylie looked on the world through suspicious eyes and wore a carapace of belligerence that concealed a profound sense of inferiority. Yet the partnership flourished because the talents of this unlikely pair complemented each other. Wylie cherished Tate's memory and always insisted on including as much of his music as possible when he mounted a pantomime. If a newspaper happened to carry an inaccurate mention of his dead friend Wylie quickly despatched an outraged correction. He tried to forget his sorrow in the multiplicity of projects that were always in his mind. One of them was a production of *A Midsummer Night's Dream* with Robey playing Bottom. Nothing came of the idea, although he did put him into his next spectacular at the Hippodrome which, Robey said, 'was the best revue I ever took part in'. It displayed him at the age of fifty-three executing an intricate step–dance which ended in an elaborate cartwheel.

Round In Fifty, despite the title, had no reference to golf and was a modern version of Jules Verne's *Around the World in Eighty Days*. Robey played the part of Fogg's spendthrift son Phil who aims to circle the globe in fifty days. Book and lyrics were written by Sax Rohmer who, as we have already seen, provided Robey with some of his early songs. Since then they had become close friends. Born Arthur Henry Ward, this unusually talented man made up his pen name, he explained, from the word 'Sax', meaning 'blade' in old Saxon, and 'Rohmer' as a homophone of 'roamer'. He was fascinated by the occult and belonged to a number of secret societies, among them the Rosicrucians. At a spiritualist séance he asked, 'How can I best make a living?' The ouija-board spelt out the word: C-H-I-N-A-M-A-N. He remembered, one evening in Limehouse, an area he frequented, seeing a mysterious Chinaman wearing a furred coat step out of a glossy limousine and vanish into the swirling fog. Like Charles Dickens suddenly thinking of Mr Pickwick, Rohmer thought of Dr Fu Manchu. The books he wrote about the adventures of his oriental hero ran into many reprintings and sold millions of copies. (Rohmer employed as his research assistant a fourteen-year-old music-hall performer whom he sent out to work on his behalf during the day in museums and libraries. At night the boy did his juggling act on the halls. He was Teddy Knox, later a star of the Crazy Gang.)

Rohmer had a variety of gifts. He wrote songs for Little Tich and ghosted the latter's autobiography. His bent for black and white drawing was not inconsiderable, and somewhere he had picked up

enough technical knowledge to compose music. Bransby Williams
was another of his clients, and for him he wrote monologues such
as 'The Pigtail of Li Fang Foo', where the expert harmonies and
progressions attest to his musicianship. Strange things happened
in his private life which gave him material for the dozen or so
very popular books he wrote about the villainous Fu Manchu.
For a time his household contained a psychic cat which, during
its stay with him, gave birth to ninety-eight kittens. Rohmer
was also afflicted with the habit of sleep-walking. Once, in the
course of such a bout, he attempted to murder his father. Later
his wife found a crude but effective solution to the problem. As
he stumbled in a soporific daze around the house she biffed him
smartly with a pillow. He never sleep-walked again.

After he had written a few songs for Robey they discovered
mutual interests. Robey's collection of porcelain intrigued him.
They both had a passion for Egyptology. One of Robey's presents
to him was a particularly fine edition of the ancient Egyptian *Book of
the Dead*. In 1910 Robey had an idea for a series of essays, although
as yet he did not possess the required literary skill to put them
into shape. Rohmer helped him do this and the volume came out
with the title *Pause!* and, on the cover, a man's hand was held up
in a drawing which had been Robey's inspiration too.

One of the best songs Rohmer composed for him was 'Bang
Went the Chance of a Lifetime!' It emerged from one of Rohmer's
own experiences. While enduring a haircut by his garrulous barber
he heard that the latter had an old picture he wanted to get rid
of. He offered it to Rohmer for five pounds, that being probably
what the gold frame was worth. His customer was not interested
and, at that moment, in any case did not possess five pounds. The
barber took the picture to Christie's where experts decided it was a
genuine portrait of Lady Hamilton by Romney and auctioned it for
sixty thousand pounds. So, with his usual acid humour, Rohmer
put together the song 'Bang Went the Chance of a Lifetime!' and
let Robey have it, though not for sixty thousand pounds. Even a
five-pound note, a large and beautifully engraved piece of white
paper, was a lot of money in those days. Sixty thousand pounds
needs to be multiplied by at least ten to give its present value.

Some of the music for *Round In Fifty* came from Herman Finck,
conductor of the orchestra at the Palace Theatre over many years.

There his rule was unchallenged since, being able to play, unlike many conductors, every instrument in the orchestra himself, he could easily dominate unruly theatre musicians. His most famous composition was the insidious 'In the Shadows' – once heard it is impossible to forget – and the music-hall songs 'Gilbert the Filbert' and 'I'll Make a Man of You'. He was given to a form of compulsive punning which today seems pathological. More amusing are his straight witticisms. An admirer of a famous Russian dancer once exclaimed, 'He can do anything!' 'But wash,' added Finck. There were, though, rare occasions when even he was speechless. On a trip to Richmond Church hoping to find the tomb of the actor Edmund Kean he asked for help from a pew-opener. ('He can't be anything else,' insisted Finck, 'look at the size of his hands!') The pew-opener had never heard of the actor and evinced boredom.

'Well, anyway, you're not keen,' snapped Finck.

'No – my name's Gibbons.'

And there was the time when 'In the Shadows' was selling millions of copies and would have sold yet more but for the activities of copyright pirates. Outside a West End restaurant a hawker laid a detaining hand on Finck's shoulder. ''Ere, captain,' he said, 'I sees you've got a musical ear – "In The Shadows" – music same as the copyright – only tuppence!'

Wylie's partner Tate was to have collaborated on the music of *Round In Fifty*. The vacancy produced at his sudden death was filled by the versatile Sax Rohmer. It was also Rohmer's idea to use filmed sequences projected on a giant screen. When Robey as Phil missed the sailing of an Atlantic liner, he was shown speeding after it in a motor launch. Another exciting episode depicted him racing along the Portsmouth road just in time to win his bet thanks to the unexpected onset of wintertime. His greatest worry was supposed to be the taxi he had left behind him in London, its meter ticking over inexorably. 'Fifty days,' he soliloquised, 'fifty days of twenty-four hours each, at tuppence a tick – how much change will there be for me out of a pound note when I get back?'

From London the scene moved to Boulogne and on to Brindisi, Hong Kong and San Francisco. A white and silver Chinese ballet featured pagodas under a crimson sky. In California, while day turned into night, an illuminated steamer glided across a lake and an orange glow became a mass of shooting stars. These splendours, combined with Robey's drawing power, ensured a run of four hundred and seventy-one performances for *Round In Fifty*.

When it was over he allowed himself a rare three-week holiday and, on his return to London, found that Oswald Stoll had invoked his contract again to star him in *You'd Be Surprised*, a revue described as a 'jazzaganza'. The public was, indeed, surprised, for the theatre into which the new revue had been booked was none other than the Royal Opera House, Covent Garden. That venerable building was no longer used as a furniture warehouse and had, thanks to Beecham and others, become the home of opera again. There was concern that a music-hall comedian should be appearing on a stage once dignified by Caruso and Melba. Would he make his entrance as a comic Lohengrin riding a swan? Would he profane the temple of art with jokes in bad taste? Both he and Stoll took full advantage of the publicity generated by the choice of setting and stirred up interest with teasing predictions of what to expect. In the event he did not appear on the back of a swan but strolled from the wings and remarked, 'I had hoped, I say, I had hoped that my peregrinations from the halls of raucous song and ill-clad Terpsichore to this temple of ancient and classic consonance would have synchronised with a general improvement in your demeanour. But alas! I fear such is not the case.'

It was not, and, in his 'desecration' of Covent Garden, he did his best to pull together an awkwardly assembled production which, too Americanised, too diffuse, ran only for a few months. By March 1924, he was back at the Hippodrome under Julian Wylie's aegis in *Leap Year*, a revue mainly written by Julian's brother Lauri. That was the year of the Empire Exhibition at Wembley, and as a topical gesture *Leap Year* included episodes from Canada, South Africa and Australia, together with a gorgeous ballet called *Emblems of Empire*. The crowds who poured into London for the exhibition brought full houses at the Hippodrome and, by coincidence, a long run of exactly the same number of performances as *Round In Fifty*.

Coming out of the theatre late one night Robey was accosted by a stately gentleman in evening dress. 'Excuse me, sir, but can you find room for a mule in this show?' he asked. His eye glittered strangely.

'I'm afraid not,' Robey answered. 'All the mule parts are filled already.'

The gentleman pressed his case. 'That's a pity. I have a mule that would make the fortune of this piece. He's a born comedian. I lent him to a pantomime at Christmas, and they talk of him still. The pantomime was *The Forty Thieves*.' The unknown went on to explain that his mule had kicked down all the scenery, kicked away the wings and the top ends of two double basses protruding out of the orchestra, sent the footlights flying into the stalls and pinned Ali Baba himself to the stage. After which the interesting animal had romped around like a blend of hystero-epilepsy and a cab accident.

'That was some mule,' said Robey tentatively as he looked around for a policeman.

Another personage materialised from among the crowd and kindly but firmly grasped the owner of the mule by the arm. 'I'm sorry, sir, but the gentleman isn't quite himself,' he whispered as he led him uncomplainingly away.

Much more annoying for Robey than the occasional madman was the imposition of an understudy. In *Round In Fifty* and *Leap Year* this was Harry Brunning, an experienced actor and keen admirer of Robey.

'Who's that fellow sitting there doing nothing?' enquired Robey at rehearsal.

'That's Harry Brunning, your walking understudy,' Wylie explained.

'I don't want a bleeding understudy,' snapped Robey. 'I've never been "off" in forty years, and I'm as fit as a fiddle now.'

But if, Wylie said, there was an emergency and no one to play his part, then the theatre would have to close and everyone, performers included, would lose a great deal of money.

'Well,' grunted Robey, 'he stares at me all the time. Makes me self-conscious, and I can't rehearse like that.'

Since he detested the very idea of an understudy – it implied an insult to himself, an unnecessary expense to the management, a slur on his ability to deliver the goods – he made things as difficult as possible for the unfortunate Brunning. He even refused to let him have copies of his songs so that Brunning was forced to crouch in some dark corner and make hasty notes as he sang them. While enduring this treatment Brunning was invited to appear at his wife's benefit night with a Shanklin concert party. Robey agreed that Brunning could be released for this engagement. 'Stay away for a bleeding fortnight,' he told him. 'Have a nice holiday. There's no chance of me being off.' On the crucial night, five minutes before curtain-up, Robey had not appeared. He was still invisible at starting time. The opening sketch, in which he featured, began, and the despairing stage-manager begged the players to gag their way through without him. At the precise moment when he was due to speak his first line Robey suddenly came on, fully made-up and in costume, and responded to his cue. It was only a gag, he told the exhausted stage-manager afterwards, and he had thought it would be a funny trick to play.

He never conquered his hatred of understudies. There was a time when he caught a bad attack of influenza and his doctor forbade him to appear. His co-star refused to go on with his understudy, so he climbed out of bed, tottered down to the theatre and told her he would play as usual.

'Oh well,' she replied, 'I'll go on too.'

'Oh no you won't,' he snarled, 'you old cow, you'll stay off and give your understudy a chance.'

[iii]

A Garden of Eden just made for two

By 1925 Robey had spent nearly a decade in revues and made a name for himself independent of the music-hall. In March that year he continued his success with *Sky High* at the Palladium. This time his exaggerated eyebrows were rivalled by those of his partner Nellie Wallace, a comedienne always billed as 'The Essence of Eccentricity', though she could more truly be described as the acme of vulgarity. It was her custom to make a curtain speech that ran like this:

> A man may kiss a maid goodbye,
> The sun may kiss a butterfly,
> The morning dew may kiss the grass,
> And you my friends . . . farewell.

The sad downward inflexion of the word farewell, says her contemporary Douglas Byng, 'took away the rather rude implication'.

On her head there perched what looked like an up-turned saucer, black in colour, moored by a piece of grubby elastic crowned with a bundle of bedraggled feathers. Large black eyebrows were painted on her forehead, and from her mouth projected a row of teeth that gave the impression of having been hung out to dry and then forgotten. Around her neck dangled a moth-eaten bit of fur, 'me little bit of vermin' as she affectionately called it. Beneath her garishly coloured jumper – 'they bring out the figure so well,' she used to explain – she wore a tartan skirt that often flew up to show expanses of red flannel. As a child trouper she had played the death of Little Willy in that lachrymose drama *East Lynne* and brought the house down with hysterical laughter. While playing Joan of Arc she made her entrance on the back of a horse which sneezed unexpectedly and sent her flying into the orchestra pit. After this she realised that the only place for her was the music-hall, where she soon became the leading grotesque of her time. At the age of seventy-eight, during the 1948 Royal Variety Performance, she sang one of her favourite numbers, 'A Boy's Best Friend Is His Mother', collapsed in the wings and died the following day.

Twitching her great parrot's beak of a nose, embroidering the melodic line with inimitable gurgles and yodels, she would desperately chant:

> My mother said always look under the bed,
> Before you blow the candle out, to see if there's a man about.
> I always do, but you can make a bet
> It's never been my luck to find a man there yet!

Then, with a mad wave of the 'little bit of vermin' and a twiddle of her elastic-sided button boots, she would pose coyly and declare: 'It's excitement, all excitement. If you're fond of anything tasty, what price me?' Sometimes, dressed in a shimmering, skin-tight evening gown, she would drop her fan and be obliged to lie full length to pick it up. Occasionally she was able to bend down, and when she did a trombone in the orchestra would emit a shattering burp which brought a look of icy outrage to her face. Alec Guinness, her childhood admirer, remembers a sketch in which she played a nurse at an operation. While the surgeon tackled a sheeted patient with a vast carving knife she would extract, now and then, improbable items from beneath the sheet: a live chicken, a flat-iron, a hot-water bottle. These she held aloft with a shout of gleeful triumph. Finally she inserted a long rubber tube and blew down it. The patient, still covered in a sheet, inflated enormously and began to hover in the air. She leaped up and down, her button boots flashing, as she tried unsuccessfully to earth it with an accompaniment of tremendous blasts from the orchestra at each attempt. Guinness, then only a small boy, sent her a bunch of yellow roses backstage. Then, overcome with the excitement, his temperature rose to one hundred and four and he took to his bed. A week later he received, in turn, a large bouquet of yellow roses with a card that read: 'I hope the little boy who sent me flowers gets better soon. Love, Nellie Wallace.'

She was eccentric in private life, too. Stanley Holloway remembered her patrolling backstage and wielding a disinfectant spray gun in search of flies. 'Filthy beasts!' she hissed. 'Dirty beasts!' Like Billy Bennett and Little Tich, she sang, in her hoarse and plaintive voice, songs that had a surreal touch:

> Tonight I'm alone, broken-hearted,
> To mother I've murmured 'Good-Byee';
> From the home of my youth I've departed
> With a tear in my bonny blue eye.
> Forget all my troubles I can't, though I've tried –
> There's only one thing left for me, suici-i-ide –
> I don't like my mother's
> > *Pie* crust;
> Eat it? No! – I'd sooner
> > *Die* fust.
> I've tied it round me neck
> And tomorrow I shall be –
> Down at the bottom of the deep blue sea.

She was, in addition, the only woman to be a successful pantomime dame. When Robey left *Jack and the Beanstalk* for *Round In Fifty* it was Nellie Wallace who took his place. As Dame Trot she ironed an overflowing bundle of unmentionable garments with Rabelaisian vivacity.

While Nellie Wallace busied herself with the low comedy element in *Sky High* Robey was concerned in a major love affair. This involved his leading lady Marie Blanche. 'Her versatility as an actress and singer was well known,' is the discreet comment he allows himself in his autobiography. The same versatility enchanted him in other spheres. She was then in her early thirties and a divorcée, with, already, a long career which included many ingénue parts in musical comedies and roles as principal boy in pantomime. Her irruption into his existence put an end to family life for him. Even by then it had become sporadic. His wife Ethel, plumply handsome in youth, had grown very fat and lost her looks. The two children, Edward and Eileen, preferred to confide their problems in her since she was a gentle and loving parent, whereas their father, though bound to them with strong affection, tended to scare them somewhat. They did not feel entirely at ease with him, and if they misbehaved they immediately repented when Mrs Robey threatened to 'tell your father'. Robey detested the thought of his son going on the stage, and when Edward appeared in amateur performances of Gilbert and Sullivan, for whose operettas he had a lifelong taste, he made sure his father never got to know about it. Eventually, with Robey's approval, he took up law, for, as he said, 'the nearest thing to acting seemed to be the Bar'. Robey agreed, observing, 'Well, the Old Bailey is a damned fine scene.' For a long time he worked under the Director of Public Prosecutions and appeared in famous cases like that of the acid bath murders. After taking part in the Nuremberg War Trials he became a jovial stipendiary magistrate at Marlborough Street police court. His enjoyment of Gilbert and Sullivan brought light relief to a career in which, as prosecutor, he had obtained seventy-four death sentences. Thirty-six of them were duly carried out on the scaffold.

At the time of *Sky High* he was twenty-five years old and a briefless barrister supported by his father. The family then lived in Victoria Road, Kensington, where Robey had laid out his collections of objets d'art in some grandeur. Mrs Robey, her beauty gone and her figure shapeless, could not compete with the glamorous young stars who were his permanent companions. She was hurt and wearied by his constant infidelities. 'Women were his one weakness,' remarked Edward, 'almost one might say an obsession.' On the surface life in the spacious Kensington house appeared normal. Robey's daughter Eileen was a gifted portrait painter and Edward showed promise as an aspiring barrister. Robey himself, though, was rarely present. He and his wife now led entirely separate lives. Much later he commented: 'We had a wonderful son and a wonderful daughter – very talented, both of them – and it was a happy life at that time, but I was away too much, I've no doubt.' They might have continued to live together in a neutral atmosphere had not two of Mrs Robey's friends urged her to issue an ultimatum about Marie Blanche, the latest in a long series of mistresses. He promised that he would have nothing more to do with her, although he had little intention of keeping his word. A year or so later Robey toured South Africa and his ship put in at Funchal, Madeira. With him was Marie Blanche. Another ship happened to anchor there at the same time. It was carrying Mrs Robey and her two friends on a cruise. At one dramatic point ashore all the parties concerned met each other face to face, Mrs Robey and her friends on one side, Robey and Marie Blanche on the other.

After this unspeakable coincidence Robey never came back to Victoria Road and never saw or spoke to his wife again. Edward, at Mrs Robey's behest, tried to use his legal skills as mediator, but his father steadfastly refused any personal contact with her. 'Indeed,' wrote Edward, 'I feel sure my father was glad of the excuse to be completely free.' Robey took a flat in one of those gloomy blocks around Shaftesbury Avenue and led an independent life. Sometimes he would meet Edward at the theatre where he was appearing, or at the Ivy restaurant for lunch, and there he would hear the latest family news. He rarely enquired after the mother of his children.

Defiantly, he starred Marie Blanche in his next production, a revue called *Bits and Pieces* which he put together himself. After *Sky High* he had been booked for a lucrative tour of the Moss Empires circuit. Since times were difficult in the variety world at a moment of recession he thought the management would have trouble fulfilling his conditions. He therefore suggested that he organise a full-length entertainment at his own expense and tour it on a percentage that would enable Moss Empires to make a fair profit. He would, moreover, be giving employment to twenty-five or so performers. *Bits and Pieces*, a loose assemblage of turns by comedians, dancers and singers, was pulled into shape at the Royal Albion Hotel in Brighton. He decided to try it out in smaller places before taking it round the big cities and chose Llandudno as the starting point. Suddenly the General Strike broke out and, a week or so before opening, it seemed as if there would be no trains to take the company and its baggage to Wales. Then, on the very day arranged for their departure, the railmen went back to work and Robey's flock arrived on time. The show went well, as it did in all the other towns, so well indeed that the management of the Princes Theatre in London offered a six-week Christmas season. Since another attraction was currently running there Robey was not allowed, under the contract, to advertise his own revue until it had ended. Ingenuity solved the problem. Having booked spaces on the sides of two hundred London buses, he filled them with the name of the theatre, a picture of a bowler and a huge pair of eyebrows, and the one word: COMING! Soon there were long queues at the advance booking office, queues of the sort he loved to photograph for his unique collection.

Bits and Pieces was so successful at the Princes that it ran well into 1927 and its original six-week booking became one of six months. Robey's own numbers included his impersonation of an orange-blossomed bride. Carolling 'The strife is o'er, the battle won', he tripped on stage to soliloquise:

I've flopped, never to flap again. Oh, and I do feel so fun-ny . . . I feel as if all me past life was running down the back of me neck. I don't know whether to laugh or cry, or mix 'em both up like a Seidlitz powder. I feel like a potato – I want to be mashed.* Mind you, I wasn't sure of him till the banns went up three weeks ago. They do say there's always three clear Sundays before an execution takes place, and I don't know whether he's got any money or not, but I *do* know he pays income tax. I suppose that's why he's taken me on – to get a bit off. Of

* Mashed = Edwardian slang for 'chatted up'.
  Masher = Ladykiller.

course, everything's so different now, and so strange. I have
to be careful what I say and do now . . . If ever I mention
him to any of my friends I can refer to him as 'Mai Husbarnd'
. . . I can say 'Mai Husbarnd' without getting funny looks from
people. And only a few weeks ago I didn't know whether to
look on him as a gift from heaven or a thundering liar. Mind
you, girls, this wedding business is no joke. Oh, no. It's a very
serious business is marriage you know. There isn't a word for
marriage . . . it's a sentence.*

Apart from the *double-entente* of 'to get a bit off' and the concluding
epigram, the material sounds almost as antiquated as those fustian
speeches of the clowns in Shakespeare, so quickly do modes in slang
and humour change. Yet this was the most popular comedian of
the day speaking, one whose every sentence was punctuated by
laughter from the audience. We miss the benefit of seeing him
and of noting how the flickering eyebrow, the prim gaze, the
telling gesture, illuminated and gave pith to the words. James
Agate, an exacting judge, who saw *Bits and Pieces* at an early
try-out in the Golder's Green Hippodrome, described Robey as
'our national comic genius'. He added:

To deplore that Robey is '*always* the same' seems to me to be the
authentic mark of futility in a critic. Of course he is always the
same and the gods be praised for it. Just as the great romantic
actor colours everything that he plays with his own peculiar
splendour so Robey casts the mantle of his own comicality
and nobody else's over every subject of his contemplation –
legs of mutton, Cassiopeia's chair, the lodger and the lodger's
landlady. The gusto of Munden, said the essayist, antiquated
and ennobled whatever it touched. I do not know what Lamb
would have thought of the story of the eel-vendor and the Bank
of England or of the ditty about the little pigs who lie in the
best of straw. Nor do I know what the audience at Golder's
Green thought. I only know that such laughter has not been
heard since the days of *The Bing Boys*. It is sometimes said that
this actor's humour is less ripe than it was – a dictum which

* Quoted in Wilmut, *Kindly Leave The Stage!* p.27 (see Bibliography).

betrays a certain unfamiliarity with the workings of Nature. Let
me declare that Mr Robey's performance on Thursday last was
the finest I have ever seen him give. And I speak for, I suppose,
some thirty years.

It is significant that, rather than the word 'comedian', Agate uses
the word 'actor'.

Agate's counterpart on the *Observer*, St John Ervine, gave a
postscript on what he called Robey's 'jug and bottle humour':

> If I say this humour is vulgar I do not mean that it is offensive.
> It is vulgar only in the sense that it is the sort of fun that bubbles
> out of good-natured, unassuming common people to whom the
> simple facts of elementary existence are the only facts. Mr Robey
> fully and funnily exploits those humours and makes us realise
> the essential cheerfulness of the Cockney to whom poverty and
> disaster are finally comic.

Bits and Pieces was to have a long life and to make him more
money than any other show had done before. In June 1927, he
took the whole company to South Africa on a three-month tour
by way of Capetown, Johannesburg, Pretoria, Bloemfontein and
other big cities. Guards of honour welcomed him at railway
stations, mayors delivered greetings, diamond tycoons entertained
him with lavish banquets. The continual warmth and dazzling
sunshine enchanted him, the Zulus fascinated him. At a kraal
near Johannesburg two thousand of them drew up in battle array,
made the ground shake with their rhythmic stamping and hailed
him in roars of 'Baas!' He took an assegai and juggled, throwing it high in the air and catching it faultlessly. At a Kaffir
war dance the performers grew more and more frenzied until
they foamed at the mouth. They gave him an elaborate white
shield and, at the end, saluted him with mighty shouts of 'King
George!'

In September the company set sail from Capetown as Robey, on
the deck of the *Edinburgh Castle*, watched the city and the mountain
dwindle into a haze of sunshine. Below, in his cases, was packed
a magnificent haul of assegais, knobkerries and battle-axes to add
to his London collections. The ship called in at Madeira where he

and Marie Blanche had their frigid encounter with Mrs Robey and her friends. Afterwards he dispelled the gloom by showing off a green parrot he had acquired. It was called Joey and could swear, fluently and expertly, in Portuguese.

London seemed dim and chilly when he reached it in September 1927. Autumn fogs were about to descend and obscure his memories of the clear sharp sun of South Africa. Bradford, when he started another provincial tour of *Bits and Pieces*, had a monochrome tinge. He missed the warmth, the colour, the brightness of his visit abroad. By the middle of 1928 he was on his world travels again and headed for Canada, still with *Bits and Pieces*. Here, as in South Africa, he felt oddly at home and was touched by the patriotism of the people he met who looked on England as their mother country. Everywhere he went there were Canadian ex-servicemen who talked to him about experiences at the Front and wartime memories of the Alhambra and the Hippodrome. As he made his long rail journeys back and forth across the country, there were often groups of them waiting for him at remote stations where the train would stop specially so that he could get out and chat with them. In Vancouver he gave a performance for returned soldiers and another at an ex-servicemen's hospital. When they sang 'Land of Hope and Glory' and 'God Save The King' his feelings about the Empire became positively Disraelian. Ontario, he discovered with pleasure, had its own Pall Mall, its own Piccadilly and its own River Thames. It soon had Robey as its own Freeman when the Mayor presented him, on stage, with a charter and a large golden key.

He had arrived in Canada 'when the maple was beginning to turn scarlet,' he wrote. 'I left when the winter snows were beginning to gather.' In between he traversed the country's plains and mountains. He saw the Rockies with their peaks and glaciers, their cascades and frozen lakes. In Alberta he visited an Indian reservation and was made a chief of the Sarcee tribe. The ceremony was conducted by Joe Big Plume who solemnly placed upon his head a massive head-dress of eagle feathers so long that it hung down his back. The words of the initiation were translated by a Sarcee maiden called Daisy Otter. Distinguished guests included the buffalo hunter Lame Bull, the ancient warrior Fox Tail, the keeper of beaver medicine Two Guns, and the former chief Big

Belly. 'You have come to us from far across the seas and your mission in life is to make people happy,' intoned Joe Big Plume. 'That is good, and the Sarcee nation is much honoured in naming you Dit-Ony-Chusan, or Chief Eagle Plume, in memory of one of our great councillors and warriors.' The new Chief Eagle Plume, whose dark single-breasted suit emphasised the vivid colours of his towering head-dress, received the document of initiation with becoming gravity.

His three months in Canada had been a raging success. 'As I look back upon the experience,' he wrote, 'I seem to see it as an unbroken happiness.' The return to England proved to be not so agreeable. In December he put on, at the Carlton, another show of his own devising called *In Other Words*, the title adopted from one of his popular songs. Both with the press and the public it turned out to be a failure. This, after so many years of triumph, was a disconcerting blow. As a professional, however, he did not repine and set to work immediately, revising, adjusting, replacing old material with new. When he tried out *In Other Words* at Manchester it redeemed itself and enticed full houses. The public, he believed, was always right, and he, as the servant of that public, must always honour its opinion.

A repeat tour of South Africa in the early months of 1929 restored him completely. When he came back to England, though, he decided he had enough of management. At the age of sixty he was tired of organising, of directing other people, of worrying over receipts, of dissipating his creative energy on administration. He went solo again and knew once more the joyous feeling of independence as top of the bill at the London Palladium and the Victoria Palace. Of his sketch based on the German music professor *The Times* wrote:

It is quite probable that Mr George Robey, who is appearing at the Palladium this week, will be remembered more for his consummate playing of musical instruments than anything else. His touch with the triangle with the whole Palladium orchestra blaring about him, his sense of the moment to hit the big drum when the slightest failing in timing would have ruined a time-honoured turn, his feeling for the *timbre* of the bells he so subtly jangles are all magnificent.

. . . The Only Girl in the World

It was a relief to be on his own again.

When I was running a show in London they charged me £800 a week for the bare walls of a theatre. My orchestra brought the expense near to £1,000 a week. Then I had to pay the staff in front and behind the curtain and there was a large advertising bill. I had to pay an expensive company and allow something for myself. I go into variety at the Palladium, just myself and a few 'props', no anxiety about receipts, no responsibility, only personal expenses, and they pay me £500 a week. Well, I ask you . . .

From the Palladium he trod a familiar path to the Holborn Empire. One evening, while on stage, he spotted a dapper little man who had slipped unnoticed into the stalls. Robey pointed him out to the audience. There were echoing cheers as the little man stood up and waved to the gallery. Later he came behind to Robey's dressing-room and spoke of the days, now thirty years ago, when as a small boy he had sat up in the gods at the Holborn and laughed at Robey's performance. Each night he followed him from hall to hall. As they talked he seized Robey's dilapidated bowler and put it on. Then he picked up the cane and waggled it. He had never, he said gravely, dreamed of such an honour. Old songs of Robey's came into his mind and he quoted lines from 'Prehistoric Man'. That evening, he added, he had enjoyed Robey's performance as much as ever. 'I laughed like a kid,' he remarked. 'I really think you are wonderful – as agile and strong as a man of twenty-five.' It was Charlie Chaplin speaking.

The return to variety had improved Robey's bank balance and he was prospering. Yet there were problems with income tax, and he found it a tedious chore to arrange all the complicated bookings which were urged upon him by eager theatre managers. In the old days he had handled these matters on his own. Now he found them an irritating distraction when there were so many other interesting things he wanted to do. Among the dates he played with a *Bits and Pieces* tour was the Royal Artillery Theatre in Woolwich. Once a garrison church, later burnt down and rebuilt as a theatre, it had been opened with military éclat in 1905 by Lord Roberts. The 'Royal Artillery Theatre and Opera House', as it was grandly named, flourished under the management of the formidable Mrs Agnes Mary Littler who ran it for thirty years until 1939. She had three children, of whom two were boys, Emile and Prince, and one was a girl called Blanche. Robey became interested in Blanche. She had inherited a good head for business from her parents, was a deft negotiator of contracts, and knew how to settle with inspectors of the Inland Revenue. She was, without a doubt, the manager he needed.

The Littler children had been brought up in their Ramsgate home surrounded by an atmosphere of theatre. At meal-times the conversation was of percentages, gross takings, programme building. Their parents spoke of bookings and contracts, of bar receipts and ticket reservations. Prince, the younger brother, followed his parents into the business and, by the late 1930s, owned or leased a number of provincial theatres and had an interest in many others. He became a very influential figure in the Stoll organisation, was chairman of Moss Empires and director of Howard and Wyndham. The shows associated with him over three decades ranged from Ivor Novello musicals and *The Barretts of Wimpole Street* to *Guys and Dolls* and *The Farmer's Wife*. Each Christmas he presented seven or eight pantomimes in the provincial capitals. All the traditional honours came his way: a CBE, presidency of the home for aged actors and actresses at Denville Hall, and chairmanship of benevolent societies. His talent for production extended also to the pedigree Guernsey cattle of which he bred a notably fine herd in Sussex. His brother Emile had a no less distinguished career. After experience in America he ran the Birmingham Repertory Theatre for Barry Jackson and went into management on his own account. A burgeoning network of company directorships linked him with many of the most famous inter-war stage hits. On occasion he ventured into authorship and part-wrote comedies with titles such as *Love Isn't Everything*. In later years he added television to his multifarious activities. Like the rest of the family he could not resist pantomime, and, in the middle of a hot summer, was happily organising snowbound transformation scenes. As a symbol of his preoccupation, he gave to his office in Birmingham the name of Pantomime House.

Blanche was helping to run the Woolwich Theatre at the age of sixteen. She quickly learned the business and, in her late twenties, had her own production company and a partnership in one of her brother Prince's concerns. Provincial tours in those days could be very lucrative. Once a London impresario had taken all the risks and scored a hit, the organisation that made the touring arrangements could look forward to a very substantial return on an investment virtually free of hazard. Blanche and Prince did very well out of touring West End successes.

When Robey agreed to appear at the Royal Artillery Theatre Blanche was very grateful. The place did not really have the seating capacity to cover his usual fee and the expense of the supporting company. Still, there were sold-out houses every night of the week. At the end of the booking she suggested to Prince that he go behind and congratulate Robey. Prince demurred, being strangely shy, so Blanche went round herself to thank the artist whom she admired deeply. Their conversation was long and friendly. He told her of the income tax problems which his huge earnings had attracted and of his tangled business affairs. She heard him sympathetically and wondered at his naïveté, for he had not realised that he should have been putting money aside to meet the demands of the tax authorities when, inevitably, they arrived. He was, she thought, despite his fame and his popularity, in a rather pathetic state. Within a few weeks she was arranging his bookings, answering his letters, compiling his tax returns, reading plays for him and even supervising his band calls. She had very quickly become 'the only girl in the world' for him.

Chaperoned by a woman relative she went to tea at Robey's bachelor flat in Shaftesbury Avenue. Having heard of his exquisite collection of china and objets d'art she expected luxury. When he opened the door she was startled: the rooms were cramped and dark. The only flicker of life came from a small coal-fire. Robey presented his guests with tea in large, thick cups. No doubt, he told them complacently, they were surprised at the speed with which he made it. Delighted at his own ingenuity, he explained that he had kept the kettle on the boil all afternoon in readiness for their arrival. Here was a man, she reflected, who needed someone to look after him not only as a star but as a human being. After that meeting in the cheerless flat they took to lunching regularly at the Ivy restaurant. On their first date, beaming nervously, Robey held her hand under the table.

Her parents did not disapprove of the relationship. Robey, in fact, took care to win them over, to charm, to please with conversation that usually had an intellectual or literary content. Blanche's father, much interested in Shakespeare and the classics, had friendly jousts in which he challenged him to identify quotations. Robey never failed. There was, however, the question of age. In 1929 Robey was sixty years old and Blanche only thirty. By marrying a man twice her age – for marriage had already been spoken of – she would, her father pointed out, have a very old party on her hands when she reached her own middle years. She conceded the argument but replied that if they could have a period of happiness together, then that was something to be very thankful for. Robey, now, was tired of philandering. Marie Blanche and the others belonged to the past. He wanted peace and security. He loved Blanche Littler and she loved him. He had become a one-woman man. Another nine years were to pass before he obtained a divorce from his wife. In the meantime he and Blanche set up house together.

He idolised her. When touring or abroad, he would write and telephone her every day.

> Whatever happens [he wrote] our lives are linked together and I know that you trust me in every way and I know you know that nothing can ever turn me away from you, you blessed gift of God to me. When I pray – as I do often now – I thank the Almighty for that lovely moment when that dear woman came into my dressing-room at Woolwich and told me that she was 'the manageress'. I have been a different man from that moment. I still do my nonsensical things but deep down a something has been stirred that will go with me to the grave and I thank you, my blessed one, for the greatest and most wonderful happiness that any man could wish for. I love you.

In Birmingham, where he was appearing at the Hippodrome and she had gone to see a new play, he took her out to an early lunch saying he wanted to show her something while she was there. Afterwards, surprised, she was escorted to the cathedral. There he asked her, 'in the presence of God and in His house', to stay with him until they could be legally married. He thanked God that they had been brought together. His promise, he said, was that he would never say or do anything to cause her unhappiness.

Again and again he would hark back to that wonderful, that unforgettable moment when the unknown young woman appeared in his dressing-room and introduced herself as the manageress of the Royal Artillery Theatre. Woolwich, for him, was not a place of street markets and arsenals, of noisy soldier cadets and dim warehouses overlooking the muddy Thames, but one of supreme romance, because it was there that he had met 'my dearest, sweetest and loveliest in all the world'. He hated leaving her to go on tour: 'It is a wrench to part again,' he told her. 'It has all been so utterly marvellous that it frightens me for fear that anything might happen to either of us. Nothing could describe the happiness that you have given me . . . Thank God for it all and you, my dearest dear, for the love you have given me.' And after a short reunion between journeys he would write in almost liturgical mode: 'Thank the Lord for quiet rest and for thy care of me. Darling, that's how I feel about my lovely day today, seeing my dear sweetheart and having that beautiful rest with my dear one sitting beside me. It was the first time that I have felt happy and comfortable this week. I was so glad to see that my babe was better and looking like her old self. Goodnight, my beloved, am looking forward to phoning tonight.'

Two years later he was writing:

My love – I can hardly believe that two years have passed and have gone! How I wish that I could have them back. They have been two years that I thank the Almighty for – and you, my dear. You have given me two years of wonderful happiness and comfort such as I have never had, and only hope to have in the continuance of your love and care of me. Bless you, my lovely sweetheart; if the future only holds half the joy and glory of the last two years I shall be satisfied.

When he embarked on a solo tour she would see him off with little presents, bunches of roses, boxes of cigarettes, which he would open eagerly in the train as it moved out of the station. 'If I lost you it would be the finish of everything for me, so please, darling, look after me,' he wrote. She was his wife, his mistress, his manageress, his accountant, his secretary, his unfailing companion. He, in turn was irresistible to her. She found him the perfect artist and the ideal husband. She regarded him with a fierce admiration. It amused her, sometimes, that when by chance she happened to speak to a good-looking young man he would become jealous and uneasy. Even if he did not know the person concerned, he would, in his agitation, invent dreadful stories about him to try to put her off an imagined favourite. He need not have worried. Her devotion to him was complete and unshakeable. He overwhelmed her. When she tried to analyse her feelings about him she could only say that he was 'awfully lovable and awfully kind'. There was something about him, she said, that drew her to him, something that attracted her magnetically. She never, ever, wanted to be separated from him.

One day after Robey's death she was driving along the promenade at Brighton with her friend the male impersonator Hetty King. As they passed the statue of Queen Victoria Blanche lifted her gaze to the grim stone features and protested, 'Look at that! *She* shouldn't be up there, that's where my George ought to be.'

'What?' said Hetty King. 'Are you serious?'

'Of course I am,' snapped Blanche. 'George's statue should be there, not hers – he was more popular than she was!' She meant every word of what she said.

Yet the marriage was not entirely one of cloying sweetness. Accompanied by Blanche on a train journey between dates, Hetty King remembered him sitting quietly in a corner of the compartment. The silky grey hair, the hands primly crossed, suggested a bishop relaxing from his pastoral labours. 'Sleeping,' Blanche whispered, 'he's sleeping.' Assured that, for the time being, her darling was out of harm, she left the compartment to freshen her make-up. As soon as she had gone he came to life and pointed at the hat-box which always accompanied him. It contained a choice selection of brandy, gin and whisky.

'Quick, quick, give me a drink, quick before she comes back.'

'I can't,' Hetty King replied in embarrassment, 'you'll have me murdered!'

'Go on, don't yap, woman,' he commanded, 'get on with it.'

So, with furtive speed, she poured his drink, and, when he had done, briskly restored the empty glass to its hiding place. At Blanche's return he was slumbering peacefully, benign as ever, in his corner.

CHAPTER IV

FROM OFFENBACH TO SHAKESPEARE

[i]

'Go on, you silly old cow'

Variety in the 1930s was going through a difficult period. The Wall Street crash of 1929 helped to intensify an economic recession already well entrenched in England and to swell the numbers of unemployed. Although seats at music-halls were comparatively cheap, audiences began to shrink. An added complication was the arrival of the sound film, which, offering comfort and spectacle far beyond the resources of theatre, posed the gravest threat so far. Robey, well aware how the wind blew, decided on an experiment with what were then known as 'talkies'.

In 1931 he made his first sound film. It was called *The Temperance Fête* and ran for a modest three-quarters of an hour. The plot came from a series of books by Herbert Jenkins, author as well as publisher, featuring the adventures of a Cockney removal man called Bindle. They were, in their time, very popular, and today may be found on the shelves of second-hand booksellers in numbers testifying to the demand that once existed for them. Bindle's wife is a gaunt, shrewish, Bible-thumping female whose only virtue is her skill at cooking exquisite meals for her lord. Their life together resolves into a sequence of battles in which he deflects her reproaches about his ungodly, beer-swilling life with good-natured witty banter. She, an ardent temperance advocate, gets him put in charge of the lemonade stall at a fête. He cannot resist doctoring the refreshment with alcohol, and the highly respectable guests, including his pious brother-in-law, a grocer of the strictest morals, career madly about in a state of unseemly drunkenness. Robey's cheerful leer and benevolent larkishness made him a good choice for Bindle. His brother-in-law, haggard and dyspeptic, was played by the cadaverous Gibb McLaughlin, an unsung character actor whose career lasted some forty years. As an ancient butler, as a Chinese ghoul, as a prune-faced maître d'hôtel, as a dried-up solicitor, he was omnipresent in British films, of which he made over a hundred and ten, between 1920 and 1960. Mrs Bindle was played by Sydney Fairbrother, a *nom de guerre* adopted by the actress, though hardly as a change for the better, in preference to her original name of Tapping. Her forte was tough old Cockney women. She was supported in *The Temperance Fête* by a player with the even more baroque name of Anita Sharp-Bolster.

A year later he was in *Marry Me*, a musical film put together under the impeccable auspices of Michael Balcon and Anthony Asquith. At the box-office it was probably the most successful film he had made to date. The leading lady, Renate Muller, had been imported from Germany in an attempt to capitalise on her popularity at home, and the film was shot in English and German, which latter language, of course, Robey spoke well. The setting, again designed to appeal abroad, was Berlin, and the action centred upon a gramophone factory where Fräulein Muller fell in love with the romantic lead Ian Hunter, a junior matinée idol of South African origins who later matured into a reliable player of charming noblemen, worldly *raisonneurs* and the third party in eternal triangles. In *Marry Me* he continued to reject the heroine, but she, on becoming his housekeeper, managed to win him back, whereupon, as Beaumarchais would have said, everything ended in music and songs. As always in British films of this period, however dire they might be, minor delights were to be found among the supporting players who on this occasion included Charles Hawtrey, the future ditherer in the *Carry On* series of films. He had slightly altered his name Hartree to resemble, one imagines, more nearly that of the famous Edwardian actor-manager, and added the suffix 'junior' to suggest an even closer relationship. It is a little startling to realise that he began his career at the age of eight in a silent film of 1922 before graduating as one of the superior schoolboys whom Will Hay, a bumbling form master, attempted ineffectually to outwit. With his high voice, petulant mouth, gooseberry eyes and clothes-horse frame he gave his best performances as a member of the *Carry On* team.

Robey himself was reasonably satisfied with *Marry Me*, in which he played the dupe of a shady matrimonial agency. Although he still did not feel entirely at ease before the camera, he was beginning to adapt the techniques of a lifetime for a medium which he regarded with caution. His next film should have been something remarkable, for it was directed by the Austrian G. W. Pabst who had already established himself as a talented film maker. *Die Freudlose Gasse*, which under its English title of *Joyless Street* sounds just as depressing, is now a classic silent film, as are *The Love of Jeanne Ney* and *Pandora's Box*, the latter starring the enigmatic Louise Brooks who contributed signally to the erotic atmosphere. A version of Brecht's *Threepenny Opera* and the technical brilliance of *Kameradschaft* confirmed Pabst's reputation. He now planned to make a film of *Don Quixote*, gallicised as *Don Quichotte*. For the knight of the doleful countenance he engaged the opera singer Chaliapin, and for Sancho Panza he chose Robey. The casting of Chaliapin was not such a surprise as it might seem. The great bass was not only a fine musician but also a much more accomplished actor than many other singers who often know little more than the notes of their part. His dominating personality and his gestures were based on a subtle dramatic technique imbued with profound musicality and intuitive stagecraft. It was appropriate that, twenty or so years before, he should have triumphed in Massenet's opera, *Don Quichotte*.

Having shivered in the rains of Keswick while making his earlier, more primitive film of *Don Quixote*, Robey looked forward to wandering through the sierras and moonlit forests known by the hero, to gliding along the Ebro, to viewing the sunny roofs of Barcelona and Saragossa. He was disappointed when he learned that all the outdoor scenes were to be shot in France around the hinterland of Nice and Grasse. To France he went, expecting his return within four weeks. Instead, he was away for twelve. The weather proved as unreliable as Keswick's had been. For days he sat cursing on a bench under the palm trees of Nice looking at hills wreathed in dark clouds, a sky grey with threats of rain, and a sea muddy as the Thames at low tide. When the sun peeped shyly forth he was despatched into the mountains in a car that sped at dizzying rates along zigzag roads narrowing to a thread at corners and seeming to vanish into air. He would rather, he thought, have climbed up on his hands and knees all the way. Often, at four o'clock in the morning, he would be hauled out of bed with the urgent summons: 'Come along! We've got to be up there in twenty minutes!' Once arrived among the hairpin bends and precipices, he would see the clouds come out again and would sit around for hours blanketed in chilly mists that descended from the heights. He was not, he reflected, destined to be a mountaineer.

When the sun finally decided on a lengthy stay, so too did all the insects of the neighbourhood. One of Robey's eyes was permanently bloodshot with mosquito bites. Wasps, who seemed to be motivated by a furious dislike of Sancho Panza, made him a favourite target and stung him with the energy of mad cats. If fine weather enabled the film crew to shoot all the classic episodes – the charge against the sheep, the tilting at windmills, the release of the galley slaves – it also brought out the snakes and the scorpions. For once Robey felt grateful when a cloud passed over the sun: at its appearance even the wasps seemed disheartened and gave up their assaults. There were consolations. His rooms in the Hotel Negresco at Nice were luxurious and the management attentive. Pabst, for all his renown, turned out sympathetic and understanding. 'We had,' said Robey, 'let me say at once, a really great producer. In making pictures, Herr Pabst is simply a Master. He has the whole art at his finger-tips; his intelligence is equalled by his imperturbability, and they're both wonderful.' The towering Chaliapin proved no less amenable. 'What an actor and singer! – and what a man! His Don Quixote in that picture was the biggest and greatest performance I have ever seen. Think of scene after scene having to be done first in French and then in English, and he hardly knowing a word of either language.' One very difficult episode occurred when Quixote, mistaking Dulcinea's inn for a castle, was supposed to sing an affectionate farewell. Each time the cameras started rolling something went wrong: Quixote's horse moved, a wasp swooped, the sun went in. Tension increased and Chaliapin's nerves became tattered. Robey moved over to him and whispered: 'Next time sing "This isn't really a castle, It's only a blooming pub!"' Chaliapin did so, everyone laughed, and when he tackled the scene again it worked admirably.

While Chaliapin awaited his call, his giant figure clad in armour, his blue eyes staring sadly at the desolate Alps, Robey would try to cheer him up by teaching him English. He educated him in the correct swear-words to be used for every situation and in those hallowed exchanges about the weather that are the Englishman's birthright. Chaliapin was an excellent mimic and reproduced them colourfully. 'You would hear him firing off his replies like cannon shots,' said Robey, 'reducing the recipient first to a sort of paralysis and then to a kind of hysteria.' He did not always get the idiom right.

'Very hot work,' observed Chaliapin.

'Yes, nerve-racking,' said Robey.

'What do you call it – nerve-wacking? Nerve-wacking – that's a new English word I have learnt.'

'No, not nerve-wacking, nerve-rracking.'

'Yes, you're right, it is that. Do you know,' turning to a bystander, 'if my friend Robey did not give me liquid I would be dead with all this work. It is very slow.'

Another source of light relief was Sancho Panza's donkey. He had been lent for the production by H. G. Wells, who at the time was living nearby.

I shall always be grateful to him for having introduced me to that friendly and fascinating quadruped [said Robey]. He was the sweetest and most intelligent donkey it has been my good fortune to meet. My only regret is that I was unable to bring him back with me and have him in my act. In the mornings I would feed him with carrots. He would look round and up at me, and bare his teeth in the nearest approach to a smile I have ever seen on any animal's face. I called him by name like a dog and he would come trotting after me.

Despite complaints about weather, the discomfort of having to maintain a permanent stubble on his chin for the part and all the other irritations he described in his long letters to Blanche, he enjoyed the experience. 'Whatever I may have told you before,' he remarked to a newspaper correspondent, 'I like this film-work.

It doesn't let you hibernate. It keeps you young. I'm sixty-three and with all this work on my hands I am as fit as a lion.' He was also ready to learn. 'I try to put in as much of myself as possible, but they don't like me to overdo it. On the stage a devastating glare is just the right thing but here they want smaller, more subtle movements and a smaller sort of humour. It's no good screwing up one's face in front of a camera. Just a wink you wouldn't notice on the stage is quite enough, they say.'

The only moment of disagreement arose when the time to shoot Sancho Panza's death scene arrived. As usual in film-making, dialogue was often written overnight and the lines were fed to Robey just before he made his entrance. They included a joke about sausages. Robey the actor objected. The reference, he felt, was wholly out of place in an episode that ought to be dignified and pathetic. Despite much argument he held to his point and carried the issue. Another actor who was present said, 'I felt then, as all artists did, that he was standing out for something real and honest, when others might have thought it too trivial, and easier to fall in with the film people. It must have taken a lot of courage at that stage of his career to be "awkward", but it was just that, wasn't it, that made him so great?'

Days became weeks and weeks turned into months. Shooting overran hopelessly and took three times the period originally forecast. Robey's litany of complaint went on: 'It's now three o'clock. The buggers dragged me out of bed at half past seven this morning. "We want you at once," they said. And now just look at it. I've been hanging about here all day and not a shot. Perhaps they'll start in an hour, or in two hours, or in two days. They say it's the weather. They always say it's the weather.' At last it all ended. Pabst was not dissatisfied with his experiment. 'More Robey than Sancho,' he commented, 'but although I would like him to be more Sancho than Robey, the public will no doubt be delighted.'

The delays over *Don Quichotte* upset all the lucrative bookings Blanche arranged for him. She had signed him up for the Hippodrome and the Palladium on his return from France, but now the dates were lost and she was obliged to buy out his contracts. At that point the film company, as film companies do, had run out of money and she could get no redress from them.

He was not the only one to suffer financially. A distinguished French composer was sought to write incidental music for *Don Quichotte*. Four such were approached, each in secrecy, and Ravel agreed to accept the commission. He was, however, dilatory and did not work fast enough. In the end the music was composed by Jacques Ibert, a brisk journeyman more accustomed to the rigorous deadlines of filming than was his senior colleague. Ravel did manage to write three songs which he hoped Chaliapin would sing. They were called *Don Quichotte à Dulcinée* and had words by the novelist Paul Morand who also provided the film script. Ravel had once contemplated an opera based on *Don Quixote*, and his Spanish links made him an interesting choice. But Chaliapin was destined never to sing his music in the film, and Ravel became yet another of the unsuccessful claimants to sue the production company. *Don Quichotte à Dulcinée*, transparently harmonised and subtly flavoured with Basque dance rhythms, have an appealing simplicity. It is ironic that the drinking song which concludes them should end with the line 'I drink to happiness', for these were the last notes Ravel composed before his mind clouded over with the brain disease that shrouded his last years in twilight.

The next composer with whom Robey was to be associated after *Don Quichotte*, though more directly, was also French but of a quite different calibre. The impresario Charles Cochran had always admired Offenbach and in 1932 decided to stage an English version of the operetta *La Belle Hélène*. He set it up with all his characteristic panache and commissioned the illustrious Max Reinhardt to direct it. The writer A. P. Herbert he asked to modernise the ancient libretto but to preserve the comic tone of the original. The sets and costumes were created by a promising young designer called Oliver Messel, and the choreography by Massine. The arrangement and orchestration of the score were entrusted to Erich Korngold, a musical boy prodigy in his native Vienna which he had been forced to leave as a young man on Hitler's accession to power. Later he became a very successful writer of lush incidental music for Hollywood films, though he still kept his hand in by composing operas and symphonies. The beautiful Evelyn Laye was to impersonate Helen. In one of his many flashes of inspiration, Cochran offered the role of Menelaus, King of Sparta and red-faced cuckold, to Robey.

Here was a fresh challenge. The revues he had appeared in up to now were loosely structured affairs. Although he had been a member of a team given set lines to deliver and prearranged business to follow, within those limitations he still enjoyed a wide measure of freedom to be his own inimitable self. In operetta, however, a sterner discipline ruled that he should fit in with stars of equal renown and follow a script that had been carefully prepared. One of his fellow actors was the comedian W. H. Berry who thought his role 'too unutterably silly' and, disliking the lack of freedom, would sulk and demand he be given a topical song to put over. Then, Cochran gratefully recalled, Robey would come along 'like a ray of sunshine'. 'You and I are the luckiest fellows in the world to be in this wonderful show!' Robey would boom.

And it was, being one of Cochran's most lavish spectacles, indeed 'a wonderful show'. *Helen!*, as they called it, presented exquisite stage pictures by Oliver Messel which included the famous scene representing Helen's bedroom all in white: white curtains, two white swans on each side of a dais in a reference to Helen's parentage, four white pillars supporting the baldacchino, and white sheets strewn over the bed. In continuance of the 'white on white theme', Evelyn Laye wore a white robe tied with a blue sash. Long and arduous rehearsals went into this beautiful production. Some lingered on until six o'clock in the morning. Robey never flagged and patiently sat waiting hours for his cue. In the meantime he cheered up the weary chorus girls and told them jokes which were so awful that they could not help laughing. ('What is it that comes out of Cow(e)s all hot and steaming – and goes plonk-plonk? A *paddle steamer*, of course!') He boasted of his physical fitness and especially of his taut stomach muscles. 'Hit me there!' he would command, banging his abdomen forcefully. 'It's like timber, it's like iron! Hit me there!' A friend remembered an occasion when he hit himself so vigorously that he fell over backwards. Once, at three o'clock in the morning, Cochran and Reinhardt could not prevent themselves from dozing off. They awoke to see Robey blithely turning double somersaults across the stage.

Robey found Reinhardt an agreeable colleague and chatted fluently in German with him. Soon he absorbed the conventions of operetta and was able to accommodate them so that they fitted his individual style. If he invented a new bit of business at rehearsal he would usually keep to it later and avoid the temptation to vary it with the last-minute improvisations he would have introduced had he been playing solo. Lines were a different matter. Each night he would find new intonations and new inflections, although he scrupulously retained the cues his colleagues were expecting. Yet he could not always resist the mischief-making that came naturally to him. There were times when Evelyn Laye heaved with painful laughter at his antics while trying to preserve a statuesque presence. At the first night he was supposed to return home, greet his wife Helen as she sat in front of her dressing-table, and plaster some of her cold cream on his rubicund face. In an unrehearsed gag he picked up the pot of cream, put in his finger and licked off the muck with enjoyment. 'Stop me and buy one!' he uttered, quoting the legendary phrase chanted by street vendors of Wall's ice-cream and raising a bellow of laughter from all parts of the house.

That first night in 1932 had a rapturous tone. The audience, carefully assembled by an impresario whose skills extended front of house as well as behind, was what gossip columnists used to call 'brilliant'. James Agate spoke warmly about this 'piece of French art, French verve, French bedazzlement, and music so French that it needed a German Jew to write it'. Of Robey, wearing a Grecian bowler hat cunningly designed by Oliver Messel, Agate commented that he was

the cynosure of every eye off the stage though on the stage nobody marks him, whence it will be realised that his perfor-mance is a miracle of accommodation like that of a trombone-player obliging with a pianissimo. The old-time roars have taken on a sucking-dove quality, a Robeyism, here more honoured in the breach than in the observance, is now an overtone. The gorgeous rhetoric of the halls has been subdued to the poet's 'Nicean barks', and the performance is irresistibly comic throughout.

From Offenbach to Shakespeare

In the *Daily Mail* Alan Parsons had more conventional praise.*

I have never heard a louder laugh in the theatre than that which greets Mr Robey. Poor King Menelaus, the general butt and laughing stock, cannot even find a throne to sit on at the conference of kings. He raises the famous eyebrows and turns appealingly to the audience, and exclaims, 'Well, I meantersay.' Ancient Sparta and London suddenly touched hands across the gulf of centuries and one felt that the whole world was kin. Mr Robey was superb throughout and I would wager that in all his life, however unfamiliar his surroundings, he has never been so happy.

The critics generally were impressed by the way in which Robey, best known purely as an entertainer, subordinated his mannerisms and proved himself to be an actor above all. The experiment had succeeded and he could claim yet another successful venture into an unfamiliar medium. Reinhardt was delighted with his comic star. 'Ultimately,' wrote Cochran, 'at the performances he attended, he would laugh so loudly as to have been conspicuous if the rest of the audience had not been doing the same. Several nights he came just in time to see George discover (in a looking-glass) Helen in bed with Paris: "There's Helen and there's *me!*"' Unfortunately, as *Helen!* entered on its run, the magnificence of what Cochran thought as near perfect a production as he ever created began to dim and receipts fell. A certain malaise permeated the cast and some of them just walked through their parts with a lacklustre air that affected everyone else.

It is hard enough to get success at any time [Cochran reflected]. But it is doubly disheartening when, having achieved a measure of first-night success, the quality of the subsequent performances

---

* He was the husband of Viola Tree, Beerbohm-Tree's daughter, and possessed the same wit as his wife and father-in-law. He had trouble grasping plots in time for his deadline, so he came to a friendly arrangement with theatrical managements whereby they gave him a full synopsis of the play in advance, thus enabling him to write at least half of his notice before the first night curtain went up.

is dissipated by the players and the run of the play consequently shortened. It amazes me that so many actors and actresses receiving high salaries fail to realise the responsibility they carry on their shoulders. They are the controllers, not only of their own destinies, but of the manager's fortune and the livelihoods of all the people employed in the theatre.

From these criticisms he excepted 'that great comedian George Robey. His performance of Menelaus was as fine as anything he did in his career, and more in the spirit of Offenbach then that of anybody in the cast.'

Helen! ended its run in the middle of 1932 and Robey went off on variety tours again. They took him to Manchester where the local chaplain of the Actors' Church Union had organised a club for the unemployed. The chaplain asked him if he would give an hour's show for the benefit of men who found themselves, through no fault of their own, in a wretched dead-end. 'Now, padre,' Robey answered, 'I'm not what you would call a religious man. But would you say doing a good turn to the down-and-outs was religion? . . . Yes, I'll come. Here are a hundred shillings for your club.' He arrived, sang song after song, performed sketch after sketch, and at the end of it all gave a cheque for twenty-five pounds to the club. In a speech of thanks the chaplain mentioned the reference to him in *Journey's End*: 'Robey was pricelessly funny.' As the unemployed men gathered round his car to see him off, Robey looked at them out of the window and tears ran down his cheeks.

He came back to London and, early in 1933, started rehearsals for a new musical comedy called *Jolly Roger*. In it he played the role of Bold Ben Blister, late Royal Navy and Sancho Panza-type companion to the hero Jolly Roger. The spectacle was an affectionate parody of nineteenth-century comic opera and told how Sir Roderick Venom, wicked governor of a Caribbean island, worked secretly in league with the Bloody Pirate, scourge of the seas, and imprisoned the handsome Jolly Roger on a charge of piracy while attempting to seduce Roger's sweetheart, the beautiful Amelia. The score was by Walter Leigh, a young composer who had studied under Hindemith and later acquired distinction writing music for revues and superior pantomimes. Had he not been killed while on active service in 1942 he would have emerged as an acknowledged master of light music, which can be just as difficult to compose as sonatas and symphonies. Even so, the music he left shows distinctive flair and craftsmanship. He had earlier collaborated with one of the authors, V. C. Clinton-Baddeley, a name that often occurs on inter-war revue programmes, in a similar comic piece entitled *The Pride of the Regiment*, or 'cashiered for his country'. The penny-plain and tuppence-coloured atmosphere of *Jolly Roger* resembles that of the ballet *The Triumph of Neptune* which Lord Berners wrote for Diaghilev. There were heroic attitudes, damsels in distress, last-minute rescues, and puns in Victorian style of an elaborateness that outdid Gilbert. Among the best numbers was a duet in which Robey played the castanets on a set of bones while attempting to frighten the Bloody Pirate and make his flesh creep:

> We drove them all frantic
> Around the Atlantic
> By murder and rapine and dirt!

His patriotic bosom swelling with pride, he also proclaimed stoutly that 'The Britisher Wins Through'. A particularly neat quartet hymned as its subject 'Barratry, Arson, Rape and Slaughter'.

Robey's adversary in *Jolly Roger* was the crooked Governor, a part filled with relish by Gavin Gordon who once declared that his favourite role was anything 'villainous'. Gordon was a versatile figure who could act, sing, dance and compose. Originally trained as an opera singer, he then branched out into the theatre. He also wrote ballets which were staged by the pioneering Camargo Society and at Sadler's Wells, the most famous being *The Rake's Progress* after Hogarth. The impresario of *Jolly Roger* was a lady called Rita John who hoped to repeat with it the triumph she obtained with *The Pride of the Regiment*. She costumed it generously and gave it a lavish setting. What she had not counted on, however, was a political issue involving Robey which gave it unexpected publicity and may even have helped to increase its run.

The try-out in Manchester and Birmingham succeeded well and the company prepared for a London first night at the Savoy. Before this could take place a message was received from Equity, the newly formed actors' union. Unless, it declared, Robey joined their ranks, it would ask the others in the cast not to work with him. This ultimatum to become part of a closed shop instantly antagonised Robey. He disliked and distrusted the notion of trade unionism. It went against all his individualistic beliefs. The issue, to him, was simple: if he had disagreements with a management he cleared them up himself. He was the servant of the management that paid him and he dealt directly with them. There was no need for intermediaries and no need for the theatre to be unionised. Equity, like that filthy jazz music he hated so much, was an alien influence, and, no doubt, a nest of left-wing agitators. The secretary of the union being then A. M. Wall, Robey dismissively remarked, 'I've heard of the Great Wall of China, and Wall's ice-cream, but who is this Mr A. M. Wall?'

A few weeks before *Jolly Roger* opened at the Savoy Equity held a general meeting in the Theatre Royal, Drury Lane. The President, Godfrey Tearle, an actor of charm and urbanity, tried to calm down the large numbers gathered there, and even the maligned A. M. Wall essayed a conciliatory note. The meeting turned restless and noisy. Militant speeches were made, the orators demanded action, and the orchestral members of *Jolly Roger* threatened not to play unless Equity's demand was met. Robey now proposed what must have seemed like a diplomatic solution that would please everyone without compromising principles. He gave Equity a cheque for ten guineas, the cost of seven years' subscription, but described it as a 'donation'. This would not do. The union returned the cheque and insisted that he join their ranks.

Although he went on grumbling about 'red' agitators and 'orders from Moscow', Robey knew he must find a way out of the impasse. Otherwise the London production of *Jolly Roger* was doomed. There was a rule that employers could not belong to Equity since a conflict of interest might arise. Why should he not become Rita John's official partner? The deed was done and Miss John wrote to Godfrey Tearle: 'I wish to inform you that Mr George Robey has taken a financial interest in *Jolly Roger*, and is a partner with me in this enterprise.' Henceforth all printed matter would carry the legend: 'Rita John and George Robey present *Jolly Roger*.' Equity professed satisfaction and Robey felt he had vindicated his position. Yet, ironically enough, Robey's action secured a long-term benefit for the union: having watched the progress of the dispute, the Society of West End Managers granted official recognition to Equity and drew up an agreed standard contract of employment.

Robey did not change his opinion. A newspaper that announced the 'friendly' solution was told: 'I feel like the bull in one of Aesop's fables. A gnat alighted on his horns and said: "I'm going away." To which the bull replied, "I did not even know you were there."' Opinion within the profession varied. Leslie Henson described Robey as 'that big obstinate bullock of a comedian'. The matinée idol Owen Nares came up to Robey one lunch-time at the Ivy and greeted him: 'You *are* a stubborn old darling, but I love you dearly.' At the first night of *Jolly Roger* he made his entrance before a house crammed to the gallery and, peering over a wall, delivered his opening line: 'Not a soul in sight.' A vast roar of laughter and applause met him. In his autobiography he primly commented:

> Came an evening in March 1933, when, in co-operation with London's youngest and latest manager, Miss Rita John, I had the privilege of presenting the new musical burlesque, *Jolly Roger*, at the Savoy, and acting the part of that genial card, Bold Ben Blister, in it. The first night audience on my first entry gave me the most prolonged ovation I have ever received. On that occasion, however, there was a principle involved, and no doubt at least half the applause was for the principle.

He was to remain, all his life, what he called a 'conscientious objector' in trade union matters.

Much helped by the incidental publicity, *Jolly Roger* lasted out a run of over five months. 'From first to last,' the *Daily Telegraph* said of Robey, 'he is pure joy, whether being made to walk the plank or rescuing beauties in distress, or giving a castanet solo on a couple of bones or sewing his little sampler. This is a really great performance.' Singing the mock duet 'Richard the Dago', or vociferating in gravel-like tones his new catch-phrase, 'As you might say', or turning an elegant cartwheel the length of the stage, whatever Robey did he dominated the show. At the end of the London run Blanche's brother Prince took *Jolly Roger* on a provincial tour with a new cast. When it came back to the London suburbs Robey again played his original part with, if anything, renewed mastery.

In the meantime he had refreshed himself by appearing in the series of cabarets at the Trocadero organised by Charles B. Cochran. These were, in effect, miniature revues which lasted from half past eleven to midnight and engaged the talents of people like Doris Zinkeisen, Oliver Messel and Diaghilev's star Massine. Rehearsals for a new cabaret began at midnight on Sunday, by which time all the customers had left, and went on until breakfast-time. Robey was paid three hundred and fifty pounds a week, then the highest salary a cabaret performer had ever received, and showed he was worth it by attracting large crowds. Again this was a new opportunity which he joyfully seized. Instead of being alone on a stage and isolated from the audience, here he was at close quarters and surrounded by them. Accordingly he adopted a more intimate approach and scaled down his music-hall style, as he had when filming.

Among the audience one evening was a judge who had worked at the criminal bar with Robey's son Edward. He enjoyed the performance so much that he went to see it twice in a fortnight. He told the comedian of this and mentioned his criminal work. Robey's eye sparkled. 'The *criminal* bar, you say?' he observed in his richest voice. 'Have you been in any nice juicy cases of incest lately?' The company of lawyers always delighted him. He loved to hear them talking shop and listened, enthralled, to their revelations of human iniquity. Among his friends was the barrister Marshall Hall, a famous hero of many courtroom sensations. Hall was a collector too, and much envied Robey's valuable array of old snuff bottles. After examining them he told Robey that he would like to burgle his house if only to make off with that part of his collection.

'And whom would you engage to defend you if you were caught?' asked Robey.

'I rather think I'd brief myself!' replied Hall. At his death he left Robey a pair of cuff-links in memory of their times together.

This was one of the anecdotes Robey told in his autobiography *Looking Back On Life*, which he published after the run of *Jolly Roger* ended in 1933. He had already, twenty-four years earlier in 1909, brought out a precocious work on the same lines called

From Offenbach to Shakespeare

My Life Up Till Now. Much had happened since then: the war, the emergence of variety, and his own steady graduation from the music-hall to films, musical comedy, operetta and cabaret, at each point modifying his technique and adapting it to the demands of new media. In *Looking Back On Life* he brought the story up to date and, at the age of sixty-four, concluded proudly:

> Up to the present day I have never failed to do my night's turn. No manager has ever let me down; and some of the letters of which I am proudest are from managers who have said that I have never let *them* down. I have never acknowledged any Masters but two – my Employers, and the Public. My Employers pay me, the Public pay my Employers, and there you are. To do one's best for them both seems to me the only straight, sane, self-respecting path, as well as, from every point of view, by a long way the pleasantest.

For a preface to *Looking Back* he called on his distinguished friend Sir James Barrie for the use of his essay on Robey's wartime auctioneering exploits. Barrie wrote of his 'faculty for making himself loved' and, perceptively, of Robey's non-conformism on stage, of his near-anarchic flavour.

> You ought not to love him, for he does almost everything that you have been taught not to do, and from his first appearance it should be evident to you that he has that moment escaped from a just captivity. He always arrives on stage with an air of triumph, as if he had eluded people who were waiting in the wings (I think they are called) to intercept him. Every time he goes off, I expect they are at once after him, for when he returns he looks more elated than ever. We have a fearful joy in him, because he is always playing truant.

The non-conformist, the truant, as presented by Robey the comedian, was at odds with respectable society. He thumbed his nose at convention and larded his patter with the grossest double meanings. There was even a sketch attributed to him in which he played, wearing mortar-board and gown, a schoolmaster teaching the alphabet to his pupil. Upon a blackboard he wrote the letters until he arrived at F. The pupil read out the letter K. The schoolmaster tried to correct him. Again the pupil repeated the letter K, and went on doing so whenever Robey prompted him. At last his exasperated mentor bellowed, 'I don't understand it. Every time I write F you see K.' A quick curtain fell on the bafflement of the innocent and knowing sniggers from the sophisticated.

And yet, in *Looking Back On Life*, this was the man who devoted a whole chapter to what he called 'Intermezzo – A Word on Honest Vulgarity'. The music-hall, he claimed, would not be in such a bad way if only it had remained loyal to its old tradition of 'wholesome, genial, honest vulgarity'. What he described as 'refinement', or 'refainement', was the enemy of healthy open laughter. 'Give me a joke that is a joke, not a Sunday-school translation of one,' he went on. 'Give me humour which will make any man laugh, but of which no man need be ashamed. I want no furtive, shamefaced allusions to things unmentionable. The vulgarity I like must be honest – such as can be presented openly. Veiled hints and suggestions are not humour – neither are they vulgar: as a rule they're just filthy, and therefore *unmanly*.'

From this he went on to the 'modern' view of sex.

I am old-fashioned enough to be unable to appreciate this new attitude towards sex. To my mind it is harmful in the extreme. That is why I prefer honest vulgarity. My attitude towards sex is to laugh at it, and, if possible, to make the younger generation laugh with me. So long as they laugh their thoughts will remain clear, and bestial suggestiveness won't have a chance with them. Honest vulgarity is neither filth nor purity. It lies somewhere between the two.

What, he enquired, was the effect of modern pruriency and nastiness on the younger generation? Did it not give them thoughts no decent mind should harbour at their age? Did it encourage boys to seek the healthy pursuits of the cricket-field, or girls the wholesome atmosphere of the tennis-court? Presumably 'honest vulgarity' did.

This odd divergence between his public statements and his music-hall practice was echoed in the account he gave of his life. Perhaps because he was aware that a Commander of the

British Empire was speaking, he emphasised the respectability of his opinions and gave a genteel varnish to the origins from which he had sprung. He situated his birthplace not in the lowly Kennington Road, where he had in fact first seen the light of day, but in the more salubrious Herne Hill, and invoked the illustrious company of Edward Alleyne, founder of Dulwich College, and of John Ruskin, who had both been associated with the area. In *Looking Back On Life*, too, he perpetuated the legend that he went to Cambridge for a university education, although, he added carefully, some of his father's speculations went wrong and he had to leave. Generally he preferred to shroud his early life in a mist of confusion. Sometimes he would speak of having passed his youth in South Africa where his family then lived. On other occasions he would hint that he had trained for the Diplomatic Service. These fantasies were, in part, due to a natural bent for joking. They also originated from a sense of social inferiority. Although the millionaires with whom he dined were often, like him, from humble backgrounds, the Dukes and Viscounts who invited him as a public figure to their receptions were not.

In practice, though, he was not a snob. He would enjoy chatting with taxi-drivers about the latest archaeological discoveries in Egypt as much as debates with shopkeepers on the progress of Manchester United up the league tables. *Looking Back On Life* contains moving tales of his encounters with private soldiers who had been wounded in action. He spoke to them tactfully, never said the wrong thing, and left them feeling happier than they had been before, despite their awful sufferings. Did it matter, after all, that he dearly loved a lord?

The dedication of *Looking Back On Life* expressed one of his most deeply felt beliefs. 'To my dear friends the British public at home and throughout the Empire,' it read, 'this book is affectionately dedicated by their faithful and grateful servant, George Robey.' He was a Victorian patriot who gloried in the British Empire and saw himself as the servant of a public which had given him fame and riches. Soon after *Looking Back On Life* appeared he had the honour of entertaining both his public and the monarch he revered in the Royal Variety Performance of 1934. He had often travelled to Windsor by royal command to amuse Edward VII with his act and, in private, choice anecdotes. At a party for

King George V and Queen Mary he had once been in full flood when he suddenly remembered that the next line in his song ran, 'I feel just as good as a jolly old queen.' He caught the stony regal eye of Queen Mary and, losing his nerve, cut the turn short. With her son he was much more at ease. 'Please, George, do Great-grandma,' the Prince of Wales would ask him. Draping a handkerchief over his head and turning sideways to reveal a daunting profile, he started talking in a low guttural voice, Queen Victoria to the life.

With him at the Royal Variety Performance were Elsie and Doris Waters, and Arthur Lucan and Kitty McShane as Old Mother Riley and her daughter. An indication of the important role now played by broadcasting was the presence of Henry Hall and the 'BBC Dance Orchestra'. Sharing the top of the bill with Robey was Billy Bennett. The latter's bawdiness had an energy that exemplified Robey's theory about honest vulgarity. Billed as 'Almost A Gentleman', he would tramp on stage wearing a soup-stained shirt-front, a too-short dinner-jacket, a seedy collar and baggy dress trousers. Once his signature tune of 'A Fine Old English Gentleman' had died away, he embarked on one of his famous recitations. The quiff plastered on his balding forehead glistened with sweat in the spotlight and his bushy moustache quivered in the draught from the wings. His rubicund features glowed hotly as he announced his parody of the popular monologue 'The Green Eye of the Little God' which came out as 'The Green Tie on the Little Yellow Dog', or 'Mandalay' in which the heroine sits in a sparrow's nest:

> She's as pretty as a picture,
>   Though she lost one eye, they say,
> Through the black hole of Calcutta –
>   Perhaps the keyhole of Bombay!
> Look as far as you can see, boy,
>   Look a little further, son,
> For that Burma girl is burning –
>   Stick a fork in, see if she's done.

He also had a version of 'Christmas Day in the Workhouse', otherwise 'Christmas Day in the Cookhouse', where an ancient soldier, his whiskers full of sparrows' nests, curses the Sergeant Major and tells him where he can stick his Christmas pudding:

> So thank you, and bless you, and b-low you, you
>   just take these curses from me,
> May your wife give you nothing for dinner, and then
>   warm it up for your tea.
> Whatever you eat, may it always repeat – be it
>   soup, fish, entrée, or horse doovers,
> May blue bottles and flies descend from the skies
> And use your bald head for manoeuvres.

For some reason, however, his act never really succeeded in Huddersfield, a town which failed to appreciate his broad humour. When friends asked why, he would reply, without a smile, 'They take me for a baritone.'

He was the son of a slapstick comedian and began his career as the back end of a stage donkey. Not wishing at first to emulate his father, he joined the army as a cavalryman and became adept at going over high jumps without stirrups or saddle, his arms tightly folded. At the end of the war he and a mate were detailed to clear out a NAAFI canteen in a French village. They gave away all the contents to the inhabitants but could not get rid of two big sacks containing Epsom Salts, in those days a volcanic remedy for constipation. 'We didn't know what to do with them,' said Billy. 'So one night we took the stuff and emptied it down the village well. After that the place became famous as a health spa.'

Most of his songs he wrote himself. They were farragoes of glorious absurdity which featured heroines so fat that in order to enter a room they had to go through the same door twice, or so statuesque that they would dive into the sea and wash people off the pier with the splash. He sang of Irish Eskimos who spent their time trying to straighten out bananas, of ocean beds lined with fish and chips, of railway engines that went in two directions at once, and of farmers who used spanners to milk cows. In bibulous tones he would propound such riddles as what made the woodbine wild and where had the kidney bean? If, he enquired, a duck has its tonsils out, where does it keep its quack? Furthermore, he would ask, can a bandy-legged gherkin be a straight cucumber's child? The mock pathos of 'She Was Poor But She Was Honest' ('It's the same the whole world over/It's the poor what gets the blame/It's the rich what gets the pleasure/Isn't it a blooming shame?'), contrasted with his parody entitled 'The Charge of the Tight Brigade' and the epic about Nell, the collier's daughter. Nell, innocent and sweet seventeen, became involved in so many complicated matrimonial adventures that in the end:

> Now Nell is her mother's new mother,
> Her father becomes her own son,
> Her mother's first child is her father-in-law,
> And her daughter's the son of a gun.

Robey thus had strong competition in what was to be his last Royal Variety appearance. Despite Billy Bennett's rumbustious antics, the screeching slapstick of Old Mother Riley and the barbed dialogue of Elsie and Doris Waters, Robey shone as the true star of the evening. The *Daily Mail* remarked:

> Mr George Robey was in the very first command variety show twenty-two years ago, and has been an institution in the comedy world ever since. He held the stage last night in the superbly assured manner of the old-time music-hall comedians, and 'brought down the house' with utmost ease. First in his familiar clergyman-plus-eyebrows guise, with his old song 'Thingummybob'. That started everyone laughing delightedly. Then that little masterpiece of burlesque in which Mr Robey appears as a Teutonic music professor, exhibiting a formidable array of instruments, of which – after much ceremony – he 'plays' only the simplest, including a super big bass drum.
>
> At Mr Robey's first excursion into pidgin German, the King began to laugh; then he whispered animatedly to the Queen – and continued to laugh heartily throughout the burlesque. It was a great triumph for a great comedian and the first big success of the evening. This ended what may be described as the music-hall performance proper – with Mr Robey well on top as the individual hit of the evening.

His triumph at the Royal Variety Performance helped to erase the disappointment he had experienced in a new musical comedy earlier that year. Called *Here's How!*, it had been specially written around him. He was cast as a brewery tycoon whom a gang of racketeers plot to cheat of his business. A Manchester try-out did well, although it was clear that without Robey the show would have failed. At the London première he was commended by the *Stage* for having made wonderful use of the few opportunities given him: 'After more than forty years on the stage Mr Robey can still hold his audience with the twitch of his eyebrow and sing and dance as drolly as ever . . . There is a scene in which he causes roars of laughter by just transferring his cane from one hand to the other . . .' The *Observer* wrote: 'He is, as ever, a law unto and an entertainment in himself . . . at his best when, putting the plot in its place, he comes nearest the footlights and furthest from his part to amuse and admonish us in the way he and we like best.' *The Times* was impressed by his

extraordinary power of being a little larger than life when he comes down-stage and of making the walls of the theatre draw in to share his confidences. And what a talent still for surprise! . . . All the other talents, one thinks, he possesses but his dancing days are done! Then suddenly he dances, step for step, kick for kick, rising even into the air and twiddling aloft in true Arab manner. Enviable being who is such a master of his craft that he can convulse an audience with a caper by the simple process of quietly moving his walking stick from one hand to the other.

At the fall of the curtain the audience demanded Robey and sang 'For He's a Jolly Good Fellow!' Without him, *Here's How!* would not have run for even the modest five weeks it achieved. A basic weakness lay in the choice of leading lady, that pretty French actress Lili Damita, who, though exquisite to the eye, was inaudible to the ear. So unfavourable was her reception that she asked the management to be released from her contract. The actress known only by her Christian name of June took her place and was welcomed by Robey with the greeting: 'Fancy, it's only

March and we have June with us!' Mademoiselle Damita went back to France and made a number of films, though she is likely to be best remembered for having accepted the formidable challenge of becoming, for a brief period, the first of Errol Flynn's several wives.

While playing by night in *Here's How!*, by day Robey had been travelling out to the film studios where he made *Chu Chin Chow*. This vastly popular musical play had started its run during the war and only closed after nearly five years of dazzling audiences with glamour and oriental splendour. The plot, based on the old tale of Ali Baba and the forty thieves, had been devised by Oscar Asche, a large, imposing actor of mixed Australian and Norwegian origins, who starred himself and his beautiful wife Lily Brayton in his own production. The score, by the popular theatre composer Frederic Norton, provided songs that lingered long in the repertory of drawing-room performers – the dainty 'Any Time's Kissing Time', the wistful 'Cobbler's Song' ('I sit and cobble at slippers and shoon/From the rise of the sun to the set of the moon') and the stirring chorus without which no musical of the period was complete, 'We are the robbers of the wood.' *Chu Chin Chow* established many records which were only to be broken in more recent years: a very long run (well over two thousand performances), a fortune in percentages for its lucky creator Asche, and a reputation as one of the most successful British musicals of its kind. The settings were of a grandeur that caused *The Times* to speak exuberantly about 'fantastic, polyphonic, polychromatic orientalism'. Beerbohm Tree, who had let out His Majesty's Theatre for the production and thereby made a lot of money, was inspired to make one of his best witticisms. Contemplating the scanty décolletage of the pretty chorus girls, he murmured, 'H'm, more navel than millinery.' Even after its long run ended *Chu Chin Chow* was constantly revived and played all over the world.

The spectacular element was especially appropriate to the cinema, and in 1923 Herbert Wilcox made a silent version. By 1934 Michael Balcon reckoned that the time had come to produce a second film. He engaged a team of distinguished writers – the playwright Edward Knoblock, the radio scriptwriter L. Du Garde Peach and Sydney Gilliatt, who later was to write and direct many famous British films – and, as director, the veteran Walter Forde who had himself been a screen comedian before retreating behind the camera. Fritz Kortner, a German actor of dark and dashing aspect, played Ali Baba's leading thief. The slave girl who foils him was Anna May Wong, the American-born actress of Chinese parentage, slight, fine-boned, with an air of oriental mystery that enabled her on occasion to portray a very effective villainess. During the time she spent in England she was adored by the musician Constant Lambert who became infatuated with her, though they only met once. Then she went back to America and died at the age of fifty-four.

Robey had the part of Ali Baba in a production designed to be a major boost for the English cinema. The sets included lavish banqueting halls, splendid palaces and exotic street scenes. He had learned by now to modify his acting for the camera, to discipline the famous eyebrows so that they made their point without exaggeration in close-ups. Greasy, unshaven, his eyes rolling slyly, he was, to the life, the downtrodden brother of the robber chief, much harried by a shrewish spouse and depressed by poverty. Among the supporting players were such well-known sights as the immensely adipose Francis L. Sullivan and the plump figure of Malcolm McEachern, later a partner in the singing team of Flotsam and Jetsam; but it was Robey who won the honours in *Chu Chin Chow*, which, at home and abroad, did well enough to justify the hopes of its sponsors. It was playing like this that inspired Alexander Korda to remark: 'I regard George Robey as capable of rivalling in popularity any film star in the world. I have been considering for some time past the possibility of presenting him as a first-rank film star.'

At the end of 1934 he went back to more familiar territory. Blanche and her brother Prince decided to revive *The Bing Boys Are Here* and produced it at the Alhambra, where, eighteen years ago, he and Violet Loraine had immortalised 'If You Were the Only Girl in the World'. The exercise in nostalgia was tinged with sadness: where were all the men in khaki who had filled the house during the war years? It succeeded, nevertheless, and, not content with going through the established routines, Robey was always seeking to introduce new ideas. He spotted two gates that led into the pit and, leaning over, tried to close with his stick one of them that was slightly ajar. Yet he could not quite reach it, and his attempts to do so were built up over the days into a piece of business that brought roars of laughter from the audience. One of his fellow players could not understand the fuss he made over this banal circumstance and suggested an easier way of shutting the gate. Robey was indignant. 'You are no artist!' he snapped. 'The whole point of this is that it is perfectly simple for me to get to the gate, but I must appear not to think of it; the essence of the humour is that I never reach it. Once I touch it, all is lost.'

Another incident that showed his knack for turning circumstances to his advantage occurred on the first night of the revival. During a café scene glasses were knocked off a table and smashed on the stage where, almost immediately, dancers were to perform their number. While the stage-manager was trying to think of a way to clear up the dangerous fragments, Robey went off and then came back bearing a dustpan and brush. He knelt down and, with finicking nicety, transformed the brushing up of shattered glass into another neat piece of business.

There were people in the audience who had not even been alive when *The Bing Boys Are Here* made its debut. They were able to see and hear for themselves what it was that had so enchanted their parents. The plot may have been a little improbable and the dialogue somewhat stilted, but the charm and inventiveness of Robey triumphed over all. James Agate wrote about his performance in the revival:

Of Mr Robey it is difficult to think with moderation. I think I was never so impressed by the fullness of this great comedian with whom, as Hazlitt says of Falstaff, it is cut and come again. He is like some bottomless tankard. Or perhaps better, some great galleon of comedy unloading its deck treasures without encroaching upon the wealth in the hold. Scientists tell us that the output of solar heat is only credible on the assumption that the sun has some private means of recouping itself. Or one might put it in the simplest form and say that here is a comedian who spends only his income without encroaching on his capital (I have heard there are such people). Whatever the explanation, there is no getting to the end of him.

On the final night of the run Robey and Violet Loraine sang 'If You Were the Only Girl in the World' for the last time together. They made their exit and then returned for an encore. On their second exit Violet Loraine was weeping and Robey himself was close to tears. They gave another encore and both came back crying. When the stage-manager indicated that they could go on again for a last repeat, Robey turned to Vi and said, 'Go on, you silly old cow!' During this last encore they neither of them were able to sing much. The tears were now cascading down both their faces.

[ii]

The chimes at midnight

In 1950, four years before he died, Robey contributed to a symposium called *If I Had My Time Again*. During the course of it he remarked:

> And now I will let you into a real secret – of a really great ambition – and one that has yet to be fulfilled and, alas, that I am pretty certain never will be. It is to play Hamlet. Yes, that very prince of parts. It is quite true – *Hamlet* is my favourite play and I have a copy always with me – even at my bedside. Now why is it that so many comedians have the desire to play the greatest of all roles? I can only theorise, but for myself I love the play and can recite it line for line backwards too, if desired – but I am sufficiently humble to know my limitations, and for one thing I could never look like the popular conception of that tragic figure, though I have every justification for bemoaning: 'O! that this too too solid flesh would melt!'

If Hamlet was beyond his grasp there were surely comic parts that he might have undertaken. On at least two occasions enterprising producers had suggested that he play Bottom in *A Midsummer Night's Dream*. Pressures of time, a crowded engagement book and a certain lack of confidence prevented him from taking up the challenge. Then Sydney Carroll, the drama critic and director, approached him with the offer to play Falstaff in *Henry IV, Part I*. Carroll had established the open-air Shakespeare productions in Regent's Park, although he intended to mount *Henry IV* at Beerbohm Tree's old theatre, His Majesty's. Robey was tempted. He discussed the matter with Blanche, as he did everything. He meditated, he argued with himself and he thought of the many lucrative engagements that would be cancelled to make way for a venture which, if it succeeded, would bring him much honour but little cash. He accepted.

While playing two performances a night of *The Bing Boys Are Here* he took with him everywhere a pocket edition which contained his part neatly underlined in red ink. Blanche gave him his cues and suggested mnemonics which helped him remember changes of scene. Even while lunching at the Ivy he would take out his copy to study it between courses. Gladys Cooper came in there one day and noticed him, a solitary figure engrossed with his book. When, at last, he could tear himself away from the words, he saw her and crossed over to speak. 'I shall never learn it!' he complained. 'Never! And the dress rehearsal is in four days! You see, I've never had to learn a part before – least of all a Shakespearean part – and I'm terrified. I'll *never* learn it!' The eyebrows wriggled frantically, the face took on an expression of comic horror. Although for many years Robey had delighted in reading Shakespeare, to play him before an audience was an entirely different matter. He felt embarrassed and frightened at rehearsals in the presence of other, experienced Shakespearean actors. Instead of moving around at his pleasure and improvising new business as he went along in reaction to the audience, with Shakespeare he was restricted by the tyranny of words that could not be changed and movements that were inflexibly designed to fit in with those of the company. Humbly he asked for and accepted direction. When he arrived for rehearsals at His Majesty's, nervous and apprehensive, the housekeeper took him to the star's dressing-room and told him to let her know if he wanted anything. He patted her arm gratefully and said, 'You shouldn't have taken all that trouble for me, my dear. I'm only an old trouper.'

The leading role was played by John Drinkwater. Today he is known chiefly as the author of biographical plays about Abraham

Lincoln, Oliver Cromwell, Mary Stuart and Robert E. Lee which had a vogue in their time. He also wrote many other plays and prose biographies. A year or so before he appeared in *Henry IV, Part I*, he had been made Commendatore in the Order of the Crown of Italy by Mussolini, whose turgid melodrama *Napoleon* he adapted into English. His career as an actor began with the Birmingham Repertory Theatre and mainly involved Shakespeare. In *Henry IV* he took his cue from the opening line: 'So shaken as we are, so wan with care', and depicted a Prince who was sober and subdued. The small but vital part of Mistress Quickly was filled by Lady Tree, relict of Beerbohm, still as tart and ready of tongue as she had been when, as the leading lady in her husband's company, she queened it in that self-same theatre. The features of the Earl of Douglas would have been strangely familiar to the television watcher of a later generation. They were those of the Scottish actor John Laurie, who, after fifty years of quietly distinguished acting in Shakespeare and the classics, was to be admired as the doom-laden Scottish undertaker in *Dad's Army* by millions more than ever saw him on the stage.

Long before the curtain went up lively argument raged about the propriety of casting a music-hall entertainer in one of Shakespeare's most hallowed roles. There were those who argued that, since the clowns in his plays were acted by well-known Elizabethan buffoons like Tarleton, it was logical in our day that they should be played by popular comedians. Others claimed that this would only be possible if it were the custom to choose music-hall performers for the comic parts in modern tragedies. Moreover, Falstaff was not just another clown like Dogberry. And besides, Robey came to the part with an inescapable reputation built elsewhere. If Nellie Wallace played Maria in *Twelfth Night* everyone would be aware of her 'little bit of vermin'. If Charlie Chaplin acted Hamlet, however perfectly, he still would not be able to expunge the memory of moustache, cane and boots.

In his dressing-room on the first night Robey was quiet and nervous. He knew he was not word-perfect. Instead of reddening his nose and blacking up the eyebrows as he was more accustomed to do, he put on a straight foundation and capped it with a white wig and white beard. He looked at himself in the mirror and said with a timid smile, 'The prisoner partook of a hearty breakfast.'

He made his first entrance to a round of applause and threw

himself valiantly into the part. In spite of his determination to be wholly Falstaff and not George Robey, it was sometimes impossible for him to remain within the limits of the fat old knight. When he spoke the line, 'What doth gravity out of his bed at midnight?' he broadened the vowel of the third word, just as he was wont to pronounce 'Nottingha-am' on the music-hall stage. If the words were slow in coming he would gain time by staring at the audience with the basilisk glance they knew from his variety act. Such episodes as the 'honour' speech, one of the great set-pieces in the play, were apt to be uncomfortable experiences.* On the other hand, at the end, where the Prince takes Falstaff for dead ('I could have better spar'd a better man'), and calls him 'embowelled', Robey sat up among the corpses and said, 'em-bow-elled!', legitimately raising a tide of laughter that continued until the scene had ended.

Attack and timing, which Robey had learned in the music-hall, were, many actors agreed, the virtues of his Falstaff. If, said Douglas Byng, a young actor ever asked him how he could learn to play Shakespeare, he would tell him to go and watch Robey. When Byng eventually saw him as Falstaff he realised how wise his advice had been. Laurence Olivier, too, praised what he described as Robey's 'whiplash diction that would hit the back of the pit with a smack'. His face, went on Olivier, and his 'wonderful comic gift' enabled him to give 'a truly remarkable performance' as Falstaff. The critics, in general, agreed. 'A richly comic impersonation . . .' wrote W. A. Darlington. 'A very fine Falstaff, which will probably be one of the best our theatre has seen. A model of clear diction.' James Agate was quite certain that

> in a fortnight's time Mr Robey will be giving one of the best Falstaffs in living memory. It is in him to do so, but the audience must do its part. He has the authentic geniality of the old fribble, the genuine twinkle which kindles as easily as a taper that has been lighted many times. He is an English gentleman in ruins

---

* The famous speech occurs when the Prince says, 'Why, thou owest God a death', and Falstaff begins, ''Tis not due yet, I would be loath to pay him before his day. What need I be so forward with him that calls on me? Well, 'tis no matter, honour pricks me on. Yea, but how if honour prick me off when I come on? How then? Can honour set-to a leg? No. Or an arm? No. Or take away the grief of a wound? No.'

. . . or shall I put it that the new Falstaff is about to be and can be all this, if the audience will let him . . . He has still to amend one or two impermissible and calculated occasions. These are when the actor slyly evokes his former self, the mask of Falstaff is dropped, the audience leaps at the gleeful discrepancy, and the ruin of the play impends. These stolen seconds – for they are no more than seconds – are a threat to the illusion the actor has laboured to create, and they must be resisted. If they are not I throw up my brief, and it is on this understanding that this experiment, magnificently successful as to nine-tenths, has my blessing.

Strangely enough, one of his music-hall techniques proved highly suitable. This concerned the soliloquies. All his life in variety Robey had been especially aware of his audience, played to it, studied it and took his cue from it. When he had a soliloquy to deliver he made no bones about walking down to the footlights, directly facing the audience, and addressing them as if he were a politician wooing his constituents and anxious to make his views perfectly understood. Was not this, it might be argued, in the Elizabethan tradition?

His fellow actors treated him with guarded respect, never quite sure, despite his willingness to learn, whether he was in a gregarious mood or not. One of them said to him, 'You're looking very well, George – it's wonderful how you keep going year after year, not looking your age at all. How do you account for that?'

Robey pondered a while. At last he replied, solemnly, 'Early piety,' and walked quickly away.

At the end of the performance he made a curtain speech and said, 'I can assure you that I have had great difficulty with the words, but as you have heard I have mastered a few of them. I have understood *most* of them . . .' and promised that if the audience came again he would give them the whole of the text. Next morning, having read the press notices, all of them laudatory, he announced that he would study the part afresh and keep his promise. In the afternoon he blithely trotted off to a nearby cinema and viewed the latest adventure of his favourite film actor, Mickey Mouse.

During the run, which ended in May, a party was held on stage to celebrate Shakespeare's birthday. Robey played the host wearing Falstaff's bulky leather jerkin and heavy padding, none of which damped his exuberance either at the celebrations or in performance. He had met a new challenge and won artistic glory. It gave him confidence to think about other Shakespearean roles. This time he put aside the obvious clown parts and addressed himself to Shylock. Here, he decided, was a figure most often, and wrongly, played for tragedy. His own concept of the role was different: he saw Shylock as a comic figure. The Jew, he argued, was a fundamentally sympathetic character made bitter by the actions of his Christian enemies. His views inspired an editorial in *The Times* which gravely debated whether *The Merchant of Venice* should be treated as a comedy or as a tragedy. Having contributed to a discussion which has flourished ever since the play was written, and which continues to do so, Robey fell quiet. It is probable that his son Edward may have persuaded him against undertaking this novel interpretation, and Falstaff remained his sole, honourable venture into Shakespeare.

Still, he went on reading Shakespeare and always kept a volume of the plays at his bed's head. The music-hall skit in which he impersonated the dramatist and gave him a ludicrously tall forehead was really a tribute of affection. In his sketch he claimed that research among Tudor documents at Hampton Court showed that *Measure for Measure* and *As You Like It* were really the names of two favourite ale-houses. During his number he also made some telling gibes at those who claimed that Bacon was the true author of the plays. (Among their leaders was an American gentleman by the name of Mr J. Thomas Looney, an opportunity too good to miss.) He also worked up an anecdote in which he told of going into a shop for a packet of cigarettes, mesmerising the girl assistant with an Ancient Mariner stare, and addressing her:

> Hast thou among thy merchandise
> A brand of cigarettes thou canst commend?
> Not so full flavoured that their fumes
> Strike harsh upon my unsuspecting throat
> Nor yet so mild that they insipid be
> Like maid's first lisp of love beneath the moon,
> Nor yet unmindful of my slender purse
> That doth but ill provide my worldly wants.
> If such a brand thou hast I now beseech
> Let not thy action lag behind my speech.

From Offenbach to Shakespeare

At which, said Robey, the girl turned to another assistant and said, 'Blimey, Liz, a packet of gaspers for Henry the Eighth.'

In another version, still dazed by too much reading of Shakespeare, he said that he had apostrophised the girl thus:

Give me not Turkish sweets of rich content
That sate the palate of some Arab queen,
Nor yet the box of wafers, carmine-tipped,
That, on a touch as light as featherdown
Break into beams of saffron-mantled light
And turn the darkness into rosy glance,
Killing soft night with artificial day,
Rousing shy creatures from their downy beds
And that too soon. Nor yet the sable weed
Sold at a price extortionate that turns
Man into puffing billy, to forsake
Wives, children, duty, and all else beside
And smoke the foolish pipe. Nor give to me
Fine grained amber at a pound a peck
That fools do know as snuff, to glut the nose
And obfuscate the sinewy sinuses,
Aping the habits of our far forebears
The old Darwinian monkeys – No, forsooth!
Give me in short, whatever else you have
– Eschewing things you'd like to give to me:
Jewels, rare spices, aromatic herbs –
A score of Woodbines, neatly in their case.
I know you have 'em, for I saw 'em there
Diapasoned in the window like a figure,
Like to a school of oysters, or a row
Of somnolent sardines, demeanour mild;
Soft looks like odalisques, whose lambent forms,
Exuding sweet self-sacrifice, desire
For immolation: let me have some fags
And let me have 'em quick: I'm in a hurry.

After three indulgent months of Falstaff it was time for him to recoup his financial losses by carrying on business as usual. In June 1935, he went into an adaptation of an old French farce called

Accidentally Yours. His co-star was Alice Delysia, the French actress long settled in England, who could overwhelm an audience with her flamboyant personality and gurgling voice alone. Among her other contributions to London theatrical life was the christening of the Ivy restaurant, from its beginning a favourite haunt of the profession. 'Actors cling together like ivy, don't you think?' she observed one evening as she contemplated the diners around her. In *Accidentally Yours* Robey played an elderly banker, immaculate with morning-coat and striped trousers, who faced the problem of how to rid himself of an unwanted mistress acted by Delysia in full frothing blast. They made excellent foils to each other and were supported by a youthful Jack Hawkins as juvenile lead. At one point Robey charmed the audience by playing bits of Strauss and Schubert on a violin he had recently made. After a Birmingham try-out the play ran briefly in London. The threadbare piece was, wrote a critic, in Falstaffian phrase 'blasted with antiquity' and redeemed only by Robey's confident mastery of farce technique, his eloquent eyebrows and his sly laugh.

A surer way of retrieving the income lost while he played Falstaff was to make films. In the theatre his earnings depended on the length of a run which could more often be short rather than long, whereas in films he was paid handsomely and in advance, regardless of whether the production was a success or a failure. During the four years that led up to the beginning of the war in 1939 his name enhanced three films of mediocre quality. *Birds of a Feather* presented him as a wealthy sausage manufacturer who rents a castle from a penniless Earl. When hidden treasure is accidentally found there, a gang of burglars plan to strike. They are foiled by a scheme which calls, among other things, for the Earl to dress up as a servant in his own house. The sausage king returns to his suburban habitat while his son marries the daughter of the newly enriched peer. Robey's flickering eyebrows and mobile lips were complemented by the bald pate and quavering jowls of an actor always very formally billed as C. Denier Warren. Though born in Chicago and playing innumerable fusspot roles as an American in British films, this chuckleheaded performer spent most of his life from the age of eight over here, having, indeed, made his stage debut as an Ugly Sister in a children's production of *Cinderella* at the Clapham Grand Theatre. Later he concentrated on radio work and had much to do with the popular wartime programme *The Kentucky Minstrels*, where his high and excitable tones created an air of urgency. In private life he was, as to be expected, a boisterous member of the Savage Club. Later research indicates that the mysterious initial 'C' eternally prefixed to his name stood for 'Charles'.

A more elaborate affair was *Southern Roses*, a musical film, which inaugurated the newly built studios at Denham. They, in their time, were the best equipped of their kind known to Europe and gloried in technical facilities much envied by others. Robey opened them, unofficially, while being escorted on a sightseeing tour round the buildings. On the way he met Nat D. Ayer, composer of *The Bing Boys Are Here*, and, with Ayer at the piano, gave an impromptu performance of 'If You Were the Only Girl in the World' to the startled executives who were accompanying him. Once again he had the part of an elderly tycoon, this time one who owed his wealth to the manufacture of paint. The film had an exotic Spanish background, and Robey was obliged to pose as the husband of a beautiful stage actress with whom the romantic hero fell in love. The real pleasures of the film, apart from Robey, were to be found among the supporting players. These included the Irish actress Sara Allgood who was usually called upon to play comfy, consoling mothers, although her range was much wider than this since she had been a famous member of the Abbey Theatre in Dublin and a star of Sean O'Casey's plays. It was perhaps this distinguished background that enabled her to dismiss Alfred Hitchcock, with whom she made *Blackmail*, as a 'cheap, second-rate director'. Also in *Southern Roses* was Athene Seyler, a lady with the face of an amiable pug and a voice of trepidant sweetness. Plump cheeks a-quiver, eyes radiating benevolence, she was, at least to film-goers, the incarnation of gentle maiden aunts, woolly-witted spinsters and tea-party hostesses. In 1989 she celebrated her hundredth birthday by reciting, on television, the speech of Rosalind from *As You Like It* with which she had won a Gold Medal at the Royal Academy of Dramatic Art eighty years previously. She remained word-perfect.

The last feature film to star Robey in the lead was *A Girl Must Live*. This had better credentials than most since the director was Carol Reed and the scriptwriters numbered among them

Frank Launder and Michael Pertwee. Yet again he was an ageing businessman, a rich furrier, who becomes the plaything of three scheming gold-diggers played by Margaret Lockwood, Renée Houston and Lilli Palmer. He is persuaded to finance a new musical comedy with the promise that he will be able to choose girls for the chorus. At first he is made much of by the ladies already mentioned, but when a handsome young Earl (Hugh Sinclair) lately returned from Australia appears on the scene, Robey is quickly dropped in the latter's favour. The film was enlivened by a bedroom episode where Renée Houston and Lilli Palmer bombard each other not only with words but also with every available piece of crockery they can find. It is, in the end, Margaret Lockwood who secures the Earl for herself. This, of course, was inevitable, since her pretence of not being interested in money is more convincing than that of her two rivals. The dialogue is pleasingly acidulous. When one of the girls boasts that the Earl cannot take his eyes off her, the other replies, 'You should realise, dear, that he hasn't seen any woman, white or black, for eleven years.' A crooked film producer who is trying to charm finance out of the Earl comments despairingly, 'D'you know, I don't think that guy *wants* to lose money!' His remark is addressed to that bland character actor Naunton Wayne, whose look of permanent surprise carried him through many films of the period, notably as the cricket-loving companion of Basil Radford in *The Lady Vanishes*. There were glimpses, too, in *A Girl Must Live*, of an unimaginably young Michael Hordern.

None of Robey's films have left any trace, although *Don Quichotte* is sometimes mentioned because of the association with Pabst or with Chaliapin. Alexander Korda, as we have seen, believed him to be a great film comedian with the potential of international stardom, and even signed him up on a three-year contract. Whether this was merely an artful public relations move to benefit from Robey's prestige or whether it represented a genuine opinion is hard to decide. You never knew with Korda. He had a habit of announcing grandiose plans and of expending large sums of money which he afterwards, quietly, recouped at a profit by selling contracts and options to shadowy figures who in turn sold them on to others without an inch of film ever being shot.

If, however, Robey was to be denied stardom he at least made good use of his film experience in a related visual medium. In

August 1938 he went to Alexandra Palace and, face to face with a monolithic camera under sizzling lights, the primitive make-up trickling down his collar, he performed for the benefit of the few thousand people in the London area who owned television sets. In the expert opinion of the late Grace Wyndham Goldie, a well-known BBC producer, he did rather well.

It was extraordinarily interesting to see Mr George Robey in television. [In those early days people appeared 'in' television, not 'on' it.] Sound broadcasting conveys so little of his comic quality that it was a pleasure and a relief to feel, the moment the familiar figure appeared on the television screen, the impact of that tremendous personality. And, surprisingly, Mr Robey's methods, the large-scale methods which dominate vast music-halls, were just as suited to television as large-scale acting has proved to be . . . It is perfectly clear that Mr Robey, whose comic effect is not contained in his voice alone but depends very largely on the relation between his facial expression and his words, is one of the people who ought to be kept for television and who should be forbidden, by his own good angel, if by nobody else, to approach the ordinary microphone.

Radio is, in a way, more difficult than television. With the latter a broadcaster can rely on expression and gesture to accompany his voice and to colour his delivery. On radio everything has to be implied by the voice alone. Robey had already made his debut at the BBC microphone in 1936. He gave a talk in a programme called *The Spice of Life*. For close on half an hour he spoke about life behind the footlights, of how he worked and of how he built up his performance. He mentioned his hobbies, his violin-making and his love of sport. There were references to his philosophy and the lessons he had learned from nearly fifty years on the stage. Then he revealed that, in his view, he was not a good 'mixer' and that he had enough of crowds while working in the theatre: he much preferred the company of no more than two people, one to tell a story and the other to hear it. His greatest thrill in life, he confessed, came from making people laugh. Whenever depression threatened, he went on, he had always found that 'Get out into the sunshine' was a helpful exhortation. All this was quite new to his listeners who had thought of him simply as a red-nosed comic. Over a thousand of them wrote letters to him as a result of the talk.

The more one studies Robey's material, which is not on the whole particularly funny in print, the more one realises that his success depended largely on the visual aspect of his performance: the incongruous dress, the grimaces, the look of the eye, the shape of the mouth. All this was denied him on radio. 'Why,' he said to his listeners, 'my stock-in-trade, my eyebrows, my red nose, my funny hats and cane, all the stage mannerisms that have been built up by years of patient study – they don't mean a thing on the air.' The one stage characteristic that did prove invaluable was his impeccable diction. Each word, each syllable, came over with perfect clarity.

Despite the absence of that all-important element, a live audience, which Robey in the theatre had long ago learned how to turn into an accomplice, he discovered that he could interest and hold his invisible listeners by adopting the intimate manner one would use in speaking to a friend. He learned that a smile on the lips could give warmth and attractiveness to a speaking voice. His first talk led to others. A short while later he did an impression of an old-time music-hall bill which was beamed across the Atlantic for the tenth birthday celebrations of NBC. Another broadcast he gave which attracted a great deal of attention was a relaxed chat on cricket and the famous players he had met at Lord's.

In June 1937, to his great surprise, he found himself a member of the General Advisory Council which had been set up by the BBC to give advice on matters of policy. At first he thought that the telephone call announcing his appointment was a practical joke. When he realised that the BBC offer was in earnest he remarked, 'I accepted it like a man claiming the Irish sweepstake. It's the biggest honour I've had – apart from Shakespeare. It's a good idea to find out what the man-in-the-street likes, you know, the human beings. I may be able to help.' He would, he promised, be that man-in-the-street. After a lifetime on the stage he had wide experience of his fellow man. 'I am taking the whole thing seriously – as it should be taken. In fact, I am a man of serious thought off the stage. Perhaps you may call me a bit of a philosopher. But I know nothing about finance – I never know how many noughts there are or what they mean.' The BBC in those days was still guided by its first director, the Calvinist Scot John Reith, who believed that broadcasting's mission was to educate and uplift the public. At its most trivial this took the form of a ruling which obliged announcers to wear evening dress while speaking at the microphone. At its best it created standards and a reputation for integrity abroad which lasted until the 1950s.

At first Robey was a little overawed by his duties and by his fellow members of the Council: MPs, academics and assorted public figures. He was, moreover, handicapped by the memory of an incident that one of his recent broadcasts had provoked. In the course of it he made some trifling jest of a mild nature which happened to upset a small group of listeners. Fifty of them wrote in protest to the Corporation. 'Just a highly distressing misapprehension,' he quickly pointed out, 'that's what it was. But then it's always my fate to be misunderstood. And, mind you, the trouble and care I took with that broadcast! I acted as my own censor and cut one thing out after another until what I was going to say couldn't possibly be misapprehended. But there you are – it seems to be a world full of wicked thoughts!' It often happened in the theatre that, given his reputation, the most guileless remark could inspire a crude guffaw on which he could immediately capitalise by reprimanding the audience with an imperious 'Desist!' and an appeal to temper their merriment with 'dignity and reserve'. On the wireless things were different. As Pascal said, 'The moment at which I speak is already far way from me,' and once the microphone had picked up a phrase it was gone beyond recall. 'I'm more than surprised,' said a crestfallen Robey, 'I'm grieved.'

A month or so after he joined the Council he had so far recovered from his minor gaffe and adjusted to the august company in which he now figured as to raise the topic of religious programmes. These were very dear to Reith's heart. On Sunday evenings the BBC regularly programmed a church service, and for one whole hour listeners had nothing else to hear but hymns and liturgy. The only alternative was to hunt for the European stations on their dial. No one, yet, had the audacity to question this feature. Robey did. Why not, he suggested, put out the service on one wavelength and, on another, give listeners an alternative by offering light entertainment or instructive talks? He received hundreds of letters, the majority of them criticising the lacklustre Sunday programme. His proposal was politely heard and quietly forgotten. In time he realised that the General Advisory Council, like so many great British institutions, amounted to little more than a genteel means of stifling discussion by creating an illusion that something was being done.

In the theatre, at that time, he was performing a sketch whose subject alone would not have been permitted a mention under Reith's austere governance. At the Holborn Empire, in *Let's Join George*, he introduced a monologue about 'The Nudist'. The *Manchester Guardian* wrote:

> Holding a yellow dressing-gown together with one hand and sometimes timidly apologising with the other, George Robey explains that he has joined a nudist colony. In his new adventure that part of Mr Robey which is feminine, which knows all about barmaids and the proper respect they deserve, becomes stronger and more assertive. The refined and almost haughty way in which he explains his unusual costume has something prudish about it. He bridles more remarkably than ever, and as one might expect from such a situation there is ambiguity about his words which he finds regrettable, lamentable.

So, too, would Reith, but in all sincerity.

By the autumn of 1936 he had been persuaded into *Certainly Sir!* at the Hippodrome. This new musical comedy should have been a success. It was produced by Jack Waller, a famous name among inter-war impresarios, and written by the same team which created such recent hits as *Yes, Madam?* and *Please Teacher!* starring the baby-faced Bobby Howes. The female lead was Renée Houston, and Robey had the part of a blackmailing butler. The plot reached dotty depths rarely plumbed by musical comedy and served as an excuse to interpolate a glamorous fancy-dress ball, a chorus of Dresden shepherdesses and a whirling nautical display. The first night audience heard with puzzlement music which occasionally borrowed the opening theme from Tchaikovsky's Sixth Symphony and, likewise, other bits and pieces from Chopin and Wagner, not forgetting Strauss. (This was an age which preferred to hear a Chopin impromptu as 'I'm Always Chasing Rainbows' and a Mozart piano sonata as 'In An Eighteenth-Century Drawing-Room.') The most successful home-grown number was Robey's song, 'I'm Not Surprised, I'm Amazed', which gave him a new catch-phrase. But even his robust presence could not save *Certainly, Sir!* from a distinctly unsympathetic reception. It was an evening he preferred to forget. The piece lingered on for only twenty performances and was the biggest flop he had ever known.

A month or so later, with some relief, he went back to his origins and played a variety programme at the Victoria Palace hopefully entitled *Laughter Over London*. He had been so long away from music-hall that his performance had an air of revelation.

Those who have seen Robey only in musical plays and revues have no idea how infinitely superior he is as a single turn on the halls, where the intimacy between performers and audience is undisturbed by alien influence [wrote a *Sunday Pictorial* columnist]. I don't believe Robey will ever know how good he is or have more than the haziest notion why. But he is as deep as Tristram Shandy. His talk on relations, excellent in matter, is classic in delivery. May he continue on the bills till he plays Falstaff again.

This was the setting closest to his heart: a shabby backcloth and a prop or two with which to dominate an audience for half an hour, alone and by the force of his own personality. In 1937, at the age of sixty-eight, he gleefully ventured into the new medium of non-stop revue. *Les Folies de Paris et de Londres* at the Prince of Wales began early in the day and went on into the next morning. He arrived at the theatre around midday, gave sixteen performances and did not leave until one o'clock in the morning. He enjoyed the experiment, and, more especially, the company of the beautiful young glamour girls whom he entertained with silly stories and jokes. They called him 'a darling'. During the long waits in his dressing-room he solved endless crossword puzzles, a distraction which had now replaced violin-making. He fulfilled the exhausting routine with unquenchable gusto and was as lively at the end of it as he had been at the beginning. After the last performance he allowed himself a shower and sponge-down. 'That,' he exulted, 'will keep me fit for another sixty-eight years.'

The years he had already completed were, thought his friends, a cause for celebration, and they entertained him to dinner at the

Criterion restaurant. In a speech afterwards he looked back on his long career and recalled his playing of Falstaff. 'People often come up to me and ask, "Was it difficult?"' he said, 'and I tell them that for forty-five years I have worked under all sorts of difficult conditions and during that time I had to find my own material. This time I went into the theatre with a script which was written by Mr William Shakespeare and I found that all I had to do was to say it.' Humour on the stage, he reflected, had not changed for centuries and never would change. The foundations of humour were as old as the world, and the things that made people laugh remained the same. 'What are the basic, never-failing ingredients of laughter on any stage in any country?' he asked, warming to the opportunity of introducing yet again his most cherished opinion.

> First of all, someone's discomfort. Audiences are no crueller than any other human beings – but let them see some poor fellow receive a brick on the jaw accompanied by a loud report, and you have the safest laugh in the world. Mothers-in-law, pawnbrokers, landladies, twins and – I am sorry to say – drink, these ingredients will never fail. The secret, I am not in the least ashamed to say, is good, honest vulgarity.

Not long afterwards, however, an untoward experience made him revise his opinion about the laughable quality of physical knocks. At Christmas 1938 he was booked to play the dame in the Birmingham Theatre Royal's production of *Robinson Crusoe*. He was always very popular in Birmingham where he had spent some of his youth as a tyro civil engineer, and there the local Rotary Club entertained him to lunch. In a speech he offered his definition of laughter. 'It is,' he said with mock gravity, 'the synchronised co-ordination of neuro-physiological reflexes, with a semi-automatic impulse of mass-inhibited suggestionism.'

The neuro-physiological reflexes were given ample scope when he appeared at the first night in his famous black bonnet and cape, a naughty glare raking the audience and daring them to misinterpret his apparently innocent remarks. Soon he had everyone singing

> Beg your parding,
> Mrs Harding,
> There's a kitty in your garding . . .

From Offenbach to Shakespeare

At a matinée a week into the run he put on, in accordance with a pre-arranged gag, a Greta Garbo mask and wig and began to edge his way off stage. Temporarily blinded by the mask, he stumbled and fell into the stalls where he landed with such force that he broke the arm-rest of a seat. Back he clambered over the footlights while the audience laughed at what they thought was part of the routine. He was in agony. Nonetheless he carried on with the dialogue, although, when he came to sing, he held his side in an attempt to allay the pain. When the audience at last realised what had happened, their applause for his doggedness held up the show. A doctor gave first-aid in his dressing-room, and when the curtain fell he was taken, still wearing make-up, to a radiologist. He had, it was discovered, injured his spine and broken three ribs. It was impossible, said the specialists, for him to play the evening performance. He argued, he stormed, he raved. The medical man was adamant. Robey, stricken with grief, groaned angrily, 'It is the first time I have ever failed an audience in my life.'

Blanche Robey sat by his bedside through the night and refused to let him be taken to hospital. Morphia injections failed to bring him sleep and he could not even lie down on his bed. Over a thousand letters arrived from anxious admirers, and flowers and gifts, for his accident had been headline news. The letter he enjoyed most was one that read: 'Funny you should have broken your ribs after making so many people break their ribs through laughing at you.'

Within a fortnight he was much better and astonishing the doctors by his quick recovery at such an age. Blanche, exhausted with the long hours of constant attendance upon him, went into a nervous collapse. It was his turn, now, to be the devoted nurse. One lesson he had learned, he said:

If ever you find me cracking jokes on the stage again about comic men who slip on banana skins, or trying to make fun out of accidents – boo! For nearly fifty years I've lived and worked in a world where it has been an article of faith that the two funniest subjects on earth are mothers-in-law and people who fall suddenly on their backs. Now I know there's nothing funny whatever about falling over, whatever the process may seem to the onlooker. I tell you this kind of experience shakes your faith in the old axioms.

While recuperating he watched Portsmouth football team in training for the Cup Tie and spent half an hour practising kicks with them. Then he returned to Birmingham and *Robinson Crusoe*, deliberately choosing Friday, 13th February, as the date of his reappearance. Had he not, in youth, been a founder-member of the Thirteen Club? Still heavily bandaged and attended by both nurse and doctor between the acts, he went on stage to find the only tonic that really worked for him: an audience. They rose to him. Twice daily he went on playing Mrs Crusoe until the pantomime ended after a record run of seventeen weeks. It had been, he said, 'apart from the little slip I made early on', quite the happiest of all the pantomimes he had played at Birmingham for more than forty years. And even 'the little slip' was a good thing so far as it brought him the kindness and sympathy of unknown friends. 'I feel it was worthwhile taking that ten-foot drop to make me cognisant with all these friends,' he remarked gratefully. He was not just a comedian. He was a national figure. Madame Tussaud's proved it by consecrating him with a lifelike waxwork model.

But had the 'ten-foot drop' resulted from the cause to which it was publicly attributed? The official version was that, his sight obscured by the Garbo mask, he had stumbled and fallen. A later report indicated that Robey was drunk. This is ironical, for he was by no means a heavy drinker. Unlike many others in his profession, he disliked the beery gatherings they enjoyed and, while buying drinks so far as social courtesy demanded, was glad to leave for home as soon as he decently could. While playing *Robinson Crusoe* he had, for some reason, drunk too much and too near a performance. So his anguish over the incident was twofold in that he, normally a temperate man, should have broken a lifelong tradition of reliability with such uncharacteristic behaviour. Although his audiences thought him as lively and masterful as ever, something of his confidence perhaps had gone. Off stage there were periods of quietness when he no longer wished to talk and was content to let Blanche fuss around him and arrange his life. Dependent on her for many years, he now relied on his wife utterly. For they had finally got married.

As always, Blanche had revelled in her charge as companion of the great comedian and famous public figure. She had surrounded him with fierce devotion and unquestioning faith. Although she was a shrewd and clear-eyed businesswoman, an unparalleled negotiator of contracts and a formidable match for any man in the theatre business, she worshipped Robey with the intensity of a young and unsophisticated girl. Only one element had been lacking to make her happiness complete: if only she could be his wife, lawful and acknowledged!

For some time she had been increasingly uneasy at her ambiguous position in Robey's life. They had lived together for eight years and she found the situation embarrassing. Since she was always the one who had to organise everything, she it was who asked Robey's son Edward if he could arrange a divorce. This, the latter thought, was not unreasonable since the marriage had broken down several years before his father met Blanche and she could not be held in any way responsible for the episode. With tact both legal and filial, he persuaded his mother to agree. She consented to the filing of a petition and, in accordance with the cumbersome divorce procedure of the day, the necessary evidence was presented and accepted. Almost a decade after he had met Blanche, Robey married her on 30th November, 1938. They emerged beaming into the chilly air on the steps of the Marylebone Register Office where the legal deed was done, she in furs and a smart new hat, he in cutaway black coat and winged collar. As the crowd of onlookers and cameramen pressed around the couple, he doffed his top hat and waved it jubilantly. At sixty-nine his forehead was now completely bald and the hair at the back of his head gleamed steely-white.

A fortnight later they were guests of honour at a celebratory banquet in the Dorchester where nearly five hundred people met to salute him as comedian and charity fund-raiser. The prospect daunted him. 'They'll expect me to be funny, I suppose,' he said, 'and I've never felt less funny.' That evening the man who described himself as 'a red-nosed comic' sat at the head of the table next to Mrs Robey and blushed with embarrassment as Lord Londonderry, Sir Patrick Hastings, Sir Seymour Hicks and other luminaries praised him in fulsome speeches. Sir Oswald Stoll called him 'a great comic general commanding British armies of laughter', 'the Hogarth of the halls', and spoke of the time when he engaged him at a salary of four pounds a week. The guest of honour recovered himself so far as to riposte, 'Yes, but when I went back to him for *The Bing Boys* the figure was so astronomical that I daren't mention it before a lot of hard-up actors.' Violet Loraine, who was sitting a few tables away, smiled sweetly. So did Dame Marie Tempest.

Lord Londonderry presented him with an engraved cigarette case in solid gold and mentioned his work as violin-maker, water colourist, footballer, war worker and friend of charities. 'We thank you,' said Londonderry, 'not only for what you have done for us but for what you have done for the nation.'

Robey took out the typewritten notes he had made for his speech, but after a few minutes he put them away and spoke impromptu. 'Don't expect a lofty speech from a very low comedian,' he warned his audience. At first he waxed reflective. 'I think memory is right to place emphasis on friendship,' he observed. 'The worthwhile part of a man's history cannot be written alone. He must have friends to look over his shoulder and help him with a cheery word. The little happy moments that stand out in a man's memory shine out on an occasion like this, like bright gems on the black velvet of the past.' He could not, however, remain serious for long, and soon he was telling jokes in his old robust manner. When it was all over he handed out to each guest the little self-caricature he usually gave to his fans. The drawings had taken him several days to complete. After such a canonisation as the Dorchester banquet it is no surprise that the unfortunate incident of *Robinson Crusoe* some weeks later should need to be disguised as a simple matter of a missed footing.

[iii]

Sir George the lean and slippered

In 1939 he reached his seventieth birthday. That year, on Whit Monday, he starred as top of the bill at the London Coliseum. His appearance was, in effect, a come-back after the débâcle at Birmingham and gave notice that, whatever people might say, the old player could still hold an audience. 'London last night saw a younger than ever George Robey for the first time since his pantomime accident,' remarked the *Daily Mail*. 'He strode on to the Coliseum stage as if he had never dashed into the Birmingham orchestra pit. Perhaps the voice was a little richer, the look of astonished reproach a little colder . . . but otherwise it was the same George Robey. The audience was amazed.' The attack was there, and the vigour, and once again he told stories of such convoluted vulgarity that the puritanical but unsophisticated Oswald Stoll, his employer on this occasion, failed to grasp them. Yet although Stoll missed the point, it did not matter: the house was full and the box-office prospered.

A few weeks after he finished his Coliseum booking he prepared for a long tour of Australia. He had often been invited to go there, but other commitments intervened, other obligations absorbed him, and only now had Blanche been able to clear his engagement book for the eighteen or so months the journey required. The itinerary led from Sydney to Melbourne and Adelaide, and then, they hoped, on to New Zealand and South Africa where he was to play pantomime in Johannesburg. Despite the threat of war that dominated Europe he was optimistic and looked forward to seeing new people and new places.

Before they departed on the long absence there were affairs to be put in order. The biggest problem was his collection of antiquities. It was difficult to know where to store them, and in addition Birmingham Art Gallery, where a large selection of his porcelain had been displayed on loan, no longer wanted the responsibility of sheltering it. He decided that many of his treasures should be sold. 'It will,' he said bravely, 'be fun trying to collect these things again when we get back.' The auctions lasted several days at Christie's and other houses. A worse possible time could not have been chosen. The public was more concerned with air-raid precautions than with valuable Chinese artifacts, and dealers and shrewd collectors found many bargains. Numerous items went for less than twenty guineas. Six Quan Yin figures reached the highest price of one hundred and fifteen guineas, although two of them on their own had cost him as much as a hundred and twenty pounds. The total proceeds amounted to the wretched figure of one thousand three hundred and seventy-four pounds, a sum much less than what he had laid out over the years. It was as well that he did not go to the sale. 'I couldn't face it,' he avowed. 'Giving up the hobby of a lifetime is no joke so I stayed at home.' The snuff boxes went, and the Chinese hardstone and the jade figurines and the mother-of-pearl sheaths and the porcelain plates. Only a vague imprint of them remained on bare walls. The glass cabinets stood empty and anonymous.

Early in June he set sail with Blanche and, on the way, stopped off in Egypt where he tried the pleasures of camel-riding. He did not relish it and thought how much pleasanter had been his elephant rides in Manchester. In Bombay, he told reporters that he was not retiring yet. There was, he added modestly, nothing outstanding about himself. 'I believe in remaining mediocre,' he explained. 'I lead an audience up the garden path and do not let them think what I am going to say. I just try to amuse people and I think I have been lucky.' As he sailed past the Cocos Islands its eleven white inhabitants cheerily radioed to him the wish that they might have an opportunity to 'stop, look and listen' to him. He promised he would entertain them on the return journey. When he docked at Fremantle he told a newspaper: 'It was about time I came to Australia but I didn't know I was coming. My wife put me on the boat and I didn't mind.' This was not such an exaggeration as might appear, for Blanche had the discreet habit of arranging everything in advance and of then presenting him with a *fait accompli*. They both agreed it was better that way.

He opened in Melbourne to warm applause. A newspaper report commented:

He marched on to the stage, looking like a seedy parson, and gathered in his audience as if he owned it. He fired off a string of absurdities, sang a couple of songs with appropriate patter, indulged in some autobiographical reminiscences, and strolled off with the audience howling 'Encore!' after him. His stuff just slips out. How? Search me, I can generally keep a critical and non-committal dial in such circumstances but he cracked mine in several places.

Interviewed afterwards in his dressing-room he was asked what he planned to collect in Australia. 'Money!' was his lapidary response.

From Offenbach to Shakespeare

As he toured the country he met, again and again, people who had seen him in England and remembered him fondly. There were cricket-playing friends, ex-servicemen with memories of the old Alhambra and even a man who had been a page-boy there and the woman who, as a girl, worked the spotlight that illuminated him at the Coliseum. Old admirers travelled hundreds of miles to watch him and letters claiming acquaintance arrived by the score every day. Nostalgia bloomed.

It faded, abruptly, when news came that war had been declared against Germany. Robey was not a profound student of politics, international or otherwise. In 1936 the *Daily Herald* had published a poem he wrote which ended with one of his famous catch-phrases:

> The most paradoxical thing of the lot
> Is the way that the Nations behave,
> It appears, from the speeches of prominent men,
> That PEACE is the thing that they crave.
>
> Yet the factories are working by day and by night
> And the atmosphere's getting more tense,
> They're turning out tons of munitions and guns
> And they say that it's just for defence!
>
> But to round off the joke, they say they're all broke
> Yet for armaments millions they've raised:
> If it's just to take part in a war that won't start
> I'm more than surprised – I'm amazed!

His views were simple. Hitler had done well in modernising Germany and would do even better by defeating Communism, which, to Robey's mind, was the real threat. Moreover, he found it hard to hate a country where he had spent such pleasant times in his youth. He liked German people, German culture and the German language. Were they, after all, such a dreadful race?

The Australian tour was abandoned and the idea of going on to New Zealand and South Africa dropped. They must, they decided, go back immediately. Passages were taken on a flying boat of the old Imperial Airways. After a three-day journey with stopovers at unwelcoming Brindisi and sullen Marseille, the aircraft flew through a terrifying thunderstorm to land at Southampton on a chill October night. The travellers, most of them sea-sick, were ferried ashore in a violently rocking boat. Robey, stoutly, declared that it had been a wonderful flight, with the afterthought, 'I don't like the air and would not do it again ever – unless they ask me to drop bombs on the enemy.'

There were awkward moments when he was questioned about interviews he had given in Sydney at the declaration of war. They were, he insisted, delivered in a jocular tone and had been misunderstood at home. Did he say that at least the Cameroons might be handed back to Germany? Well, yes, so long as they gave us Heligoland in exchange. Had he declared Hitler to be a great man? Only because he had done a great thing for England by giving us a kick in the pants and waking us up from our false security. But now Hitler had become 'a mad dog' and the cause of slaughter. Robey had never imagined that he would plunge Europe into another war.

Back in wartime England he confined himself to ENSA functions, shows in hospitals and turns at remote anti-aircraft sites. There were to be no spectacular charity events of the kind he sponsored in the 1914–18 war. In any case he did not have the energy and Blanche was determined to shield him as much as possible. He went through the old routines efficiently though a shade mechanically. For the new generation he was little more than a dusty name. When he distributed the little caricatures he drew of himself they looked at them uncomprehendingly and then threw them away. One awful night in a northern town the audience was unimpressed by his reputation and bored with humour that seemed old-fashioned. They gave him a disrespectful reception.

At the age of seventy-three, in December 1942, he played his last pantomime, the Bristol Hippodrome production of *Robinson Crusoe*. With Blanche he travelled down to Bristol in one of those wartime trains that halted for interminable and mysterious waits in the middle of the countryside and dawdled cautiously through blackouts. Sustained by an occasional nip of brandy in his freezing carriage, he arrived to find the city a victim of bombs, perhaps even more so than London. Certain areas were completely desolate and many churches had been blown up. There were few people to be seen on the quiet streets except for troops.

'Pantomime at its Best', exclaimed the Hippodrome posters. 'A Riot of Fun and Colour.' 'Fourteen delightful scenes . . . a star company of 60 artistes.' Fun and colour were what the inhabitants of that devastated city craved most of all after their experiences in the blitz. Robey gave them a generous allowance twice a day, twelve times a week. He might tire more often these days, he might doze off between calls, but somehow, when on stage in front of an audience, he seemed to draw energy from them which straightened his drooping frame and gave his step some of the old nimbleness. Despite his seventy-three years he bounded, capered, flounced coquettishly in his dame's skirts and, with a strong clear voice, rebuked the giggling audience in words they had been waiting for, words they knew by heart: 'Let there be merriment by all means. Let there be merriment, but let it be tempered with dignity and the reserve which is compatible with the obvious refinement of our environment.' And then he might give them one of the old favourites:

> Poor thing, poor thing –
> And I thought of when I placed her wedding ring,
> It was too bad to provoke her,
> And I didn't want to choke her,
> So I sloshed her with the poker – poor thing!

Blanche had invited their old friend the critic James Agate to see the show. He arrived for the Saturday evening performance of 16th January, by which time in the run Robey had well and truly hit his stride. Agate looked back over the years during which he had known an artist whom he believed to be the greatest of his kind since Dan Leno. He thought of Goldsmith's Mr Hardcastle who remarked: 'I love everything that's old, old friends, old times, old manners, old books, old wine,' and to those, he decided, he would add old actors. There was a patina on Robey's quips, and a beauty in those ageing Widow Twankeys and Mrs Crusoes. The hey-day in the blood was tamer, and whereas previously the impression was one of riot, now you had a sense of pranks recollected in tranquillity.

'It is a matter of forty-five years since I first saw this great player assume bonnet and dolman,' Agate reminisced:

I saw him just above the horizon, decorating and cheering the elevated sphere he just began to move in, glittering like the morning star, full of life and splendour and joy. And never, as Burke didn't say, were these optics dazzled by a more delightful vision. In those far-off days an elephant used to call for the star at his lodgings and squat on the kerb till a sufficient crowd had collected, when a frock-coated figure, collarless but with brow circumspectly cinct, and carrying an odd little cane, would mount on to the animal's back and ride down to the theatre indifferent to the mob, wrapped in his own thoughts, and as if this were his usual mode of conveyance.

I remember that in this early pantomime there was a cow alleged to be ten years old, that the principal boy said, 'Isn't she a picture, Mother?' and that George, wearing a blue and white check apron, said, 'Yes, a picture by Teniers!' Did I miss, the other evening, some of the old exuberance? Possibly. But will anybody insist that Beethoven in his Third Manner retained everything of the frolicsome First or tempestuous Second? To Robey, too, must be allowed his third period. After the storm comes the calm, and it is conceded that those over-the-wall squabbles with Mrs Moggridge belong and may now be relegated to the order of happy, far-off things and battles long ago.

Next day Agate was entertained to Sunday lunch by members of the *Robinson Crusoe* company. Robey, he thought, seemed a little tired, so he did his best to keep the talk going. Robey whispered to him, 'I'll bet the folks around are saying, "There's Robey making 'em laugh!"' There was a touch of wistfulness in his voice. Agate found him modest as always. He confessed that he once declined an offer to play one of the Ugly Sisters in *Cinderella* because the other was Fred Emney. 'Fred *was* a woman,' said Robey. 'I should have been merely a red-nosed comedian in petticoats.'

Later, back in London, when *Robinson Crusoe* was over and Robey had put off his dame outfit for ever, he and Blanche gave Agate lunch at the Ivy. It was a special occasion at which Robey presented the critic with one of his famous canes. The cane, promised Agate, would star in his collection of walking sticks, beside that of Charlie Chaplin, mounted on royal blue velvet and glass-cased. Robey went on to complain about modern audiences being over-influenced by radio. 'They don't laugh at one joke for fear of missing the next,' he argued. Agate did not dare tell him that audiences laughed as much as ever when they were genuinely amused: the sad truth was that ageing comics like Robey did not know their humour failed to work as it did back in the years when they were at the top of their form. During lunch Robey, in an undertone, recited the Ghost's speech from *Hamlet*, starting at 'I am thy father's spirit' down to 'list, list, O, list!'. He then took it up from 'Sleeping within mine orchard' to 'remember me'. His recitation was word-perfect. When, Agate asked, had he studied it? 'Before I went on the stage,' Robey answered. 'It is to this speech that I owe my enunciation.'

Later that year he appeared in *Seventy Years of Song*, a pageant organised at the Royal Albert Hall by Charles B. Cochran, a fellow veteran who also found wartime and increasing age a burden. This cavalcade of popular song had a large orchestra under Geraldo and a cast of several thousands. Eva Turner sang 'One Fine Day', Hutch played 'Alexander's Ragtime Band', Ivor Novello intoned 'Keep the Home Fires Burning', and massed troops from the army, navy and royal air force marched and countermarched throughout the vast spaces of the hall. There was a final chorus of 'Land of Hope and Glory' chanted by many hundreds, but the most popular item was 'If You Were the Only Girl in the World' given by Robey and his old-time partner Violet Loraine who had come out of retirement to assist him. The ancient song had not lost its power to charm or to move the emotions.

Suddenly, it seemed, he had become a back-number. Older people remembered him fondly. Younger people thought him old-fashioned, and, when they saw him perform, could only just discern that something of his presence still lingered. They could not believe that this had been the great comedian of their fathers and their grandfathers. Blanche arranged little tours for him from time to time, enough to occupy without overtiring him. It kept him happy, she told friends, and preserved his self-respect. In 1944 Laurence Olivier asked him to appear in the film of *Henry V*. As we have seen, Olivier admired Robey's diction and technique. 'His countenance and his wonderful comic gift,' Olivier believed, made his Falstaff 'a truly remarkable performance. Having seen that performance it needed no great stretch of imagination on my part to cast him for the little bowdlerised scene in *Henry V*.' The episode, specially interpolated, showed Falstaff on his deathbed. Robey created an atmosphere rich with pathos.

In 1945, the year the war ended, he took part in another film called *Waltz Time*. It was a musical set in old Vienna featuring the singers Richard Tauber, Anne Ziegler and Webster Booth, and Harry Welchman, that long-lived survivor from musical comedies of the early 1900s. Albert Sandler, a well-known Palm Court performer, played the violin, and Hans May, who had composed the score, acted a small role. The beautiful Kay Kendall also played a minor part. Peter Graves was an officer in the Viennese Imperial Guard who is taught a lesson by the Empress when he flirts elsewhere, and the intricacies of the plot were resolved in a final triumphant waltz. Robey, as Vogel the innkeeper, had little to do except smile benevolently.

Seven years later, at the age of eighty-three, he was to make his last film appearance in *The Pickwick Papers* as Tony Weller. At first he turned down the part. 'I'm not so young as I used to be,' he explained, 'and film-making is a big strain.' Then he read the script and began to see possibilities. He changed his mind. In a cast which also included Hermione Gingold, Joyce Grenfell, Donald Wolfit, Athene Seyler and, as Mr Pickwick, the portly James Hayter, Robey was the essence of the old Cockney coachman, ample, asthmatic, scarlet-faced. It was his last appearance in a medium he never really enjoyed. On stage he was master of the situation, in full control of every effect. In films there were too many other people getting between him and the audience. 'All right,' he once said,

I've been all right in pictures, but it doesn't mean anything. Consider: in the silent days the first gentleman of the screen was Rin Tin Tin and then when talkies came in the first lady of the screen was Shirley Temple until she became too old at about seven and was usurped by Lassie. But the whole thing is in the cutting and the editing and I will not have it that I'm a good film actor. My personality may suit a picture, but acting has nothing to do with it.

Directors and editors imposed their own ideas. What people saw on the screen was Robey filtered through a box of tricks, not Robey pure and undefiled.

The days passed quietly at the flat in Buckingham Gate where he lived with Blanche. Often he would potter out, encased in a thick black overcoat and leaning on his wife's arm, to feed the ducks in St James's Park. He liked to talk over old memories with James Agate. Who, Agate asked him, was the greater artist: Vesta Tilley or Marie Lloyd? 'I should put Marie first,' Robey decided. 'She had to create it all out of herself, whereas Tilley had her wonderful masculine props to rely on. But they were both tremendous artists, and it's a very near thing.' As for the men in his time, he reckoned, 'Dan Leno first. After him Tom Costello, Harry Randall, Little Tich, Chirgwin, Eugene Stratton, Will Fyffe.' He spoke, too, about his travels and of the African chieftain who had given a diamond bracelet to his wife and bestowed a kiss upon him. 'I think he liked me best,' said Robey grinning.

When he was seventy-eight Blanche decided to revive a musical play for children called *The Windmill Man*. It would give Robey something to do, she thought, and a short season at the Imperial Theatre in Brighton would not overtire him, especially as she cast his old friend Bransby Williams in the larger role. Robey, she planned, could fit in his German music professor act. The two veterans arrived punctually for rehearsals. The producer, who had been held up elsewhere, arrived late to find his two stars fast asleep on stage. On waking up they reproached him sorrowfully: here they were, nearly eighty, and their young producer had let them down! Moreover, as he was to find, they performed immaculately, although Robey needed Blanche. She escorted him carefully from his dressing-room to the wings, watched over him during the performance, and then took him back again. 'It's good for the old man,' she murmured.

Somebody said to him, 'It's still wonderful to watch you, George.'

Robey looked vaguely into the distance and replied, 'It keeps you occupied, doesn't it?'

By 1948 London had become too noisy, too wearisome, and the Robeys moved house to Sussex where they set up in Hove. There was not enough room to house what remained of Robey's antique collection or much of the period furniture amassed over the years. Two hundred items went to the sale-rooms, among them Chinese hardstones and objects exquisitely wrought in porcelain, coral, rock-crystal, green jade and mother-of-pearl. They raised the inconsiderable sum of two hundred pounds.

That year he fêted his seventy-ninth birthday: he was no longer a famous comedian, he was a national monument to be preserved and revered. The Greek scholar Gilbert Murray sent him many happy returns. There was a festive luncheon at the Dorchester. In his contribution to *If I Had My Time Again* he had decided that, if life was to be re-lived, he had enjoyed it so much that he would do it in exactly the same way. There had been sadness and bitterness and pain, but would he have known true happiness and fulfilment without them? He sought happiness in the laughter and applause of audiences, and there he had found it.

He had, he admitted, been fortunate. Nearly all the things he wanted to do he had done. In football he achieved his ambition by appearing with professional teams like Chelsea, Millwall and Aston Villa. On the cricket field he played opposite some of the greatest figures of his day, names he had always hero-worshipped. He taught himself to make violins, to paint pictures which were exhibited at the Royal Academy and which gained him a diploma from the Institute of Painters in Water Colours. His connoisseurship of Chinese art was peculiar and extensive. During the 1914–18 war the vast sums he raised for charity brought him the award of the CBE. He had no advice to offer apart from telling his readers to attempt new things, to be inventive, to have widely diverse interests. They should, he added, never have to search for happiness: it lay within their own hearts and minds, within their own selves. He ended his chapter with a favourite quotation from *As You Like It:* 'And this our life, exempt from public haunt, finds tongues in trees, books in the running brooks, sermons in stones, and good in everything. I would not change it.' Although his own life had been by no means exempt from public haunt, at least he claimed to have found good in everything. No, he would not change it.

There was something a shade inhuman about the smooth trajectory of the career he planned and made. No dramatic leap took him from obscurity to fame. By the age of twenty-one he was already a familiar name and within a short time he had glided up to the top of the hill. He did not suffer the early struggles of a Little Tich or the desperate poverty of a Charlie Chaplin. From a comfortable bourgeois youth he sprang fully armed into the arena. Mistakes were made, small setbacks were suffered, but on the whole he knew many more triumphs than disasters. He learned very quickly, and the result was a career that lasted for longer than that of any other comparable music-hall star. Dan Leno and Marie Lloyd were burnt out at a relatively early age. Robey went on and on, ever confident and unfaltering.

He always stood slightly aloof from his music-hall colleagues. While others would gather round the bar he chose to go home and relax with his collections and his painting. He drank little in a profession noted for bibulousness and preferred the company of a few close friends. The discipline he imposed enabled him to honour his engagements and fulfil his contracts. The physical fitness he prided himself on, the footballing, the cricketing, the athletics, kept him equal to the exhausting demands of his performance routine. He was largely self-taught, and, as a confirmed autodidact, never lost his passion for new knowledge and new words. Thus he relished polysyllables and delivered them on stage with an enjoyment that caused him to roll the phrases around in his mouth before, reluctantly, discharging them at the audience. 'Superfluous' came high among his favourite words, and so did 'modicum'. A term like 'machicolated' brought a devilish gleam to his eye. Constantly teasing the audience with Dickensian orotundity and then puncturing it with slang of one syllable, he calculated the laughter he roused with the efficiency of a chronometer.

The paradox of his career is that in private life he was the most conventional of men, strong for Empire, straightforwardly patriotic and respectful of the established order. On stage, however, he was a medieval Lord of Misrule, red-nosed and leering, for ever encouraging his audience to put the most disgraceful construction on his ambiguous remarks. His personality was such that he could, in his long-lived prime, make that audience think precisely what he wanted them to think. He dominated them. It had something to do with the look in his eye, the way he made his entrance, the pose he adopted as he stood boldly in front of them and, for twenty minutes or so, held them with nothing more than the force of his personality. He did not go quite as far as Max Miller, who, also possessing this gift, would occasionally turn his back on the audience, so confident was he of keeping them, and rattle the scenery in his exuberance. But Robey could have, had he wanted to do so. His mastery showed itself in other ways. A spectator once took exception to a particularly blatant double meaning, and, offended, rose from his seat and made for the exit. Robey fixed him with his stare and walked across the stage in parallel. When the man reached the exit Robey stopped too and jocularly remarked, 'Ai say, you don't think ai really meant *that*, do you?' The man was acutely discomfited, the audience laughed at his embarrassment, and Robey kept control of the situation.

The scripts he used, even more than the songs he sang, now have a faded air. They contain slang that is out of date and turns of phrase that are no longer funny. We have to accept the magic of his character, the crystal diction that could convey the slightest nuance to 'the last man in the gallery'. The voice, plummy, sometimes rasping and underlined with a faint Cockney mocking drawl, was assisted by immense eyebrows that flickered in sympathy, a mouth that twisted unctuously, and eyes, glittering eyes that seemed to hypnotise an audience and speak as eloquently as his very tones. With all these went the reproving glare, the tetchy huff when it seemed people were taking liberties with what he said, the shocked innuendo that looked as if it burst forth despite his best intentions, the frozen astonishment which appeared so genuine but which served only to husband the laughter still further, the abrupt command 'Desist!' And then, when guffaws had reached the point of hysteria, he would suddenly stop. The moment was judged with precision and, artist that he was, he would leave the audience wanting more.

For he was an artist in the correct sense of the word. An actor far more than a simple comedian, he proved it by gracing with facility a number of different spheres. Although he rightly described himself as a stand-up comedian and always believed that the supreme test was to hold an audience with nothing but a backcloth and a prop or two, he went on to act in plays, musical comedies, operettas, revues, films and Shakespeare. In all of these he showed versatile brilliance as an actor. If his films were undistinguished that was because he came late to the medium and did not find a director who knew how to use his particular gifts. The other media could offer him an audience, and that was all he needed to get the enchantment working again. As Lucifer Bing, as Menelaus, as Falstaff, so long as he knew there was an audience watching him he could work on them and captivate them.

All that was over now as he sat tranquilly in Hove playing with jigsaw puzzles and going for little walks jealously supervised by Blanche. He was the idol of her life, the man to whom she devoted her whole existence, her *raison d'être*, to be guarded and cossetted like a precious jewel. She was proud to be known as Mrs Robey, and she bridled at the slightest aspersion that might be cast on his sacred name. Any acquaintance who dared breathe a criticism against him was immediately cast off. He was, for her, the greatest actor, the greatest comedian and the greatest man alive. Although, in earlier years, he might have found her protectiveness a little stifling, now, in old age, he was grateful for it. His eightieth birthday came in 1949 and, with it, the ceremonial congratulations to which he had become inured. He had known, he said, most of Shakespeare's seven ages and was already into the phase of the lean and slippered pantaloon. He did not, he confessed, want to know the next age. Two years later he appeared in a television programme about his life. On this occasion he declaimed a monologue which he had specially written with tongue in cheek:

So you ask for a tale of my life, Sir,
You would delve in the depths of my past?
Very well, I will tell you of the weakness
That bought me to ruin at last.
It wasn't women and Woodbines and wine, Sir,
That brought on the state I am in.
It was my passionate love for a woman,
It was Gertie and Gold Flakes and gin.
She came of a very old fam'ly –
They'd a mansion at Tooting-le-Bec –
And she loved with a proud haughty passion –
I've her finger-nail marks on my neck!
Then he came, ah, curse him! ah curse him!
And I watched the low cad importune 'er.
He held that poor girl in a thrall, Sir,
He was more like a man than a crooner.
And the rest? It's the old sordid story,
An object of shame and derision,
And now I've come down to the lowest,
A comedian – on television!

When he was eighty-two he took part at the Palladium in a benefit performance for the family of Sid Field, the comedian who died tragically young. He sat on stage in company with the other stars who were appearing. 'Keep an eye on George, will you?' said Blanche to Arthur Askey. 'And see that he gets up when his name is announced.' She watched from the wings, a few steps away, and Askey gave Robey a nudge at the right moment. The old man got up and walked lightly to the centre of the stage. He sang 'I Stopped, I Looked and I Listened' and 'If You Were the Only Girl in the World', every word and nuance in place, as he had sung it when he was young. Blanche, in the wings, never took her eyes off him and mouthed the words in sympathy. Then Askey brought him safely back to his chair. 'Great, great artist,' murmured Danny Kaye who was also on the programme. 'They say I'm cruel to make him go on,' remarked Blanche, 'but I'm doing the right thing. He couldn't live without it.' How could she do otherwise when, each evening at home, like an old war-horse scenting battle from afar, he would automatically take out his make-up box? For the whole of his adult life he had been accustomed at that time to put on greasepaint. It was a habit too hard to break. Even if no stage beckoned, the sight of his red nose and black eyebrows emerging from the mirror comforted him and tranquillised him.

A month later, in July 1951, he went off on an extended provincial tour called *Do You Remember?* with other old-timers like Wee Georgie Wood, Hetty King and the film comedian Buster Keaton. They came to Sheffield where a member of the audience produced a photograph of him taken forty years ago as captain of an international soccer eleven. On that occasion he had scored a goal against a combined Everton and Liverpool team. 'I could do it again,' he said proudly, opening his shirt to reveal stomach muscles flat as a board. The tour went on to its last night at the Alhambra in Bradford. It had been successful, though not without tension among the performers, some of it caused by Buster Keaton who refused to mix with the other easy-going music-hall veterans and kept severely to himself in his lonely dressing-room. Before the curtain went up for the last time Robey visited members of the company and asked them for contributions to a silver salver which would be inscribed with their names and presented to Keaton.

'You know you don't like Keaton, George,' said Wee Georgie Wood.

Robey grinned. 'I know, but the bastard will be going back to America and if he takes a silver salver with all our signatures on, *he* can't say we don't like him.'

At home he busied himself with crossword puzzles and jigsaws. Sometimes he would draw the little caricatures of himself he liked to hand out. At other times he accompanied Blanche on her shopping expeditions and to the hairdresser where he waited for her with consummate patience while he finished the day's crossword. When they came home he would settle happily to unravelling knotted string and unpicking various materials. Occasionally he would give entertainments in old people's homes and help with charities. 'What amuses me is the number of times I'm asked to do shows for old people,' he wryly commented. 'I look around my audience, most of them younger than I am, and wonder if they shouldn't be entertaining me!'

The last full-length show in which he appeared was *Touch Wood and Whistle*. It was a revue produced by Blanche who toured it around the London suburbs after a first night at the People's Palace, Mile End. He sat before his brightly lit mirror and, with a steady hand, deftly put on his make-up as he had thousands of times before. The foundation was laid over face and neck with a plump stick of Leichner Number Three greasepaint. Red was added to his nose and crimson-lake liner to either side of the mouth. The eyes were swiftly outlined in black and the eyebrows accentuated in the shape of the moon's quarter. It was the work of a few minutes. In his dressing-room after the show he took a brisk cold sponge-down as usual. On the tour he played the Woolwich Royal Artillery Theatre, where, at the centre of the cast, he lined up for the final curtain, straight-backed, alert. The place was full of nostalgia for him and Blanche, and there was something very appropriate in his taking his farewell there.

His old age was serene, even though from time to time he railed against jazz music, which he had never learned to accept, and crooners whom he loathed. He abominated microphones, too, and when confronted with one on the music-hall stage he dismissed it contemptuously. At the Finsbury Park Empire in his last years he was affronted to see a microphone rising up amid the footlights. After a comic double-take he made a rude gesture at it. The microphone sank back, then snaked up again twice, each time being rejected with a gag from Robey. At last it gave up and Robey went on with his act, perfectly audible throughout the whole of the vast auditorium. 'Desist! I am not here as a source of public flippancy. I'm surprised at *you*, Ag-er-ness!' Jazz, crooners, microphones and trade unions were the only disturbers of his old age, although he did tend to be strangely upset by what he took to be the suggestiveness of some younger comedians – strangely, because his own ideas of what constituted 'honest vulgarity' were illogical. But every man is entitled to at least one bee in his bonnet, and the escape clause in Robey's argument is to be found in the last sentence of a remark he made towards the end of his life: 'I'm not a prude,' he said, 'as you know, and I've cracked some saucy ones in my time. But I've always tried to be *modest* in my vulgarity. I have never said a thing I wouldn't say in front of a family. And if people take the wrong meaning – that's their business.'

The Christmas of 1953 saw him make his last appearance in public. At a charity performance of Bertram Mills Circus he put on his comedian's dress and drove round the ring in a small coach drawn by a pair of lively ponies – too lively, for the frail figure was bounced and shaken and afterwards complained of pain. A specialist diagnosed a slipped disc and he spent Christmas Day in bed. 'It has been terribly hard to keep him in bed,' sighed Blanche. 'It has to be gentle persuasion. Sometimes I promise him an extra cigarette.' Someone asked if he would be making any New Year resolutions. He puffed hard on the extra cigarette. 'Let's see,' he replied. 'Ah yes, I resolve to keep on going the same old way!'

A week or so later, while he was still confined to his bedroom, the New Year Honours list of 1954 announced his knighthood. It seemed, at first, that the venerable English tradition of bestowing honour at a time when the recipient was too old and too weary to enjoy it had been faithfully observed. He was, however, made a similar offer in recognition of his wartime charitable work as long ago as 1919. He had modestly refused it, thinking 'Sir George Robey' too incongruous an appellation for a red-nosed comic. This time, wreathed in affection and antiquity, he accepted. 'Of course I'm delighted with the honour,' he told journalists. 'But why me? I'm delighted because my wife Blanche can share it. She deserves it. We are never apart. She goes with me everywhere. What a partner she is.' He stroked her hand affectionately.

On the eve of the ceremony he drove up to London with Blanche from Hove and stayed overnight in a hotel. At eight o'clock on the morning of 16th February Prince Littler, Blanche's brother, sent his Rolls-Royce to collect them. Robey, in morning-coat and grey waistcoat, top hat anxiously clasped in his hand, was smuggled out through a luggage lift to avoid the large crowds that had gathered in the hotel foyer and in the street. On arrival at Buckingham Palace officials met him with a wheelchair, once the property of Queen Mary, took him up in a lift, and conveyed him into the white and gold splendour of the Investiture Room. Just before he trundled in, Blanche, for luck, slipped his cane into his hand. Clutching the symbol of his stage fame, he received the accolade from Queen Elizabeth the Queen Mother who deputised in the absence of the monarch on a tour abroad. She leaned over him. 'How very pleased I am to confer this knighthood upon you. I know the Queen would have been doubly pleased to do so.' She touched his shoulder with the sword. 'I am delighted to be here,

Ma'am,' said Sir George Robey CBE. As he came away from the ceremony he met the physician Lord Webb Johnson who had also received a decoration. 'Hello, George!' said Webb Johnson. 'It's fifty years since I first saw you. That was in pantomime in Manchester and you rode down to the theatre on an elephant.' Robey beamed. Stirred by the memory, he got out of his chair and reminisced with his old acquaintance. The display of china in the long corridor aroused his collector's instinct, and he went over to examine it more closely. Before he realised what he was doing, he had walked all the way to the lift. He ended the day exhausted. 'We shall keep him in bed for a few days,' said Blanche, 'and get him home and really fighting fit.'

She was too optimistic. From that time onward he declined. In June he was seen on television as the celebrity guest in a panel game called *What's My Line*. He seemed confused by the questions the contestants put to him, and Blanche discreetly answered on his behalf. Frail, ghost-like, he peered uncertainly at the camera as if he did not know where he was. Each celebrity guest was allowed a secret wish. 'I wish,' he faltered, 'I wish I were George Robey twenty-five years ago.' At his eighty-fifth birthday in September he put on his MCC tie, a source of pride for fifty years. That was the only celebration he allowed himself. Too weak even to feed the birds in the garden, one of his last few pleasures, he stayed permanently in bed. He brightened at the news that his son Edward had been appointed a Metropolitan Magistrate and entertained him and his sister Eileen to tea in his bedroom. Then he settled down surrounded by a mountain of letters and telegrams to read the greetings that always streamed in on such occasions. People had not forgotten him.

Life ebbed gently. By the middle of November he lay in a semi-coma. Blanche was at his bedside every night, ready to speak whenever he emerged from the mist that enveloped his brain. Once he startled the nurse with a fruity comment uttered in the tones of his stage patter.

On the evening of 28th November Blanche asked him, 'Do you know who it is here?'

'Yes,' he replied, 'my little sweetheart wife.'

He spoke no more. His hands began to twitch abruptly at the bedclothes. She put into the clutching fingers his little cane and gently twisted them round it. He opened his eyes. A vague smile appeared and tears coursed down his face. Next morning, sunk in her arms, he died.

There was a funeral at the Downs Crematorium in Brighton on 1st December. Clear sunshine sparkled over wet grass as the coffin was borne in. Upon it lay the famous cane decorated with anemones and a heart-shaped wreath from Blanche with the inscription: 'For my beloved husband – the kindest, gentlest and most thoughtful man – twenty-five roses, one for each year since we first met and I fell under your loving spell. The long day ends and the eyebrows rest for evermore.'

Much grander was the memorial service at St Paul's where bishops rubbed shoulders with former principal boys and the Lord Mayor's representative mingled with Robey's long-time taxi-driver and pantomime dames in mufti. Douglas Fairbanks read the lesson from Ecclesiasticus: 'Let us now praise famous men . . .' The organist, while the mourners assembled, played 'The Death of Falstaff' from the incidental music William Walton composed for Robey's episode in *Henry V*. But really it was Blanche who had had the last word with her twenty-five red roses.

LIST OF BOOKS BY ROBEY

My Life Up Till Now, Greening, 1909
Pause, Greening, 1910
Jokes, Jibes and Jingles, Paxton, 1911
My Rest Cure, Richards Press, 1919
After-Dinner Stories, Richards Press, 1920
Thereby Hangs a Tale, Grant Richards, 1921
The Lady In Question, Eveleigh Nash and Grayson, 1922
An Honest Living, Cassell, 1922 (reprinted 1922 and 1924)
Family Affairs, John Long, 1924
Mental Fireworks, John Long, 1925
Don'ts, John Long, 1926
Bits and Pieces, Jarrolds, 1928
In Other Words, Jarrolds, 1929
Looking Back On Life, Constable, 1933

Gramophone records

A detailed list of more than one hundred and forty records made by Robey between 1902 and 1931 will be found in the monumental reference work compiled by Brian Rust and Rex Bunnett and entitled *London Musical Shows On Record 1897-1976*, General Gramophone Record Publications Ltd, 1977. (Revised edition by Robert Seeley and Rex Bunnett, 1990.)

Films

While Robey's silent films are, apparently, gone beyond recall, the sound films are listed under title entries in: David Quinlan, *British Sound Films: The Studio Years, 1928–1959*, Batsford, 1984. Dates, production and cast details, running times and brief plot synopses are provided.

BIBLIOGRAPHY

Agate, James, *Alarums and Excursions*, Grant Richards, 1922.
— *Ego 2*, Gollancz, 1936.
— *More First Nights*, Gollancz, 1937.
— *Brief Chronicles*, Jonathan Cape, 1943.
— *Ego 6*, Harrap, 1944.
— *Immmoment Toys*, Jonathan Cape, 1945.
— *Ego 9*, Harrap, 1948.
Barker, Felix, *The House That Stoll Built*, Frederick Muller, 1957.
Beerbohm, Sir Max, *Mainly On The Air*, Heinemann, 1947.
— *Around Theatres*, Rupert Hart-Davies, 1953.
Behrman, S. N., *Conversations With Max*, Hamish Hamilton, 1960.
Booth, J. B., *A Pink 'Un Remembers*, Werner Laurie, 1937.
— *Life, Laughter and Brass Hats*, Werner Laurie, 1939.
— *The Days We Knew*, Werner Laurie, 1943.
— *Palmy Days*, Richards Press, 1957.
Busby, Roy, *British Music Hall*, Paul Elek, 1976.
Byng, Douglas, *As You Were*, Duckworth, 1970.
Calthrop, Dion Clayton, *Music Hall Nights*, Bodley Head, 1925.
Cardus, Sir Neville, *Full Score*, Cassell, 1970.
Cecil, Lord David, *Max. A Biography*, Constable, 1964.
Cochran, Sir Charles B., *I Had Almost Forgotten . . .* Hutchinson, 1932.
— *Cock-A-Doodle-Doo*, J. M. Dent, 1941.
— *Showman Looks On*, J. M. Dent, 1945.
Cotes, Peter, *George Robey. 'The Darling of The Halls'*, Cassell, 1972.
Disher, M. Willson, *Winkles and Champagne. Comedies and Tragedies of the Music Hall*, Batsford, 1938.
Felstead, S. Theodore, *Stars Who Made The Halls*, Werner Laurie, 1947.
Gänzl, Kurt, *The British Musical Theatre*, Volume 2, 1915–1984, Macmillan, 1986.
Gielgud, Sir John, *Backward Glances*, Hodder and Stoughton, 1989.
Green, Benny, *The Last Empires. A Music Hall Companion*, Pavilion/ Michael Joseph, 1986.

Guinness, Sir Alec, *Blessings in Disguise*, Hamish Hamilton, 1985.

Herbert, Sir Alan, *A.P.H. His Life and Times*, Heinemann, 1970.

Howard, Denise, *London Theatre and Music Halls, 1850–1950*, The Library Association, 1970.

Irving, Ernest, *Cue For Music*, Dennis Dobson, 1959.

Jacob, Naomi, *'Our Marie'*, Hutchinson, n.d.

MacInnes, Colin, *Sweet Saturday Night*, MacGibbon and Kee, 1967.

MacQueen-Pope, W., *The Melodies Linger On. The Story of Music Hall*, W. H. Allen, n.d.

— *Ghosts and Greasepaint*, Robert Hale, 1951.

Mander, R., and Mitchenson, J., *British Music Hall*, Studio Vista, 1965.

— *The Theatres of London*, New English Library, 1975.

Marshall, Michael (ed), *The Book of Comic and Dramatic Monologues*, Elm Tree Books, 1981.

Milton, Billy, *Milton's Paradise Mislaid*, Jupiter Books, 1976.

Newton, H. Chance, *Idols of The Halls*, Heath Cranton, 1928.

Olivier, Lord, *Confessions of An Actor*, Weidenfeld and Nicolson, 1982.

Parker, John (ed), *The Green Room Book*, T. Sealey Clark, 1908.

— *Who's Who In The Theatre*, Pitman, 1914, and subsequent issues.

Play Pictorial, various issues featuring Robey and productions in which he appeared, Stage Pictorial Publishing.

Pulling, Christopher, *They Were Singing*, Harrap, 1952.

Robey, Edward, *The Jester and The Court*, William Kimber, 1976.

Scott, Harold, *The Early Doors*, Nicholson and Watson, 1946.

Shaw, G. Bernard, *Shaw's Music*, Volumes 2 and 3, Max Reinhardt/Bodley Head, 1981.

— *Our Theatres in the Nineties*, Volume 3, Constable, 1948.

Short, Ernest, *Fifty Years of Vaudeville*, Eyre and Spottiswoode, 1946.

Stage, The Stage Year Book, the *Stage*, 1914, and subsequent issues.

Traubner, Richard, *Operetta*, Gollancz, 1984.

Van Ash, Cary, and Rohmer, Elizabeth Sax (ed Robert E. Binney), *Master of Villainy*, Tom Stacey, 1972.

Vanbrugh, Irene, *To Tell My Story*, Hutchinson, 1948.

Williams, Bransby, *Bransby Williams By Himself*, Hutchinson, 1954.

Wilmut, Roger, *Kindly Leave The Stage! The Story of Variety, 1919–1960*, Methuen, 1985.

Wilson, A. E., *Prime Minister of Mirth. The Biography of Sir George Robey, CBE*. Odhams, 1956.

INDEX

Index

Index

Index